D1522160

POETRY AND HUMOUR FROM COWPER TO CLOUGH

POETRY AND HUMOUR FROM COWPER TO CLOUGH

Mark Storey

ROWMAN AND LITTLEFIELD
TOTOWA, NEW JERSEY

© Mark Storey 1979

First published in the United States 1979
By Rowman and Littlefield, Totowa, N.J.

Library of Congress Cataloging in Publication Data
Storey, Mark.
    Poetry and humour from Cowper to Clough.
    Includes bibliographical references and index.
    1.   English poetry--19th century--History and criticism.   2.   English wit and humor--History and criticism.   I.   Title.
PR589.C6S84   1979   821'.7'09   78-23875
ISBN 0-8476-6133-4

Printed in Great Britain

Contents

Preface

De Quincey recalls an episode that Coleridge used to tell with relish about his shortsighted father:

> Dining in a large party, one day, the modest divine was suddenly shocked by perceiving some part, as he conceived, of his own snowy shirt emerging from a part of his habiliments, which we shall suppose to have been his waistcoat. It was *not* that; but for decorum we shall so call it. The stray portion of his supposed tunic was admonished of its errors by a forcible thrust back into its proper home; but still another *limbus* persisted to emerge, or seemed to persist, and still another, until the learned gentleman absolutely perspired with the labour of re-establishing order. And, after all, he saw with anguish, that some arrears of the snowy indecorum still remained to reduce into obedience. To this remnant of rebellion he was proceeding to apply himself — strangely confounded, however, at the obstinacy of the insurrection — when the mistress of the house, rising to lead away the ladies from the table, and all parties naturally rising with her, it became suddenly apparent to every eye, that the worthy Orientalist had been most laboriously stowing away, into the capacious receptacles of his own habiliments, the snowy folds of a lady's gown, belonging to his next neighbour; and so voluminously, that a very small portion of it, indeed, remained for the lady's use; the natural consequence of which was, of course, that the lady appeared almost inextricably yoked to the learned theologian, and could not in any way effect her release, until after certain operations upon the Vicar's dress, and a continued refunding and rolling out of snowy mazes upon snowy mazes, in quantities which, at length, proved too much for the gravity of the company. Inextinguishable laughter arose from all parties . . . ('Autobiographic Sketches', 1854)

Laughter (the sign, as Byron knew, of a rational animal) rings through the nineteenth century; but we tend not to think of the major poets of the century in terms of the comic. In the literary histories Wordsworth, Coleridge, Blake, Keats, Shelley, Tennyson, Arnold appear in their customary roles as egocentric bards: they are lucky to get as far as the index in most studies of comedy. What I am offering in this book, very modestly, is an exploratory re-appraisal of the nineteenth-century poetic tradition, in terms of the relationship between poetry and humour.

Misrepresentation has tended to cloud the issue. L. J. Potts, for example, in a standard book on comedy, writes:

> Between Congreve and Meredith, Byron is the only comic poet I can think of (I do not speak of comic verse merely, but of poetic imagination, and I count Pope as a satirist rather than a comic writer); and great as Byron is, his poetry is too isolated to bridge so many years.

J. R. Caldwell, in his significantly labelled essay, 'The Solemn Romantics', admits that 'the humorist, if not humor, flourished', but proceeds to argue that all the major Romantic poets were engaged in an 'evangelical humorlessness'. David Farley-Hills, more recently, has said, 'we may be forgiven for imagining that some of the great Romantic writers, emulating Jesus, never laughed'. This apparently well-established attitude is extended with even more rigour to the Victorians. In my innocence I find it odd that no one has tried to refute it.

There have been some attempts to re-open the debate. Richard Boston has put part of the record straight for the Romantics as people, in *An Anatomy of Laughter*, but he has little to say about their poetry. R. B. Martin's essay, *The Triumph of Wit*, looks at the theoretical premises of the Victorians' changing attitudes to humour and wit, but it scarcely goes beyond these to the complexities of the literature of the period. In his book on comedy, Allan Rodway dismisses a large part of the nineteenth century out of hand as 'too authoritarian to be ideal for comedy'. As Rodway's book shows, one of the problems in any such discussion tends to be nomenclature. In my discussion I have decided to use the word 'humour': if this seems too vague a word, the choice is deliberate. For the nineteenth century tended to think in terms of humour rather than comedy at a time when previously accepted categories and definitions were losing their significance. Humour was a concept that applied to life as much as to literature.

It is virtually a commonplace of literary history that it is with the Romantic poets that we first need to make crucial connections between life and work. Critical purists might jib at such necessities, but I think we have to make out of them what virtues we can. The popular notion of the Romantics as solemn bards with their heads in the clouds can be readily undermined when we look at their letters, diaries, memoirs, and reminiscences. What Hobhouse observed of Byron — that his laugh was his most distinguishing characteristic — seems to have been true of most of these poets. John Clare's perceptive accounts of the famous *London Magazine* dinners, where Reynolds, Hazlitt, Lamb, De Quincey, Coleridge and others would gather, are full of the sense of fun, wit and humour generated by these writers. The smile that Hazlitt noticed forever flickering on Wordsworth's lips was infectious. Keats was fascinated by wit of all kinds, by the fruitfulness of the pun, by the inherent absurdity of a 'werry romantic' view of life. This pervasive sense of humour inevitably impinges on the poetry in many ways. Even if Shelley scorns satire, that does not prevent him from writing 'Swellfoot the Tyrant', in which the story of Oedipus is retold in the context of the pigsty, or his version of 'Peter Bell'; John Clare's *Child Harold* and *Don Juan* reflect the genuine Byronic mixture of his Romanticism and energetic humour; Wordsworth, in 'Resolution and Independence' com-memorates Chatterton, but also Burns; Thomas Hood is caught between the urge to be a 'serious poet' and his need to be inventively comic. Hood's work can be seen as an image of the pulls that operate on so many of the major figures of the nineteenth century: the relationship between his work and that of Keats is of the utmost suggestiveness.

What I want to argue, quite simply, and against the prevailing view, is that all the major Romantic poets are directly concerned with the implications of humour and what happens if it is allowed into poetry. My argument consists in the tracing of this line of humour, in its various manifestations, up to the Victorian poets, especially up to the neglected but major Arthur Hugh Clough. Clough is one of those interesting mid-Victorian figures who have received some close and careful attention in recent years; but few have been prepared to admit him into the pantheon of great Victorian writers. The tendency has been to over-emphasise what critics are pleased to call the 'modernity' of Clough, as though that in itself were his chief virtue. But 'modernity' is a red herring. When we see Clough in the Romantic and Victorian contexts, we can see him not as an aberration merely, an anticipation of things to come, but as the supreme representative of one line of poetical thinking. One of the major problems for the

Romantics had been their struggle to fit themselves into their poetry: this raised crucial questions of form, of diction, of the very role and nature of poetry as understood at the turn of the century. There were no easy solutions. It is one of the main arguments of the first part of this study that humour provides one essential means of accommodating the self, especially the Romantic self, in poetry. Clough, it seems to me, takes up the challenge inherent in Romantic poetry, and fuses the apparently discordant elements of the serious and the comic. He has to do this, if he is to reconcile the conflicting claims of a poetry of the self, and a poetry of the community and age in which he lives.

There are obvious omissions in this essay: the last thing I have tried, or been able, to be, is comprehensive. If Crabbe is mentioned, it is only, alas! in passing, but not because I think him unimportant. The very fact of his writing as he does, when he does, is a crucial pointer to the way we need to redefine our historical consciousness of the early nineteenth-century poets. Jane Austen and Byron were right (Leavis has made this point well) to recognise his place in the literary tradition. At the same time his unique voice ('Pope in worsted stockings' is an unfair dismissal of his achievement and idiosyncrasy) belongs to a previous age, and I found that I could not fairly discuss him within the confines of my argument. His shadow, though, looms large, and we need to be aware of it. The more obviously humorous writers — Reynolds, Hood, Frere, Calverley, Praed (the list can be extended almost indefinitely) — have also been taken more or less for granted: it has never been my intention to offer comments or insights on these writers. It has been enough, for my purposes, to register their substantial presence. Browning might seem an even more culpable omission, especially when I am making particular claims for Clough amongst his Victorian contemporaries. There are indeed obvious links between Browning and the Romantics (Byron especially), and if Clough had learnt much from Browning there would have been a strong case for discussing his poetry in that light. But Clough was only minimally aware of Browning, and was doing something very different. Browning, in any case, has been well served by critics, in a way that Clough (until recently) has not. Critics should be proselytisers, and I offer no excuses for championing Clough, merely apologies for doing it inadequately.

Birmingham   M. G. S.
December 1977

Acknowledgements

There are many people (apart from the innumerable scholars and critics who hover behind the following pages) who have helped me indirectly, and who would be surprised if I were to name them. I hope at least some of them know who they are. Others I should like to thank publicly, and hope they will not suffer by association with a book none of them has seen before. This book grew out of earlier work on John Clare, and I am glad to be able to record my gratitude, as I could not previously, to the following: F. W. Bateson, John Fuller, Eric Robinson, Geoffrey Summerfield, Margaret Grainger, David Powell, Alexander Bell, Judith Levin. Whilst I was in the English Department at the Queen's University of Belfast, successive generations of students provided continual and invaluable stimulus; Louis Muinzer of the Extramural Department gave me a welcome chance to try out some of my ideas on an unsuspecting group of people one summer. My former colleagues at Queen's were always more than tolerant of my absorption first in Clare and then in the wider topic that was to become the substance of this book. I shall never be able to thank them properly for their friendliness throughout the seven years I was there. I hope it will not seem invidious to mention especially Margaret Cardwell and Peter Devlin, who were most directly involved in the same area of teaching and research. Queen's University was also generous with grants for travel, and without that assistance this book would have taken much longer to get started. Since coming to Birmingham I have been lucky to have the support of my newly acquired colleagues in the English Department. Hazel Hanlon deciphered my hieroglyphs with exemplary patience and tact.

This book was written before, during and after a move back across the water from Belfast. The inevitable domestic upheaval was not alleviated by my commitment to poetry and humour, and my family will be justified in wondering, now that they see what I was up to all those hours, whether I should not after all, like Philip Hewson in Clough's *The Bothie*, have been subduing the earth. I have relatives of various shapes and sizes to thank for their interest and forbearance, my parents especially: but my wife and children have, as usual, suffered more than most for a book that can never be adequate recompense. As, in the nature of things, I cannot say it will not happen again, I hope they know how much the book owes to them.

1 'The Peculiar Province': Theories of Humour

I

An obituary writer in 1819 commemorated one of England's poets with this anecdote:

> When the Duke of Kent was last in America, he took a stroll into the country, and entering a neat little cottage, saw a pretty girl with a book in her hand; 'What books do you read, my dear?' said his Royal Highness. The girl with the most artless innocence replied, 'Sir, the Bible and Peter Pindar!'[1]

There had been a time, thirty years before this, when Peter Pindar had been a household name in England; it is rather typical of the transitional nature of the period in which he lived and died that he should be remembered in this coyly sentimental fashion. Such a response, whilst helping to explain at least partially his initial appeal and whilst looking ahead to some of the softnesses of the Victorian age, neglects some of the strengths of late eighteenth-century satire. It is salutary to be reminded that Peter Pindar died in the year that saw the publication of Wordsworth's *Peter Bell* (and its parodies), the year before Keats's volume of 1820 (which was to sell only 500 copies, and those none too quickly). Peter Pindar (and Alexander Walcot's chosen *nom de plume* says quite a lot about the man and his age) was one of many poets in the eighteenth century who turned to comic verse as an outlet for their muse. The list of such writers is almost endless; Peter Pindar was really the last such figure, before the emergence of Thomas Hood, to make a name for himself. He represents a particular type of poetry that we need to be aware of, existing under the surface of English letters – but sufficiently near that surface for someone with as many problems of literary adjustment as John Clare to know his work, and to be able to make

1

critical and appreciative comments on it. It is as though there is a
whole sub-culture of satiric poetry, often burlesque or parody, the
fag-end, perhaps, of the great age of Augustan satire, but still with
some life in it.

In his book on the origin of the *Lyrical Ballads*, John Jordan has
commented on one aspect that in 1798 would have struck many
readers as strange, and that was the almost complete lack of satire in
this avowedly experimental volume.[2] As Jordan shows, satire was
still a force to be reckoned with. The work of mid-eighteenth-
century writers such as Charles Churchill and Christopher Anstey
(even Cowper had allowed himself to be satirical) was continued by a
group of writers who composed a mock-epic poem, *The Rolliad*,
which appeared in book form in 1785 — a much harsher view of the
world than that exhibited in Peter Pindar's *Lousiad* of the same year.
The Rolliad is very much an in-joke, an imagined poem with an
imagined body of criticism already attached to it (on the lines, rather,
of *The Dunciad*): it is witty and astringent, committed against Pitt's
government and Pitt's minions. The perpetrators of this immensely
elaborate performance were a group of pranksters, each with his own
axe to grind, each well qualified in some or other profession: George
Ellis, the antiquarian, for example (later to comment intelligently on
Byron), French Laurence, a successful lawyer, Richard Tickell
likewise. After the success of *The Rolliad*, other works followed:
Probationary Odes for the Laureateship, *Political Miscellanies*. Then in
1797, the mantle of this group seemed to fall squarely on the
shoulders of a new journal, *The Anti-Jacobin*.

For the better part of a year, this magazine appeared each week,
wreaking havoc on political and poetical reputations. William
Gifford, known already for his mock-epics *The Baviad* and *The
Maeviad*, was the editor, and under his guidance English satire
developed parody into a fine art, initially at Robert Southey's
expense, but in the event anyone was good for a laugh. George Ellis
was still active, and he was joined by George Canning and John
Hookham Frere, whose finest hour was yet to come, when his
Whistlecraft got into Byron's hands and sparked off the metrical
inventiveness of *Beppo*. Between them, these four provided cruel, and
necessary, reminders to the dying years of the century that the
strengths of Augustan satire could still be drawn upon. Our
perspective on that period is altered as we register the vituperative
qualities which a great many still looked for, and valued, in literature.
But it was not simply that: a whole tradition was being invoked.

T. J. Mathias, in some ways Gifford's natural successor, wrote of his ambitions, 'I offer the poetry to those, who are conversant with the strength, simplicity, and dignity of Dryden and Pope, and to those persons alone . . .';[3] he could be brazen because of his moral confidence. Now, of course, we can see that some, at least, of that confidence was misplaced. Dryden and Pope certainly had things to teach poets at the turn of the century, but there were fundamental differences in context that had eventually to be recognised. Nonetheless one of the most fascinating aspects of this period, in which the major Romantic poets emerge and flourish, is the complexity of attitudes towards the age of satire treasured by Gifford and Mathias, but which Peter Pindar saw as essentially in need of some mollification. And those attitudes need to be set in the wider context of the debate on the purposes of poetry, and more specifically the debate on the place of the comic in literature.

The precise functions of comedy have taxed and teased writers, critics, philosophers, psychologists, theoreticians and ordinary mortals from Aristotle onwards. It would be presumptuous of me to try to say in a few pages what it has taken numerous large volumes to fail to elucidate; and yet in order to understand the questions which were being put at the end of the eighteenth century, and the connection between theoretical questions and poetic practice, we need to know why it was then that these particular questions were being asked.[4]

Perhaps the most interesting fact about comedy, apart from its irksome ubiquity, is the unease it has occasioned (the two facts are of course connected – especially when the connection is most vehemently denied). Most theoreticians have been able to arrive at a working definition of tragedy; but their resulting sense of confidence has not very convincingly transferred itself to any working definition of comedy. When confidence has been asserted, it has usually been with a rhetorical stridency determined to keep comedy in its proper place. The moralist lurking within most critics' breasts has always felt rather threatened by comedy. What Aristotle had to say about it was to be eagerly taken up by a host of later writers:

Poetry soon branched into two channels, according to the temperaments of individual poets. The more serious-minded among them represented noble actions and the doings of noble persons, while the more trivial wrote about the meaner sort of people; thus while the one type wrote hymns and panegyrics, these others began by writing invectives . . .[5]

Aristotle makes the point that Homer is the 'supreme poet in the serious style', but also, in 'his treatment of the ridiculous, he was the first to indicate the forms that comedy was to assume; for his *Margites* bears the same relationship to our comedies as his *Iliad* and *Odyssey* bear to our tragedies'. Although he does not expand on the implications of this, it is a fairly crucial acknowledgement that the supreme epic poet was supreme also in comedy. Neoclassical theorists of the eighteenth century (though not Fielding, as his Preface to *Joseph Andrews* shows) tended to forget that there was classical precedent for comic poetry alongside that of epic or tragedy. But Aristotle's use of the word 'ridiculous' needs some emphasis, as it is a concept that reappears in later theorising. It is a matter of morality:

. . . comedy represents the worse types of men; worse, however, not in the sense that it embraces any and every kind of badness, but in the sense that the ridiculous consists in some form of error or ugliness that is not painful or injurious; the comic mask, for example, is distorted and ugly, but causes no pain.[6]

Here again, Aristotle anticipates the way the argument will rage; but he is specifically making the point, with which later writers were often to disagree, that there is no pain involved in comedy. The disadvantages of his discussion stem from its brevity, and from the confusion between aesthetic and moral propriety. Underlying the argument is the assumption that comedy is an inferior form.

The history of Greek drama might well belie that theoretical point. Just as the Greeks had, in Aristophanes, a supreme comic dramatist, so the less ebullient Romans had a strong tradition of comedy and satire which it was hard for Horace, of all people, to deny in his poem about poetry. Horace emphasises the nature of poetry as craft, with its own disciplines and proprieties, which are upheld in theory but often violated in practice:

A comic subject is not susceptible of treatment in a tragic style, and similarly the banquet of Thyestes cannot be fitly described in the strains of everyday life or in those that approach the tone of comedy. Let each of these styles be kept for the role properly allotted to it. Yet even comedy at times uses elevated language, and an angry Chremes rails in bombastic terms; while in tragedy Telephus and Peleus often express their grief in prosaic language, and each of them in his poverty-stricken exile renounces his usual rant and his sesquipedalian words when he wants to move the spectator's pity with his lamentations.[7]

Beneath this allowance for flexibility lies the basic principle of decorum:

> . . . if your speeches are out of harmony with your feelings, I shall either fall asleep or burst out laughing . . . Tragedy scorns to babble trivialities, and, like a married woman obliged to dance at a festival, will look rather shamefaced among the wanton satyrs.[8]

Horace discourages incongruity. It is this overstepping of well-defined boundaries that is to become, in English critical theory, a major issue.

The debate on literature in England from the Renaissance onwards was often an embattled affair. Even the exuberance of the Elizabethans was countered by the need to defend the stage against its moralistic attackers. More often than not, it was the alleged immorality of the comic muse that caused all the trouble: the Puritan ethic could not tolerate the disruptive, iconoclastic tendencies of comedy. The threat to established order was too great, and the only acceptable defence of comedy was one which claimed for it the powers of correction. Satire especially found itself in an uneasy position, uncertain to what extent it could rely on moral justification: poets and critics had to question whether it was legitimate to employ what seemed an essentially destructive force for morally constructive ends. Hobbes declared that laughter was a reflection of inferiority, masquerading as superiority, a sign of those 'who are forced to keep themselves in their own favour by observing the imperfections of other men. And therefore much laughter is a sign of pusillanimity'.[9] Hobbes had many staunch supports in the seventeenth and eighteenth centuries, theorists who quoted and expanded on his formulation in their increasingly desperate attempts to keep comedy in its place. One of the ironies of the debate is that an age which seemed so anxious to declare itself against comedy and satire should produce so many comic and satiric masterpieces.

In the course of the eighteenth century, to speak very generally about an immensely complicated subject, two dominant arguments emerged. The Earl of Shaftesbury exemplified the more rigorous attitude favoured by those who demanded of literature a stern, corrective responsibility; behind his attitude lies the notion of laughter as ridicule, and we remember Aristotle's use of that word (and also that he was careful to dissociate it from any sense of pain).[10] It was no doubt this emphasis on laughter as ridicule that prompted several writers to postulate a kind of laughter that would be both corrective and unharmful. This was the second argument, in which malice would give way to benevolence (a term used even by Milton), and then to a much more open view of comic possibilities, whereby an apparently absurd, or at least confusingly inexplicable, world actually invited a comic response. As David Farley-Hills puts it, with reference especially to Rochester: 'the comic provided a profound insight into the nature of things. . . . Not surprisingly . . . the Restoration tends in fact, if not in theory, to take laughter seriously'.[11]

When Addison addressed himself to the problem of wit and humour (the implicit opposition between the two terms was there virtually from the beginning) he relied, as did Steele, quite considerably on the distinctions Isaac Barrow had made in 1678 between grave mirth and wild laughter.[12] Addison develops the notion of 'cheerfulness' as a preferable alternative to mirth, and its subsequent popularity as a critical term is an indication of the development of thought on the subject in the eighteenth century and beyond. A man can be of good humour, good cheer, without descending to the level of mere wit: one of the most characteristic emanations of this type is the hermit in Johnson's *Rasselas*, who combines cheerfulness with lack of levity. What Addison says theoretically is echoed in Lord Chesterfield's practical views:

> Cheerfulness and good humour are of all qualifications the most amiable in company. When there is no malevolence in the heart, there is always a cheerfulness and ease in the countenance and the manners. By good humour and cheerfulness, I am far from meaning noisy mirth and loud peals of laughter, which are the distinguishing characteristics of the vulgar and the ill-bred, whose mirth is a kind of sham. Observe it, the vulgar often laugh, but never smile, whereas well-bred people often smile, and seldom or never laugh.[13]

We can see how easily moral distinctions become both aesthetic and social distinctions of crucial significance. When everyone knows where he stands in the hierarchy, all is well; similarly, when each department of literature knows what is expected of it, there is little danger. It is when people and literature begin to behave unexpectedly that the troubles begin. Wit comes to be seen as low and common, requiring the restraining influence of the benign philosophy of the *Tatler* and *Spectator*, wherein Addison and Steele urge moderation with such grace and elegance.

Addison sets, against the Hobbesian notion of laughter as 'sudden glory', a type of laughter that is natural and healthy:

> I shall conclude this Essay [*Spectator*, No. 249] upon Laughter with observing, that the Metaphor of Laughing, applied to Fields and Meadows when they are in Flower, or to Trees when they are in Blossom, runs through all Languages; which I have not observed of any other Metaphor, excepting that of Fire, and burning, when they are applied to Love. This shows that we naturally regard Laughter, as what is in itself both amiable and beautiful.

What Addison had been reaching towards intuitively received philosophical support from three essays published in 1725 by Francis Hutcheson, who saw that laughter and ridicule had to be separated before the argument could proceed beyond the usual Hobbesian dismissal. Where Hutcheson is important historically is in his exploration of the possibilities (hitherto denied by most theorists) of wit, especially in the way he recognises the validity of mock-heroic and burlesque. To define wit's legitimacy in these terms is of course to limit its function, but it is at least allowing it some room. And once burlesque is acknowledged as an appropriate form, then the inherently unsettling qualities of that form begin to assert their own ramifications. Writers such as Bishop Hurd (1751) and George Campbell (1776) move from wit towards the idea of the conjunction of disparates, and eventually incongruity. Once that point has been reached, the attack on laughter is itself increasingly under attack. By the middle of the century the argument has advanced to the stage where Alexander Gérard, in his *Essay on Taste* (1759), can state the advantages of incongruity with some confidence, so much so, in fact, that 'ridicule' itself has lost its bad odour:

> . . . we must not omit that sense, which perceives, and is gratified

by the odd, the ridiculous, the humorous, the witty; and whose
function often produces, and always tends to, mirth, laughter, and
amusement. Though inferior in dignity to the rest, it is far from
being despicable. It has a province, less important indeed than that
of the others, yet both useful and agreeable.

The emphasis on humour as something natural, something that
springs from us as if from the soil, was bound to encourage a
confidence in its possibilities as against the more mechanical concept
of wit. When theories of the nature of poetry were asserting the role
of feeling and passion, they were much more likely to embrace the
idea of a sympathetic, even passionate, humour, than the idea of a
rather cold, calculated wit. It comes, sometimes, as a surprise to realise
how much theoretical talk, even at the beginning of the eighteenth
century, was concerned with feeling, with emotion in poetry: Dr
Johnson's attack on the worst excesses of the Metaphysicals with their
'heterogeneous ideas yoked by violence together' is matched by his
inability (or refusal) to see, in the artifice of 'Lycidas', any expression
of real grief.
     It would be quite wrong to suggest that the argument becomes
completely one-sided. Satirists especially could see the disadvantages
of a creed that gave pride of place to a warm-hearted, sympathetic
humour; wit, with its cool detachment, was necessary to satire. A
glowing, fireside cheerfulness was always in danger of minimising the
force of a moral discrimination. Against such reservations could be set
the obvious advantages of a view of literature that recognised
humour as liberating and democratising. John Dennis actually
rejoiced in the 'lowness' of humour, for

> 'tis among People of the lower sort, that by the means of Passion
> and Humour, Nature appears so admirably conspicuous in all her
> Charming diversities: Since therefore Humour is the chief business
> in Comedy after the Fable . . . it is very plain that low Characters
> are more proper for Comedy than high ones, and that low
> Comedy is to be preferred to the high.[14]

It was this concentration of humour on low characters that had made
Shakespearean comedy possible. Sir John Falstaff comes to represent
the ideal comic figure – warm, jolly, human, his heart in the right
place; in Victorian times he becomes ossified into the ubiquitous
Toby jug. But the eighteenth century does not succumb entirely to

easy sentimentality: there are other figures in the pantheon of comic heroes who are immediately appropriated by theorists of various persuasions. Don Quixote stands behind the genial, bumbling but by no means mild character of Parson Adams in Fielding's *Joseph Andrews* — and is acknowledged on the title page; he stands, too, behind Sterne's Uncle Toby in *Tristram Shandy*. Fielding's prefatory remarks on the nature of 'comic-epic' in prose point to a strong consciousness of traditional form, and a determination not to be hamstrung by it. What might appear to start out, with *Shamela*, as mere parody or burlesque, becomes an exploration of the nature of comedy which involves frequent crossing of the boundaries of propriety. Even within the self-generating tradition of warmth and geniality (which does not preclude savage irony and satire) Fielding demonstrates some of the uneasy conjunctions of modes and manners that life offers. As Stuart Tave has shown with admirable clarity, the eighteenth century — novelists, critics, readers — to some extent sees in *Don Quixote* what it wants to see in it. Fielding and Sterne capitalise on a particular way of looking at an established classic; as Fielding is thereby enabled to create in Parson Adams one of the archetypal benevolent humorists of the eighteenth century, so Sterne seems to sum up not simply the outlook of an age, but the outlook of a nation. He vindicates comedy's claim to be, as Hugh Blair put it, the 'peculiar province' of the English.[15]

Those who were prepared to allow themselves the indulgence of Sterne's incongruities and strangenesses had ample precedent: against all the irate theorising on the inadmissable mingling of dramatic modes stood the example of Shakespeare, who had combined so brilliantly what was frequently thought of as 'the grave and the gay'. Once again it was a question of practice belying solemnly earnest theory, and typically it is Dr Johnson in mid-century who openly acknowledges Shakespeare's triumph in the face of critical theory. Shakespeare had made tragicomedy possible, he had shown 'the real state of sublunary nature . . . in which, at the same time, the reveller is hasting to his wine, and the mourner burying his friend.'[16] Things knock against each other in Shakespeare's world: Johnson's canny phrase for this is 'unavoidable concatenation'. Johnson is really saying that this is a truer picture of life, and a specifically English one, which recognises the proximity of tears to laughter. If the English are naturally inclined to humour, they are equally inclined to moroseness, to the spleen and its effects. Sterne's note to Garrick, 'I laugh till I cry, and in the same tender moments *cry till I laugh*', is not far

removed in tone and sentiment from Cowper's observation that he
wrote 'John Gilpin' basically to cure himself of a brooding melancholy: 'the most ludicrous lines I ever wrote have been written in
the saddest mood'.[17] Once this kind of comment becomes
commonplace – as it does towards the end of the century – then we
have clearly moved a long way from those early strictures on
laughter, those safeguards against the dangers of humour of any kind.

It is perhaps especially important that Cowper's *cri de coeur* is in
many ways so representative of his age. If humour and pathos are seen
as inseparable reflections of each other in the life of the times, that is
because, increasingly, they seem so to the individuals coping with the
intractabilities of their own lives. And mention of Cowper is a
forceful reminder that much of the debate, after the Restoration, had
centred on novelists and dramatists: that was where the issues seemed
most crucial. But Cowper's sensibilities are shared by his fellow poets,
and by the poets of the turn of the century. It becomes poetry's turn to
take a full part in a debate which by its nature suggests that the age of
satire is past. The distinctive quality of the period – with its basis on
the one hand in literary tradition and on the other hand in personal
division – is pinpointed by Henry Mackenzie, author of *The Man of
Feeling*, who in 1780 speaks of the modern Hamletesque man of the
age who 'feels in himself . . . a sort of double person'.[18] We are back
with Hamlet and the gravediggers, back with Tristram and Yorick.
But we should not miss the anticipation of the divided spirit of a later
age, the anticipation of Clough's Dipsychus.

II

None of the Romantic manifestos on poetry is brimming over with a
sense of poetry's obligations to comedy: Wordsworth and Shelley
sustain a high solemnity, critics like Hazlitt and De Quincey show
that they have similar priorities. It is left to Peacock, in *The Four Ages
of Poetry*, to blast a broadside against the whole lot of them. But what
these writers have to say about poetry is of some importance for a
discussion of humour's place: because, whether they like it or not,
they have to acknowledge humour's presence – whatever they
choose to call it – just as they have to acknowledge, and sort out their
reactions to, the literature of the Augustan age.[19]

The Romantics' relation to the Augustans was not a simple matter
of polarities: Peacock's longing glances back to an age when, as he

thought, poetry engaged with issues of the day was sanctioned by many readers and critics. Scott's 1808 edition of Dryden was amongst other things a statement of faith, even whilst he lamented Dryden's lack of interest in the 'pathetic'. The famous Bowles–Byron controversy over Pope found Bowles having to fight hard for his anti-Augustan principles: if Warton's conviction that 'WIT and SATIRE are transitory and perishable, but NATURE and DESIGN are eternal' had theoretical and emotional support, that did not stop a large part of the reading public from turning naturally to Dryden and Pope.[20] William Roscoe's edition of Pope, published in 1824, suggested that Pope was still the favourite:

> Whatever may be the homage we pay to others, there is no author whose works have been more universally read, or are more fully remembered . . . no poet, excepting Shakespeare alone, whose works are quoted on so many different occasions.

Not everyone agreed. But even Matthew Arnold thirty years later had to admit that the Augustans had set the standards by which literature was to be judged.

Hazlitt and Wordsworth, in their respective ways, illustrate one of the difficulties: for Wordsworth, poetry 'is the breath and finer spirit of all knowledge . . .'; for Hazlitt, it is 'the universal language which the heart holds with nature and itself'.[21] Such great claims are hard to substantiate convincingly, except by rhetoric: one of the implications, we can now see, would seem to be that poetry, in its attempts to embrace every aspect of life, has to come to terms with more than the simply high-minded. This is a realisation that slips in only gradually: when the claims of poetry are pitched so high, there is, initially, little room for comedy.

It is no surprise to find Hazlitt calling Dryden and Pope 'great masters of the artificial style of poetry', and in using that word 'artificial' he indicates their inferiority to the natural, unaffected writers of his own generation.[22] When writing about Shakespeare and Jonson he says quite openly, 'I do not . . . consider comedy as exactly an affair of the heart or the imagination; and it is for this reason only that I think Shakespeare's comedies deficient'.[23] The plays of Wycherley, Congreve, Vanbrugh, Farquhar slot much more readily into his notions of comic decorum, whereby comedy is a 'graceful ornament to the civil order; the Corinthian capital of polished society'.[24] Such comments are typical and representative, and if Hazlitt had said no more on the subject it could be left there. But he is fascinated by it, and apart from giving a major series of lectures on the English comic writers, he writes a piece 'On Wit and Humour' which is of some importance.

Here he applies his observations, in the first place, to life, which is 'a tragedy or a comedy – sad or merry, as it happens.' He emphasises the way a child's tears and laughter are almost interchangeable (and echoes David Hartley's psychological formulations):

> Man is the only animal that laughs and weeps; for he is the only animal that is struck with the difference between what things are, and what they ought to be. We weep at what thwarts or exceeds our desires in serious matters: we laugh at what only disappoints our expectations in trifles. We shed tears from sympathy with real and necessary distress; as we burst into laughter from want of sympathy with that which is unreasonable and unnecessary, the absurdity of which provokes our spleen or mirth, rather than any serious reflections on it. [25]

Hazlitt seems to be continuing in the well-established, traditional belief that laughter is a secondary activity, often associated with a complete lack of feeling for what is being laughed at. 'One rich source of the ludicrous', he says, 'is the distress with which we cannot sympathise from its absurdity or insignificance.' This again had been a fairly common view. But Hazlitt does not appear to go so far as to believe that laughter is morally indefensible. He recognises the element of incongruity in anything we laugh at — 'the disconnecting one idea from another, or the jostling of one feeling against another'; this is rather important, in that it is the device Wordsworth relies on in some of his *Lyrical Ballads*, one which Byron deploys in so much of his poetry, even in *Childe Harold*. Hazlitt proceeds from this point to a fascinating observation, demonstrably true, but surprising in its context, that

> we laugh at a thing merely because we ought not. . . . The consciousness, however it may arise, that there is something we ought to look grave at, is almost always a signal for laughing outright: we can hardly keep our countenance at a sermon, a funeral, or a wedding.

This last point rebounds on Hazlitt, at his own wedding. Charles

Lamb writes to Robert Southey in 1815 to say that he was 'nearly turned out several times during the ceremony. Anything awful makes me laugh. I misbehaved once at a funeral.' Lamb actually says that he cannot, on such occasions, 'muster up decorum', which is a significant reminder of decorum's role in literature and life.[26]

Hazlitt's alertness to incongruity enables him to regard lying as a species of wit or humour: 'To lay anything to a person's charge from which he is perfectly free, shows spirit and invention; and the more incredible the effrontery, the greater is the joke'. This might seem a curious observation from one who takes a highly moralistic view of life and art, but it is typical of the Romantics' love of jokes and horseplay; typical, too, of Hazlitt's equivocal attitude. He goes on to demonstrate how wit is essentially a diminishing act, the 'eloquence of indifference'; humour is the 'growth of nature and accident; wit is the product of art and fancy'. But Hazlitt does not sustain this distinction with consistency; he dismisses both qualities just about equally:

> Wit and humour appeal to our indolence, our vanity, our weakness, and insensibility; serious and impassioned poetry appeals to our strength, our magnanimity, our virtue, and humanity.

There in a nutshell is the extremist view that had held sway for so long: it is a surprise to find Hazlitt voicing it. His confusions are clearly rather central. He can conclude a definition of wit by declaring, 'I protest (if required) against having a grain of wit';[27] and yet he shows himself alive to wit's possibilities, to the close relation between the sublime and the ridiculous, so much so that 'reading the finest passage in Milton's Paradise Lost in a false tone, will make it seem insipid and absurd'.[28] He can see the role of wit in Shakespeare, can say that 'Lear and the Fool are the sublimest instance I know of passion and wit united'. Even here, though, it is perhaps the fact that wit is saved by passion that matters.

In 'Merry England' Hazlitt continues to nibble at his fascination with the incongruities the English character presents him with: 'To be sure, it is from a dull, homely ground that the gleams of mirth and jollity break out'. The English

> have that sort of intermittent, fitful, irregular gaiety, which is neither worn out by habit, nor deadened by passion, but is sought with avidity as it takes the mind by surprise, is startled by a sense of

oddity and incongruity, indulges its wayward humours or lively impulses.[29]

In his eyes, 'English common people are a sort of grown children'. This is quite important, because it preserves that sense of humorous innocence, that finds its fullest flower in early Blake and Wordsworth: 'a degree of barbarism and rusticity seem necessary to the perfection of humour'. In spite of his comments elsewhere on the failings of English comic drama, Hazlitt focuses attention on a distinguishing characteristic of the English as a race:

> Now it appears to me that the English are (or were) just at that mean point between intelligence and obtuseness, which must produce the most abundant and happiest crop of humour. . . . The ludicrous takes hold of the English imagination, and clings to it with all its ramifications. . . . It is possible that a greater refinement of manners may give birth to finer distinctions of satire and a nicer tact for the ridiculous: but our insular situation and character are, I should say, most likely to foster, as they have in fact fostered, the greatest quantity of natural and striking humour, in spite of our plodding tenaciousness, and want both of gaiety and quickness of perception.

This seems to me a crucial statement, which illuminates in particular the type of humour that we find in Wordsworth, and makes the right connection between that and the fictional tradition represented by Fielding; and also between this and the poetry of Hood, Frere, and the other nineteenth-century humorous writers: 'I flatter myself that we are almost the only people left who understand and relish *nonsense*'. Hazlitt here looks ahead to the importance of Edward Lear and Lewis Carroll, but he is reflecting, too, the intense interest in his own day in the mockery of parody and burlesque.

Charles Lamb was another nineteenth-century writer acutely aware of the conflicts of his age, and not always able to resolve them satisfactorily. But Lamb does not suffer from some of Hazlitt's inconsistencies, so that he can push the argument forwards, for example in the direction of painting, as when he considers Hogarth. Protesting against the description of Hogarth as a 'mere comic painter' he writes:

. . . but to suppose that in their *ruling character* they appealed chiefly to the risible faculty, and not first and foremost to the very heart of man, its best and most serious feelings, would be to mistake no less grossly their aim and purpose.[30]

In his discussion of 'The Harlot's Funeral' Lamb shows how sympathetically aligned he is with the prevailing mood of the age, which is ready to acknowledge laughter whilst recognising its multifarious qualities:

> It is easy to laugh at such incongruities as are met together in this picture, — incongruous objects being of the very essence of laughter, but surely the laugh is far different in its kind from that thoughtless species to which we are moved by mere farce or grotesque.[31]

It is characteristically open of Lamb to proceed to examine the dangers of names and theories — simple categorisations had, after all, been the bane of so much theoretical discussion of laughter and comedy. Lamb argues against the current view that historical painters are necessarily better than painters of 'common life'. Should we not ask, he goes on, 'whether from that very common life a great artist may not extract as deep an interest as another man from that which we are pleased to call history'. Lamb is echoing the thoughts of several earlier writers who saw the importance of the particularities of 'low' or 'common' life, and who had argued for comedy's place in literature on the grounds that it was best suited to the portrayal of such particularities. Lamb can also be seen to be extending the argument of Wordsworth's Preface to the *Lyrical Ballads*: in his theoretical writings Wordsworth had avoided making any connection between low life and humour, but significantly his poetry frequently and disarmingly asserted that connection. Lamb's astuteness shows in the balance he keeps between apparently contradictory views: he can praise Hogarth's sense of beauty (quoting Coleridge in support), but elsewhere he can observe, with reference to *The Excursion*, that Wordsworth's originality is a disservice to him at a time when writers have to hug the shores of 'sentiment and sympathy'.[32] What was true of *The Excursion* had been even truer of the *Lyrical Ballads*.

Certainly those shores were well charted by Carlyle and De Quincey, both of whom turned to Jean-Paul Richter as the epitome of the humorous writer. It is hard to avoid the irony of seeing two English critics, at a time when the Englishness of humour had been established so satisfyingly, looking to a German for their ideal. Yet in the end what each writer has to say is characteristic rather than strikingly original. In his first essay on Richter, in the *London Magazine* for December 1821, De Quincey goes straight to the point:

> The characteristic distinction of Paul Richter amongst German authors, – I will venture to add, amongst modern authors generally, – is the two-headed power which he possesses over the pathetic and the humorous.[33]

De Quincey qualifies this: it is in fact a 'one-headed Janus with two faces', for

> the pathetic and the humorous are but different phases of the same orb; they assist each other, melt indiscernibly into each other, and often shine each through each like layers of coloured crystals placed one behind another.

The tone and the simile are revealing, as is the reference he makes to Mistress Quickly's account of Falstaff's death. Humour has been softened, it has in fact lost its power to surprise, even to delight unashamedly. We are very close to the 'milk and water' view of the comic. What De Quincey has to say later about the difference between wit and humour merely reinforces this impression:

> Whilst wit is a purely intellectual thing, into every act of the humorous mood there is an influx of the *moral* nature: rays, direct or refracted, from the will and the affections, from the dispositions and the temperament, enter into all humour.

Humour, it transpires, is essentially *diffusive*, and that word seems to be doing more than echo the eighteenth-century emphasis on warm benevolence – it is practically denying humour a focus. De Quincey rejoices in Richter's presence:

> Everywhere a spirit of kindness prevails: his satire is everywhere playful, delicate, and clad in smiles, – never bitter, scornful, or malignant [unlike Pope, charged with hypocrisy, histrionics and insincerity].

The affirmative vision of Carlyle likewise finds in Richter an ideal example of humour as an expression of character, 'as it were the central fire that pervades and vivifies his whole being'.[34] Mackenzie's man of feeling is reborn: 'in his smile itself a touching pathos may be hidden, a pity too deep for tears. He is a man of feeling in the noblest sense of that word'. Carlyle's definitions take us back to a previous age; for him the

> essence of humour is sensibility; warm, tender fellowfeeling with all forms of existence. . . . That faculty of irony, of caricature, which often passes by the name of humour, but consists chiefly in a certain superficial distortion or reversal of objects, and ends at best in laughter, bears no resemblance to the humour of Richter. . . . The humour . . . issues not in laughter, but in still smiles . . .

With so many writers erecting defences against the 'inborn levity of nature' that Carlyle distrusted in Voltaire we might well wonder how any poets had the courage to indulge in levity of any kind. As with the eighteenth century, the theories were often belied by the practice; eventually the critics had to alter their stand. An interesting figure in the debate is Leigh Hunt. In 1846 he wrote a conventional enough piece on 'Wit and Humour', but later, in his essay 'On the Combination of Grave and Gay' (1854) he leaves the usual categories behind in favour of a more pragmatic approach to literature's contradictions:

> What might have seemed nothing but levity, is found accompanied with the best kind of gravity. The man whom we might have feared as a satirist, we think we might count upon as a friend.[35]

For this reason, Shakespeare is preferable to Milton. Hunt even suggests that the real surprise is that literature does not more often evince such a combination of grave and gay: contrasts are important, 'since each ought naturally to be supposed to intensify each'. But when he goes on to discuss his own age, it becomes apparent that the 'wit' he admires is not a direct relation of the 'wit' he had eight years earlier found so alarming:

> The wits reigning among us, the Dickenses, Jerrolds, and Thackerays, are remarkable for their combination of grave and gay, for

the vein of tenderness which forms so beautiful an undercurrent to
their satire; and for that love of the general good, and that freedom
from personality for its own sake, which has exalted the character
of satire itself, and shown how it can be rendered a true instrument
of reformation.

The savageries of satire have been almost entirely eliminated. This
passage is particularly instructive in that we can see how Hunt is
moulding his contemporaries to his own expectations. His complacent view of Victorian satire is compensated for, at least in part,
when he castigates the oppressive pomposity and gravity of his fellow
Victorians; but his championing of 'vivacity' does not extend to
poetry, and so he condemns Wordsworth's *Peter Bell* for 'affecting a
vivacity that leads him to expose himself'.[36] It is interesting that what
Wordsworth might well have thought of as evasion or playfulness, is
seen by Hunt as exposure. A similar conflict between theory and
practice occurs in his remarks on Byron, whose poetry is one 'not of
imagination but of passion and humour'. *Don Juan*, however, whilst
seeming to conform to the prescriptive mixture of grave and gay,
goes too far:

> If *Don Juan* is pernicious in anything, it is in that extreme mixture
> now and then of the piteous and the ludicrous, which tends to put
> some of our best feelings out of countenance.[37]

This, of course, is precisely Byron's intention: Leigh Hunt's advocacy
of the combination of grave and gay is shown up, sadly, as a safety
valve against disruption. His 'Effusion upon Cream' says it all:

> In English poetry, as in English prose, there is plenty of wit, plenty
> of humour, plenty to make you laugh, after a fashion; but the
> fashion is rarely of a sort to make you happy — that is to say, not
> thoroughly so, not thoroughly contented either with yourself or
> with the writer. English animal spirits, for the most part, are too apt
> to turn sour, or run into satire.[38]

2 Laughing Songs: Blake and Wordsworth

I

In *English Bards and Scotch Reviewers* (1809) Byron turned the tables on Wordsworth, and equated the bard, in 'The Idiot Boy', with the hero of the story; Wordsworth in turn pronounced Byron 'somewhat cracked'.[1] Most of the major Romantic writers laid themselves open to similar charges of folly or lunacy. Blake is the prime example, because he seemed so totally incomprehensible to most of his contemporaries; his madness seemed so overwhelmingly evident both in his life and in his work. B. H. Malkin's description of him in 1806 as an 'engraver who might do tolerably well, if he was not mad' set the tone for much of the contemporary reception.[2] If looking through these heated, often outraged, reactions reminds us of the candour and obtuseness of the literary world in the early nineteenth century, it also serves to bring home to us the nature of the issues involved. The established world of order, of decorum, of accepted values, was being threatened; and when the connection between a man's art and his character was increasingly stressed, the threat was to morality and therefore even more alarming. Small wonder that attacks were as often as not focused on a writer's character. The *Antijacobin Review* in 1808 was all for locking Blake away: 'Whatever license we may allow him as a painter, to tolerate him as a poet would be insufferable'.[3] The cry of horror, 'This will never do!' which had greeted Wordsworth's *Excursion* in 1814, was echoed in 1821 when Blake produced some wood-engravings for an edition of Virgil.[4] Wordsworth and Blake seem to have presented similar problems to their contemporaries, and there are points of contact in their early work to emphasise this fact. Just as Wordsworth was, in 'The Idiot Boy', to make play with the very notion of the Romantic ballad as epitomised in Bürger's *Lenore*, so Blake, with his 1796 frontispiece to an English version of the Bürger poem, earned the scorn of the *Analytical Review*, who pronounced it, as indeed many, in so many words, pronounced Wordsworth's poem, 'ludicrous, instead of terrific'.[5] In their different ways, both poets were challenging accepted orthodoxies; in both Blake's *Songs of Innocence and of Experience*, and Wordsworth's *Lyrical Ballads*, the challenge involves the use of humour. It seems to me that the problems these poems bring us up against are indicative of the way we find ourselves having to respond to much nineteenth-century poetry.

By inventing a new process of illuminated printing, Blake inevitably disabuses us of the neat classifications we like to hide behind. It is no longer possible to consider merely the words of the *Songs*, isolated from their context both within a collection, and in terms of words and images reflecting and commenting on each other: the same is true of the longer, so-called prophetic, works. *America* and *Europe* especially demand a response both visual and verbal. Quite often, the images on the plates act as grim, sardonic rebuttals of the words they apparently attend, unsettling because they are no less powerful than those words, no less sharply etched. With such powerful primary tools at his command, Blake revels in the oppositions they invite, in the ironies of such clashes; his work bursts with passion, with anger and intensity. His vision is savage and satirical, quixotic and unpredictable. The creation of a mythology is directed to a particular end, and for all its complexities and contradictions, it derives its force and conviction from that pungent belief in himself as artist, and from his awareness of the absurdities of the world that man has made for himself. As most readers of Blake have found, though, his passions and convictions carry him into turbulent waters, his private obsessions fail to make the leap back across the chasm of the imagination that he is exploring. We end up, sooner or later, with work that seems remote and unyielding, the product of a mind that thought it had better things to do than bother about readers (a fair point, when the laborious printing process precluded a large following).

The relationship between writer and reader underwent a number of crucial shifts at the end of the eighteenth century. But the Romantic artist liked to cling on, whatever he might be asserting elsewhere, to the notion of himself as someone different, someone inspired, bardic. For Blake, there was sufficient literary sanction for this in the poetry of Gray, Collins, Edward Young (many of whose works he illustrated) for him to feel confident in donning their singing robes; the Biblical and hermeneutic traditions he was steeped in merely reinforced the confident tone. For all their obtuseness, contemporary critics, whether of his writing or his engraving, could recognise sublimity when they saw it. But Blake would not oblige even here: Bulwer-Lytton unwittingly put his finger on Blake's inherent difficulty when he referred, in 1830, to the illustrations to Young's *Night Thoughts* as 'so grotesque, so sublime'.[6] Hazlitt is reported by Crabb Robinson to have made the same point rather better, but no less misguidedly: 'he has no sense of the ludicrous and as to a God a worm crawling in a privy is as worthy an object as any other, all being to him indifferent . . . he attempts impossibles'.[7] It is precisely this fine dividing line between the sublime and the grotesque, between the serious and the ludicrous, that plays such a large part in the work of Blake and Wordsworth, indeed of most of the major Romantic writers – and also, in our responses to them. Recognition of where that line comes is, of course, hard to sustain. Many of Blake's protestations in his letters, especially about his paintings, have all the earnest bombast of the divine prophet having to cope with ignorant fools. Wordsworth can often be found taking himself and his art so seriously that it is hard to see how the façade will hold. Hazlitt was right – a 'sense of the ludicrous' is necessary; but if a writer is to 'attempt impossibles' that sense has sometimes to be kept on a tight rein.

The best answer to Hazlitt, in Blake's case, is to quote the following lines, sharp reminders of the earlier scatological tradition that stretched back to the Restoration:

> When Klopstock England defied
> Uprose William Blake in his pride;
> For old Nobodaddy aloft
> Farted & Belch'd & cough'd;
> Then swore a great oath that made heaven quake
> And call'd aloud to English Blake.
> Blake was giving his body ease
> At Lambeth beneath the poplar trees.
> From his seat then started he,
> And turned him round three times three.
> The Moon at that sight blush'd scarlet red,
> The stars threw down their cups & fled,
> And all the devils that were in hell
> Answer'd with a ninefold yell.
> Klopstock felt the intripled turn,
> And all his bowels began to churn,

And his bowels turned round three times three,
And lock'd in his soul with a ninefold key,
That from his body it ne'er could be parted
Till to the last trump it was farted.
Then again old Nobodaddy swore
He ne'er had seen such a thing before,
Since Noah was shut in the ark,
Since Eve first chose her hellfire spark,
Since 'twas the fashion to go naked,
Since the old anything was created,
And so feeling, he beg'd me to turn again
And ease poor Klopstock's ninefold pain.
If Blake could do this when he rose up from a shite;
What might he not do if he sat down to write?

Not great poetry, but full of relish in invective, in the native traditions of coarseness, in the vernacular that recognises no prim distinction between body and spirit. It is a poem very much thrown off, a defiant *graffito*: it is not a poem Wordsworth would have written. Here we see Blake's affinity with the strong line of the eighteenth-century cartoon – rude, abusive, direct; we see, too, his affinity with Swift, with Rabelais. Hazard Adams has remarked that 'in both theory and practice Wordsworth is the original and Blake the traditionalist'.[8] That too easy opposition will not stand as more than a partial truth; but it is a useful corrective, especially when set alongside another of Adams' observations that 'in one sense, at least, Blake wrote poems that the reader himself creates'.[9] For a poet ostensibly proud and determined and prophetic this is a curious development. It is certainly what happens in many of the *Songs*, in which Blake almost seems to be withholding essential information: that languorous pride will not allow him to spell things out. To read the *Songs of Innocence and of Experience* is a perplexing process, because of the constant shifts within the structure: it transpires that the very progression of the work (if we can think of it in such stable terms) is entirely provisional. Various songs move from *Innocence* to *Experience* and back again, the order of songs is altered. On top of this, the transparency of so many of the songs, their simplicity, requires support from Blake's other poems, which seem only too ready to give it. Hence the endless explications of apparently simple poems. By leaving so much out of his lyric poetry, Blake invites the reader to extrapolate as best he can; the engravings act as insurance against any easy reductionism. Just as in the 'prophetic' works the obscurity of reference and range baffles the reader not into submission but into an occasionally damaging separateness from the poetry, so in these lyrics the unique combination of directness and evasion can leave the reader suspended, taunted. There is an important sense in which Blake 'in his pride' enjoys this whole process. His is ultimately a teasing art, disturbing in its exploitation of the reader's need to be satisfied.

We just have to refer the image in 'The Tyger' of the stars throwing down their spears to the image in the Klopstock poem ('The stars threw down their cups & fled') to realise that Blake's sense of the ludicrous is acute, and throws into confusion any neat attempts to sew up his serious poems for him. 'The Tyger' has been particularly prone to this sort of critical reading, perhaps because it is so tantalising. Readers have wanted to define it, when what it calls for is the openness of response advocated by Anne Mellor, when she refers to 'Energy' as the 'open form' (as opposed to the closed form of *Innocence*).[10] The essential point about the poem is that it is a series of questions. The illustration emphasises this – a wide-eyed, rather docile-looking animal at the foot of the page, slightly different from copy to copy, but never a ferocious beast. Excuses have been offered for the disparity between text and image, but none of them convinces: the fact is that the meek tiger, standing on all fours like a rather sad cat waiting for his supper, teases us, as does the naked tree with its withered branches (hardly forest-like), and the hint of a human face peeping through at the top. David Erdman's meticulous work on *The Illuminated Blake* shows how obsessively Blake fills in every part of the plate, constantly surprising us with his fecund invention. Each curlicue of script, each flourish of a letter or a word, is transmogrified into something else. This is art in which we get no outside help, and we cannot appeal, by any means always, to internal consistency.

This last point is borne out by the history of some of the Songs. The *Songs of Innocence* have always seemed to me much harder to grasp, to accept, than the *Songs of Experience*: they require, in one obvious sense, less explication; but they make more strenuous demands on the credulity of the reader. The context, as Robert Gleckner has suggested rather differently, is crucial;[11] but when that context is itself shifting and indefinable the problems increase. Three poems that find their way into *Innocence* first appear in a strange unfinished work (unpublished in Blake's lifetime), usually given the title *An Island in the Moon*. Although it can be dated, roughly 1787, mystery surrounds the origins and intentions of this extravaganza. Clearly some particular people are being mocked – perhaps a group of scientists – but behind the piece there seems to lie at least tacit acknowledgement of the sort of entertainment popular at the Haymarket; in other words, Blake's ear has caught the intonations of music-hall farce.[12] Fortunately there is no need here to be dogmatic about the work's hazy origins. It is not surprising, really, that few critics have mentioned it. Northrop Frye calls it 'a satire on cultural dilettantism';[13] David Erdman, in the most perceptive discussion I know of the piece, indicates that it is more than this: 'Quid the Cynic . . . makes game of everyone's ambitions, including his own, and mingles laughter at the pursuers of the main chance with laughter at the pursuers of art.'[14] Blake is challenging the bases of artistic endeavour, attacking ambition that is inseparable from envy and egotism (Blake had earlier written of Envy: 'her poisonous breath breeds satire – from which none are free . . . 'tis Envy that inspires my song'). This is art of the absurd, curiously suspended between the obvious Swiftian heritage and later Dickensian comedy with its eye for the crucial detail:

In the Moon is a certain Island near by a mighty continent, which small island seems to have some affinity to England, and, what is more extraordinary, the people are so much alike, and their language so much the same, that you would think you was among your friends. In this Island dwells three Philosophers – Suction the Epicurean, Quid the Cynic, and Sipsop the Pythagorean. I call them by the names of those sects, tho' the sects are not ever mention'd there, as being quite out of date; however, the things still remain, and the vanities are the same. The three Philosophers sat together thinking of nothing. In comes Etruscan Column the Antiquarian, and after an abundance of Enquiries to no purpose, sat himself down and described something that nobody listen'd to. So they were employ'd when Mrs Gimblet came in. The corners of her mouth seem'd – I don't know how, but very odd, as if she hoped you had not an ill opinion of her, – to be sure, we are all poor creatures! Well she seated [herself] and seem'd to listen with great attention while the Antiquarian seem'd to be talking of virtuous cats. But it was not so; she was thinking of the shape of her eyes and mouth, and he was thinking of his eternal fame. The three Philosophers at this time were each endeavouring to conceal his laughter (not at them but) at his own imagination.

Inconsequential conversation takes up the bulk of the piece, which is divided, erratically, into chapters; characters with idiotic names (Tilly Lally, Mrs Gittipin, Mrs Nannicantipot, Mrs Sistagatist, Gibble Gabble) come and go aimlessly, part of the general drift, the flotsam and jetsam of a topsyturvy world. To pass the time, people offer to sing songs:

> 'The trumpeter shit in his hat,' said the Epicurean.
> ' – and clapt it on his head' said the Pythagorean.
> 'I'll begin again,' said the Cynic.

Beginning again is, like Michael Finnegan, what *An Island in the Moon* is constantly doing, as though in anticipation of Byron's persistent question 'And then?' in *Don Juan*; people talk to fill in the interminable interstices of living. Aradobo is implored to 'say something', and so he launches out, like some suddenly unleashed Lucky:

> In the first place I think, I think in the first place that Chatterton was clever at Fissie Follogy, Pistinology, Aridology, Arography, Transmography, Phizography, Hogamy, Hatomy, and hall that, but, in the first place, he eat every little, wickly – that is, he slept very little, which he brought into a consumption; and what was that he took? Fissic or somethink, – and so died!

Song begins to oust conversation as pastime; the scatological vein is well to the fore. Neither the 'Roman anus' of Scipio Africanus nor Hamlet's soliloquy on life and death is sacred: everything is mocked. (That the Hamlet reference is so irreverently woven into the fabric of the piece is an important indication of the way literature might be going.) The tone suddenly changes, when Mrs Gittipin asks for a song from Mr Obtuse Angle. The incongruity of his song in this context is extraordinary – and the company's response is fifteen minutes total silence:

Upon a holy thursday, their innocent faces clean,
The children walking two & two in grey & blue & green,
Grey headed beadles walk'd before with wands as white as snow,
Till into the high dome of Paul's they like thames' waters flow.

O what a multitude they seem'd, these flowers of London town!

Seated in companies, they sit with radiance all their own.
The hum of multitudes were there, but multitudes of lambs,
Thousands of little girls & boys raising their innocent hands.

Then like a mighty wind they raise to heav'n the voice of song,
Or like harmonious thunderings the seats of heav'n among.
Beneath them sit the rev'rend men, the guardians of the poor;
Then cherish pity lest you drive an angel from your door.

After the stunned silence, Mrs Nannicantipot sings what is later to
become the 'Nurse's Song' in *Innocence*, and Quid follows this with 'A
Little Boy Lost', which also reduces everyone to silence, until Tilly
Lally sings a nonsense rhyme about a cricket match, with the ball
getting covered in dog's droppings.

   An Island in the Moon is incomplete, and stops when Blake seems to
have had enough. Clearly not too much should be made of it. But the
presence of these songs, which later appear in *Innocence*, in this
outlandish and bewildering context is a fact of some importance. No
explanatory commentary is going to elucidate the juxtaposition of
such disparate elements. The basic seriousness of these songs ('The
Lawgiver all the while sat delighted to see them in such a serious
humour') stands out so starkly against the prevailing tone of absurdity
that they acquire a strange resonance which Blake deliberately leaves
hanging in the air. They are disruptive, dissonant notes in a score that
is otherwise at least fairly consistently ribald, raucous and irrespon-
sible. But characteristic of the piece as a whole, and of the songs
within it, is the general lack of knowledge we have as to an
appropriate response. We are subjected to a process of total
disorientation. This is a technique Blake later tones down, but never
entirely discards, as other poems – such as 'The Tyger' – indicate.
Irreverent humour can frame beautiful lyric utterances, simultaneously authenticating and questioning that very lyricism.

   Bernard Blackstone has suggested that *An Island in the Moon*
provides Blake with 'a means by which he made plain to himself and
to us his realisation of the immensely divided character of his own
time', and that it is, to that extent, 'an extended epigram'.[15] When we
come to read Byron, we might well be reminded of this possibility:
we are witnessing a variety of moods and modes that is bewildering,
that seems to reflect certainly some basic need, whether it be
connected with the age, or the poet's own psychology. When the
poet is driven so much in on himself, on his own resources, he is in a

sense much more vulnerable. This in turn makes the reader vulnerable: the one's defences become the other's defencelessness. The claims of the poet's own individuality, and of his age, are often in conflict. It is certainly interesting to read a later nineteenth-century comment (1839) in which *Innocence* is approved, for there Blake 'transcended Self, and escaped from the Isolation which Self involves', so that the poems 'belong to the ERA as well as to the Author'.[16] This is a recurrent problem. Wordsworth faces it, both in *The Prelude* and in *Lyrical Ballads*. Like Blake, he too finds himself challenging orthodoxies, and using varieties of humour to do so.

II

Several recent critics have pointed out that Wordsworth not only had a sense of humour, but was prepared to exploit it in his poetry. As Stephen Parrish has indicated, Wordsworth wrote a number of poems in the light, ballad fashion popularised in the eighteenth century, at least in Wordsworth's mind, by Shenstone and, more importantly, Burns; Jared Curtis has written well on the lightness of touch characteristic of several lyric poems of 1802. Most recently and most magisterially Mary Jacobus has written about the *Lyrical Ballads* and their relationships with, and departures from, tradition; in the course of her study, she examines the role of humour in a number of poems, in particular 'The Idiot Boy' and *Peter Bell*.[17] All I can do here is to touch on some of the areas that seem to me of special interest in connection with any investigation of the uses of humour in poetry.

Most of the poems mentioned by Stephen Parrish present no real problems, since they slot fairly easily into a particular genre of light, domestic, burlesque ballad: they make few claims for themselves, few claims on their readers, other than those of warmth and sympathy (Wordsworth, for the most part, carefully skirts the cutting edge of satire). But a handful of poems has always caused difficulty. When Coleridge came, in *Biographia Literaria*, to write about the *Lyrical Ballads*, their origins and reception, he was especially annoyed at the way in which critics had seized on these few poems, and used them as sticks with which to beat Wordsworth's other work:

> . . . that a downright simpleness, under the affectation of sim-
> plicity, prosaic words in feeble metre, silly thoughts and childish
> phrases and a preference of mean, degrading, or at best trivial

associations and characters, should succeed in forming a school of imitators, a company of almost *religious* admirers . . . and that this bare and bald *counterfeit* of poetry, which is characterized as *below* criticism, should for nearly twenty years have well-nigh *engrossed* criticism, as the main, if not the only, *butt*, of review, magazine, pamphlet, poem and paragraph:— this is indeed a matter of wonder!

(Chapter IV)

Coleridge is loading the dice here. It is all very well for him to scorn (as he does in an interesting footnote) the parodist and the imitator; what he fails to do is to account adequately for the need to parody and imitate. Elsewhere, though, in his listing of the faults in Wordsworth's poetry, he comes closer to the real point at issue, when he complains of the 'INCONSTANCY of the *style*'. Coleridge is really talking about decorum, about the need for a writer to prepare his readers for shifts in tone and stance:

There is something unpleasant in the being thus obliged to alternate states of feeling so dissimilar, and this too in a species of writing, the pleasure from which is in part derived from the preparation and previous expectation of the reader.

(Chapter XXII)

There is clearly a connection between this 'incongruity' (Coleridge uses the word) and the 'matter of factness' that he goes on to complain of as the second major defect in Wordsworth's poetry, and it is a connection that Wordsworth would have regarded as crucial. His Preface to the *Lyrical Ballads*, his notes to particular poems, make clear his intense concern for things as they are, even if this necessitates incongruity. The usual constraints of classical decorum will be swept aside if they interfere with Wordsworth's idiosyncratic view of the world. It is when this happens that the parodist picks up his pen (completely undaunted by Wordsworth's anticipatory scoffing of parody in the Preface — he realised what he was exposing himself to): the glut of imitations of many of the *Lyrical Ballads*, and of *Peter Bell* when it appeared in 1819, announced the establishment's (and the wits') response to the threat Wordsworth had posed to accepted criteria. What Hazlitt said about Wordsworth's Muse was right:

It proceeds on a principle of equality, and strives to reduce all things to the same standard. It is distinguished by a proud humility. It relies upon its own resources, and disdains external show and relief. It takes the commonest events and objects, as a test to prove that nature is always interesting from its inherent truth and beauty, without any of the ornaments of dress or pomp of circumstance to set it off. Hence the unaccountable mixture of seeming simplicity and real abstruseness in the *Lyrical Ballads*. Fools have laughed at, wise men scarcely understand them.[18]

Hazlitt sees Wordsworth's genius as 'a pure emanation of the Spirit of the Age . . . (his poetry is) one of the innovations of the time'.

This twist to Hazlitt's thesis is unusual, and perhaps hard to sustain with total conviction: in any case, he is interested as much in the political implications of Wordsworth's poetry as in the aesthetic. In fact, he sees an important connection between the two. But he is also anticipating the reactions of later critics to Byron, when they were to comment on the appositeness of *Don Juan* to its age. One of the corollaries of this view, of course, is that the age does not necessarily appreciate its own emanation. As Hazlitt says:

It may be considered as characteristic of our poet's writings, that they either make no impression on the mind at all, seem mere *nonsense-verses*, or that they leave a mark behind them that never wears out. . . . To one class of readers he appears sublime, to another (and we fear the largest) ridiculous.[19]

Here Hazlitt has in mind *The Excursion*, which he likens to a 'splendid banquet in the company of clowns, and with nothing but successive courses of apple–dumplings served up';[20] but what he says is in large measure true of the way so many responded to the *Lyrical Ballads*.

As with his comments on Blake, Hazlitt is quick to make revealing connections between the poetry and the man who writes it. He captures Wordsworth's paradoxical nature:

. . . the air somewhat stately and Quixotic. He reminds me of some of Holbein's heads, grave, saturnine, with a slight indication of sly humour, kept under by the manners of the age or by the pretensions of the person. He has a peculiar sweetness in his smile, and great depth and manliness and a rugged harmony, in the tones of his voice. His manner of reading his own poetry is particularly imposing. . . . His language may not be intelligible but his manner is not to be mistaken. It is clear that he is either mad or inspired . . .[21]

These inherent contradictions, which refuse to allow any settled impression to emerge, are emphasised when Hazlitt recalls his first meeting with Wordsworth. Again he describes him as 'Don-Quixote-like'.

> He was quaintly dressed (according to the *costume* of that unconstrained period) in a brown fustian jacket and striped pantaloons. There was something of a roll, a lounge in his gait, not unlike his own Peter Bell.[22]

The fiery eye was offset by 'a convulsive inclination to laughter about the mouth, a good deal at variance with the solemn, stately expression of the rest of his face . . .'. The next day they all went over to Alfoxden, where Wordsworth recited *Peter Bell* to the assembled throng. Hazlitt comments:

> There is a *chaunt* in the recitation both of Coleridge and Wordsworth, which acts as a spell upon the hearer, and disarms the judgment. Perhaps they have deceived themselves by making habitual use of this ambiguous accompaniment.

Hazlitt's astuteness is nice, his qualifications reticent yet pointed: he sees how the ambiguity of contemporary response could be a reflection of the poetry's inherent ambiguity, one that, far from being the central point of a particular poem, has acted as a diversionary tactic, taking the poet away from what mattered. Obviously – and Hazlitt realises the implications without pursuing them – an essentially oral poetry (often composed out loud on a walk) loses its distinctive flavour once it is solidified in print, once the speaking voice with its 'mixture of clear gushing accents . . . a deep, gutteral intonation, and a strong tincture of the northern *burr*, like the crust on wine', becomes mute print. Translated into words on a page the verse is both fixed there, baldly and bluntly, but also disconcertingly set loose: its moorings in an oral tradition no longer serve much function. As with Blake's songs and prophecies, so with these Wordsworthian ballads, the singer is important, we need his help: without it, we are likely to lose our bearings.

But the resulting ruffled composure is quite often what Wordsworth is aiming at. He is attacking on several fronts simultaneously: the historical, the aesthetic, the moral. In this he is much less open than Blake, he is inviting a more defined, less equivocal response. Wordsworth, after all, did say 'I wish to be considered as a teacher, or as nothing.' 'Each of' the *Lyrical Ballads* 'has a worthy purpose'. This rather chilling didacticism is less disarming when seen in practice but more disarming, too, in that the teaching is pervasive and inescapable. Mary Jacobus puts the point well in a comparison between *Peter Bell* and 'The Ancient Mariner': '*Peter Bell* affirms normality; its laws are stable and its values unambiguous. One poem ['The Ancient Mariner'] disturbs – the other reassures.'[23] But that normality, that lack of ambiguity, is asserted in a way that defies categorisation: the values emerge from one of the most curious poems in the English language. What is true of *Peter Bell* is true, to a lesser extent, of poems such as 'Simon Lee', 'The Idiot Boy', 'The Thorn', all of them poems Wordsworth himself was pleased with, all of them controversial, open to ridicule.

'Goody Blake and Harry Gill' is an instructive poem to begin with, showing, as Mary Jacobus has it, an 'unexpected convergence of English didacticism and German sensationalism.'[24] The German element she relates to Bürger's rather grotesquely ornate ballads which had made such a stir when they began to appear in English translations towards the end of the eighteenth century. The moral intention is clearly there in Wordworth's poem. 'A True Story' announces the sub-title, with all the implications of such a fact; the poem ends with an address to country readers, 'Now think, ye farmers all, I pray/Of Goody Blake and Harry Gill!' But it is a peculiarly searching form of morality, based on an initial question which draws us into the story at a late stage, makes us want to know about Harry Gill, but allows us to keep our distance sufficiently to observe the comedy at his expense – to put it another way, the comedy keeps the distance for us. It is, after all, hard to recite these lines in a neutral tone:

> Oh what's the matter? what's the matter?
> What is't that ails young Harry Gill?
> That evermore his teeth they chatter,
> Chatter, chatter, chatter still!
> Of waistcoats Harry has no lack,
> Good duffle grey, and flannel fine;

He has a blanket on his back,
And coats enough to smother nine.

In March, December, and in July,
'Tis all the same with Harry Gill;
The neighbours tell, and tell you truly,
His teeth they chatter, chatter still.
At night, at morning, and at noon,
'Tis all the same with Harry Gill;
Beneath the sun, beneath the moon,
His teeth they chatter, chatter still!

We rise to this irresistible challenge, but are thrown off the scent by a long account not of Harry (dismissed with perfunctory, archetypal qualities) but of the old Goody Blake, living alone in poverty and hardship, relying for warmth on whatever wood she can gather (coal does not get this far, Wordsworth points out in one version). The climax of the poem consists of the confrontation of these two, when Harry leaps out on the trespassing Goody with a triumphant shout, 'I've caught you then at last!' The circumstantial detail that has led so carefully up to this point gives way to the emblematic scene of Goody's curse on her captor:

She prayed, her withered hand uprearing,
While Harry held her by the arm —
'God! who art never out of hearing,
O may he never more be warm!'
The cold, cold moon above her head,
Thus on her knees did Goody pray;
Young Harry heard what she had said:
And icy cold he turned away.

Humour, like the eager warmth from Harry's excited face, drains away from the poem at this central moment; when we return to Harry's teeth, the full grotesqueness of his predicament is striking. The moral judgement is harsh; and yet Wordsworth salvages sympathy for this wretched man with his echo of Lear's fool, and that in turn reminds us of the world of mixed modes that the poem so dauntlessly occupies. It is a challenging poem, becoming darker as we read through it: all seasons merge into one perpetual winter, sun and moon are interchangeable (as they are to be in 'The Idiot Boy'). What struck us initially as quaint and perplexing is revealed as frightening and logical. We are left to feel rather foolish for having found those chattering teeth at all funny:

> 'Twas all in vain, a useless matter,
> And blankets were about him pinned;
> Yet still his jaws and teeth they clatter,
> Like a loose casement in the wind.
> And Harry's flesh it fell away;
> And all who see him say, 'tis plain,
> That, live as long as live he may,
> He never will be warm again.
>
> No word to any man he utters,
> A-bed or up, to young or old,
> But ever to himself he mutters,
> 'Poor Harry Gill is very cold.'
> A-bed or up, by night or day;
> His teeth they chatter, chatter still.
> Now think, ye farmers all, I pray
> Of Goody Blake and Harry Gill!

This poem seems to me a very good instance of what R. F. Storch has said about these ballads, that 'they mock the reader at the very moment that they show originality of insight into the human condition.'[25]

In 'Simon Lee' Wordsworth advances further into the no-man's-land that he wishes to make his own, that twilight territory where apparent confusion leads to the final clarity he values. Again he is concerned with extremes, with old age and its attendant horrors: it is as though the challenge of this theme necessitates the stylistic, emotional extremes of a poem that begins so jauntily and ends with such a haunting epigram on the nature of suffering, age and gratitude. As with 'Goody Blake', 'Simon Lee' works towards that conclusion, whose complexity is rolled up into the inscrutable ball of those last four lines, an oblique undermining of the social philosophy so many readers might have expected:

> — I've heard of hearts unkind, kind deeds
> With coldness still returning;
> Alas! the gratitude of men
> Has oftener left me mourning.

But by this stage in the poem, no one any longer knows what to expect: Wordsworth has already announced that he has led us up the garden path:

> My gentle reader, I perceive
> How patiently you've waited,
> And I'm afraid that you expect
> Some tale will be related.

Our expectations are to be confounded:

> It is no tale; but, should you think,
> Perhaps a tale you'll make it.

It is interesting that in later versions of the poem Wordsworth retreats from the grotesqueness of the opening; even if he does not go as far back as the sentimentality of Robert Southey, he softens the edges, as in this Miltonic echo which points the contrast between past and present:

> But, the heavy change! — bereft
> Of health, strength, friends, and kindred, see!
> Old Simon to the world is left
> In liveried poverty.

Wordsworth had, in 1798, mingled past and present much more cavalierly, and expanded on that initial note of inconsequential jollity, which appears to announce that we're in for something (it's not clear what) undemanding:

> In the sweet shire of Cardigan,
> Not far from pleasant Ivor Hall,
> An old man dwells, a little man,
> I've heard he once was tall.
> Of years he has upon his back,
> No doubt, a burthen weighty;
> He says he is threescore and ten,
> But others say he's eighty.
>
> A long blue livery-coat has he,
> That's fair behind, and fair before;

> Yet meet him where you will, you see
> At once that he is poor.
> Full five-and-twenty years he lived
> A running huntsman merry;
> And though he has but one eye left
> His cheek is like a cherry.

In 1805, this is contracted:

> In the sweet shire of Cardigan,
> Not far from pleasant Ivor-Hall,
> An old man dwells, a little man, –
> 'Tis said he once was tall.
> Full five and thirty years he lived
> A running huntsman merry;
> And still the centre of his cheek
> Is red as a ripe cherry.

The effect of the first version especially, in all its expansiveness, is different from that of 'Goody Blake': it seems to be teasing us more, underlining absurdities, giving us several simultaneous perspectives – Simon's, the community's, the poet's. And yet, by the end of the poem, we have come to feel we know Simon Lee: it is as though his tears of gratitude can only be understood through this filter of humour with which the poem begins. The comic is invoked because it is implicit in the situation: Wordsworth is absolutely determined that we do not fall into the sentimentalist trap either of the aesthetes who still think of the conventional pastoral as a mode with a future, or of the *laissez-faire* do-gooders. Just how well he succeeded was borne out at the time by Southey's rather desperate efforts at 'rewriting' these poems, to lend them the necessary emotional and moral coherence any right-thinking person would assume they lacked.[26] It is rather sad to see Wordsworth's response to Southey's impudent tinkering in the revised version: but similar sail-trimming occurs in 'The Thorn', where Wordsworth, after fifteen years, gives in to public pressure, and alters the famous couplet:

> I've measured it from side to side,
> 'Tis three feet long and two feet wide –

to something innocuous and more overtly 'poetical'.[27] And 'The

Thorn' is important in this discussion because it shows something of Wordsworth's uneasiness: he uses a dramatic 'character' to tell the story, and this can explain some of the obtuse comicalness of the verse; but the basic tenor is serious, measured, probing. If there is bafflement, it is confronted and accepted — not mocked, or glanced at with wry amusement.

'The Idiot Boy' is the most extended of these poems, apart from *Peter Bell*. Again, the account by Mary Jacobus is indispensable for what she tells us about Wordsworth's playing with convention, about his deliberate burlesque at Bürger's expense; so that an ostensibly simple ballad — and enjoyable as such — turns out to be a very literary, sophisticated joke. But it reaches far beyond the light fantastic of, say, Cowper's 'John Gilpin', with which it is sometimes compared. Here again, the poem works towards that astonishing conclusion (which in fact provides the poem's starting point), the boy's report of his travels:

> 'The cocks did crow to-whoo, to-whoo
> And the sun did shine so cold!'
> — Thus answered Johnny in his glory
> And that was all his travel's story.

The greater length of this poem allows Wordsworth much greater variety, much more scope. We are in the world of burlesque, but also of mock-epic. But it is a mockery that works both ways, reducing the opening preparations, mock-Homerically, to flurry and fiddle-faddle, and yet elevating that same fuss and palaver to the level of true feeling. We are continually checked in this way: Johnny's final glory can only be fully understood in this light, whereby his crazy, topsyturvy vision comes out in response to the women's persistent questionings. His glory, like his story, is both triumphant and absurd. The 'glee' with which Wordsworth reportedly wrote this ballad is evident in practically every stanza — comic rhymes, mispronunciations, the situation itself — all contribute to the buoyant effect. But it is a deceptive buoyancy, necessary to counter any suggestion of tearful identification, too-easy sympathy from the reader, and yet not always a reliable guide to how we should respond. It is impossible not to find amusing those lines when Betty has raced to the doctor's, to get news of Johnny, only to discover he has not even got that far:

> This piteous news it so much shocked her,

> She quite forgot to send the Doctor,
> To comfort poor old Susan Gale.

This diverts attention from Betty's genuine anguish, whilst at the same time allowing it some room. But it is, equally, impossible not to find the reunion of mother and son not merely joyous, but also curiously saddening and moving amidst the joy:

> 'Oh, Johnny, never mind the Doctor;
> You've done your best, and that is all:'
> She took the reins, when this was said,
> And gently turned the Pony's head
> From the loud waterfall.
>
> By this the stars were almost gone,
> The moon was setting on the hill,
> So pale you scarcely looked at her:
> The little birds began to stir,
> Though yet their tongues grew still.

In these stanzas, Wordsworth's beautiful rhythmic modulations adjust the tone, reining in the verse, containing the happiness and the sorrow sufficiently to make it breathtakingly moving without being cloying. In any case, this trinity of Betty, Boy and Pony is rudely interrupted by the remarkably recovered Susan:

> And who is she, betimes abroad,
> That hobbles up the steep rough road?
> Who is it, but old Susan Gale?
>
> Long time lay Susan lost in thought;
> And many dreadful fears beset her,
> Both for the Messenger and Nurse;
> And as her mind grew worse and worse,
> Her body – it grew better.

And so the comic level is regained, and we are forcibly reminded of the point of the whole exercise, reminded of the narrative tricks Wordsworth has been playing on us. Susan is a bit-player, but a necessary part of the dramatic design. She, like Betty, cannot really understand what has been happening. That is why the conclusion is so remarkably weighted: the boy, in his triumph, in his 'wit' and 'glory', is isolated from them, a complete mystery, rather like the aged, destitute Matthew in 'The Fountain' (one of Wordsworth's most powerful poems), who has confronted his alienation from nature, the impossibility of comfort, and yet that confrontation releases his songs, so long locked up within him. But those songs are themselves ambiguous, witty, crazed, baffled:

> And, ere we came to Leonard's rock,
> He sang those witty rhymes
> About the crazy old church clock
> And the bewildered chimes.

Peter Bell belongs to that odd category of poems that accumulate mockery about themselves like shabby garments, so much so that John Hamilton Reynolds's parody beat the genuine article to the post in 1819. Reynolds's brilliant dissection of Wordsworthian mannerisms, and later the same year, Shelley's more personal attack, have earned attention at their original's expense. It is now extremely difficult to view the poem as it really is, to separate it from the layers of scoffing it actually invites; the tortuous history of its composition and delayed publication adds to the problems of response. It is just as important to register the fact that it is published after the consolidation of Wordsworth's reputation in 1814 with the publication of *The Excursion*, as it is to acknowledge that in origin it is intended as some sort of answer to 'The Ancient Mariner'. It points up some of the fundamental differences between Wordsworth and Coleridge as to what poetry could or should attempt, differences that emerge in Coleridge's critique, in the *Biographia Literaria* (1817), of Wordsworth's theory and practice. The high seriousness of Wordsworth's argument in the Preface to *Lyrical Ballads* requires the counterbalance of *Peter Bell*, a poem both humorous and yet intensely, highly serious in purpose. Manifestos, of course, have a tendency towards overstatement, and if the Preface needs qualifications and riders, then *Peter Bell* can be seen to be pushing a particular line of argument too far in the other direction. For all my sympathy with Wordsworth's intentions (and a whiff of the intentional fallacy cannot be avoided here), I think those intentions, and the self-consciousness that goes with them, get, to some extent, in the way of the poem.

The humour of *Peter Bell* is of a different kind from that

encountered in the other narrative ballads. It has a whimsical quality, a wish to make a virtue out of its own gracelessness, that is not always convincing. The Prologue announces the main concerns of the poem, and the problems we are faced with as readers: we are brought up, very forcibly, against the poet striking a particular, rather fey, attitude. We might call this playfulness, but that italicised *have* protests a bit too much:

> There's something in a flying horse,
> There's something in a huge balloon;
> But through the clouds I'll never float
> Until I have a little Boat,
> Shaped like the crescent-moon.
>
> And now I *have* a little Boat
> In shape a very crescent-moon:
> Fast through the clouds my Boat can sail,
> But if perchance your faith should fail,
> Look up – and you shall see me soon!
>
> The woods, my Friends, are round you roaring,
> Rocking and roaring like a sea;
> The noise of danger's in your ears,
> And ye have all a thousand fears
> Both for my little Boat and me!
>
> Meanwhile untroubled I admire
> The pointed horns of my canoe;
> And, did not pity touch my breast,
> To see how ye are all distrest,
> Till my ribs ached, I'd laugh at you!

The point of this artifice, this elaborate concern, is that the soaring realms of possibility, the flight (literally) of fancy, is not what the poet wants: he recognises that his place is on the earth he knows and loves, and it is to this earth that he returns, to 'tell the tale /Of Peter Bell the Potter'. Characteristically, he begins *in medias res*, so that the audience within the poem has to interrupt, to tell him to start at the beginning. But his beginning is a savage image of brutality, Wordsworth's version of the shooting of the albatross, a stark fact with all the directness and simplicity the ballad form gives it. And when the

Squire makes a point about common sense, about the decorum of story-telling, we are made very conscious of the poem's manipulative character:

> All by the moonlight riverside
> Groaned the poor Beast — alas! in vain;
> The staff was raised to loftier height,
> And the blows fell with heavier weight
> As Peter struck — and struck again.
>
> 'Hold' cried the Squire, 'against the rules
> Of common sense you're surely sinning;
> This leap is for us all too bold;
> Who Peter was, let that be told,
> And start from the beginning'.

Peter Bell is immune to the effects of nature: he is wild and hard. The poem explores nature's redemptive processes, even on someone so apparently lacking in common feelings: the ass he discovers in the woods is to be the means of this redemption, the ass on whom he vents his full fury, the ass who is indifferent to that fury. Wordsworth captures the absurdity of the central event, consciously echoing the repetitions of 'The Ancient Mariner':

> All, all is silent — rocks and woods,
> All still and silent — far and near!
> Only the Ass, with motion dull,
> Upon the pivot of his skull
> Turns round his long left ear.
>
> Thought Peter, What can mean all this?
> Some ugly witchcraft must be here!
> — Once more the Ass, with motion dull,
> Upon the pivot of his skull
> Turned round his long left ear.

This is evidently ridiculous; but Wordsworth does not leave it at that. The ass's effect on Peter is described in great detail; Peter falls in a trance; when he awakes, he is led by the ass to discover the ass's dead master, the corpse now four days in the river. From this point onwards the poem is one of conversion, couched in Methodistic, pious terms, undercut, nevertheless, by that unnervingly comic movement when the ass grins at Peter Bell, and he, in 'jocose defiance' grins back.

> Let them whose voice can stop the clouds,
> Whose cunning eye can see the wind,
> Tell to a curious world the cause
> Why, making here a sudden pause,
> The Ass turned round his head, and *grinned*.
>
> Appalling process! I have marked
> The like on heath, in lonely wood;
> And, verily, have seldom met
> A spectacle more hideous – yet
> It suited Peter's present mood.
>
> And, grinning in his turn, his teeth
> He in jocose defiance showed –
> When, to upset his spiteful mirth,
> A murmur pent within the earth,
> In the dead earth beneath the road
>
> Rolled audibly! . . .

Peter Bell, like 'The Idiot Boy', is a poem of pathos, whatever else we may say about it. The widow and the child suffer loss, with which they have to come to terms: their doing so is part of Peter's lesson. But the use of humour here seems to me less satisfactory, more consciously worked-in, the contrasts and oppositions not allowed to speak for themselves. Wordsworth overplays his hand, overdoes the arch playfulness of a narrator toying with reader and subject. The delay in publication might, amongst other things, reflect Wordsworth's uneasiness, as do some of the changes he makes to the original version. *Peter Bell* seems a very important and interesting example of the way in which humour plays a large part in Wordsworth's vision, and yet what a precarious balance he has to maintain between the humour and the pathos. As R. F. Storch has hinted, Wordsworth's attempt to 'write about the self in a detached way' links the poem with the hesitations and uncertainties that are central to the language and structure of 'Tintern Abbey' and *The Prelude*.[28]

Wordsworth moves away from the achievement of 'The Idiot Boy', 'Simon Lee', even the 'The Thorn'; we can see in *Peter Bell* the disadvantages of a mode too self-consciously humorous, however necessary that humour is to the central point he is making. That is Wordsworth's problem. He faces it in a different form in the first version of 'Michael', which was, surprisingly, to have been a rather rollicking ballad, as far removed as one can imagine from the sobriety of the finished blank verse poem.[29] It is as if, in mapping out the poem, he grasped the essential point that there were limits to what could be done with the 'pastoral ballad'. It is inconceivable that 'Michael' could have its overwhelming power if it had been cast in any other mould. Perhaps, in the end, there is something a bit too consciously 'experimental' about the ballads I have discussed: as I have suggested, our response is bound to be a literary one, not one based on the simple pieties being propounded, nor on the immediacy of the rustic world caught in verse. But the humour is there, we cannot baulk it: it is crucial to our understanding of Wordsworth's vision. As we shall see, *The Prelude*, too, finds uses for humour: as the poet and the narrator merge, as the voice telling the tale becomes of paramount importance, then the resort to humour of one kind or another takes another turn, and serves as camouflage or revelation. This process can be seen, embryonically, in 'Tintern Abbey', where occasionally the doubts and uncertainties are couched in language that, with its convoluted syntax, gives itself away. In *The Prelude* Wordsworth really has to face squarely the problem of concentration on the self, and on his era, and the interaction of the two. Someone who ends up taking himself as seriously as does Wordsworth finds that a sense of his own absurdity is an important part of that process. Just as the *Lyrical Ballads* — and Blake's *Songs* — represent various experiments with tradition, various departures from the expected in which humour is welcome and necessary as a controlling (and a liberating) factor, so when poets come to write about themselves, they are virtually creating a new form, which seems to call for a lively and sensitive awareness of humour and its possibilities.

3 The Accommodating Self: Cowper to Keats

Carlyle had, in dismissing Voltaire for his 'entire want of Earnestness', pointed to the dangers of ridicule (and therefore of wit), which was 'by nature selfish and morally trivial; it cherishes nothing but our own vanity'.[1] This of course is an echo of the Hobbesian view of laughter. (But the argument could be put the other way round – in other words, egotism was the prime target of ridicule.) Certainly Hazlitt's obsession with egotism is of importance to the general drift of the argument, as it reflects some of the rampant confusions of the time. The relationship between humour and the idea of the self is not examined in the nineteenth century in any systematic way, but it is clearly lurking behind much of the debate.

Hazlitt's ambivalent attitude towards Byron stems from his distrust of the 'flaunting pretensions of a modern rhapsodist'.[2] He can call him a genuine poet, an excellent satirist; and yet castigate him for his timidity, cowardice, lack of adventurousness, all of which derive from his being 'more solicitous to please himself than the public'.[3] Byron's is a mind

> preying upon itself . . . There is nothing less poetical than this sort of ideal absorption of all the interests of others, of the good and ills of life, in the ruling passion and moody abstraction of a single mind, as if it would make itself the centre of the universe, and there was nothing worth cherishing but its intellectual diseases. It is like a cancer, eating into the heart of poetry.[4]

Hazlitt cannot accept that one way out of this obvious dilemma is the one employed by Byron in *Don Juan*: in his eyes it is the prostitution of art, dandyism at its worst (the irony that Byron uses this word of himself in *Beppo* passes Hazlitt by). Hazlitt laments: 'it is as if the eagle were to build its eyry in a common sewer . . . (it is a poem) written about itself'.[5]

The denigration of Byron as 'the pampered egotist' (anticipated in *Don Juan*, XI, 2) is matched by Hazlitt's account of Wordsworth's *Excursion*: 'An intense intellectual egotism swallows up everything'.[6] This is similar to Keats's formulation of Wordsworth's prevailing characteristic, 'egotistical sublime'. It is that attempted combination of self and sublimity which is so problematical. Coleridge captures the contemporary dilemma to a nicety:

> With what anxiety every fashionable author avoids the word I! — now he transforms himself into a third person, — 'the present writer' — now multiplies himself and swelling into 'we' — and all this is the watchfulness of guilt. Conscious that this said I is perpetually intruding on his mind and that it monopolises his heart, he is prudishly solicitous that it may not escape from his lips.[7]

Coleridge had no use for such pussyfooting — egotism was for him an essential part of creativity: one of his notes runs, 'Poetry without egotism comparatively uninteresting'.[8] But few poets had the self-confidence to subscribe to such doctrine with consistency. Even Wordsworth, who could declare that the poem which was to become *The Prelude* was the result not of 'self-conceit' but of 'real humility', had to admit when he had got as far as the seventh book, 'it seems a frightful deal to say about one's self'.[9]

The claims of the self demanded a hearing, but not everyone could achieve Coleridge's paradoxically unselfconscious self-analysis. Byron puts his own dilemma well, and in doing so seems to speak for his age: 'To withdraw *myself* from *myself* (oh that cursed selfishness!) has ever been my sole, my entire, my sincere motive in scribbling at all . . .'[10] In his letters he is constantly checking a drift towards egotism, and can most successfully do this when he reminds himself that 'Nature stampt me in the Die of Indifference'.[11] Hazlitt's phrase 'the eloquence of indifference' is seen to have relevance not simply in theoretical terms, not simply in terms of Byron's work, but in terms of one of the major problems of late eighteenth- and early nineteenth-century poets. What Hazlitt called Byron's 'unaccommodating selfishness' can be given a new twist if we transpose the terms, and see poetry as an attempt precisely to accommodate the self. This can be seen as one of the main preoccupations of the first generation in particular of Romantic poets, but Keats, Shelley and Byron are really working in that same tradition, which stretches back to the mid-eighteenth century and beyond, as a consciousness of self begins to manifest itself in various ways not anticipated in the poetry of previous ages.

One of the fundamental problems that faced late eighteenth- and early nineteenth-century poets was a formal one: there was no longer any consensus as to what literature could achieve, or how it might achieve it. It is obviously wrongly simplistic to see the Romantic poets merely in terms of reaction to the previous generation, to accept, in other words, say, Keats's dismissal of the heroic couplet in 'Sleep and Poetry' as if it were more than a personal truth. Nonetheless, it is true that the shift in sensibility which distinguishes the literature of the turn of the century is reflected in a search for new forms, new ways of saying. We can talk of the Romantics' self-confidence, their assertive belief in their own vatic powers; but the confidence and buoyancy of the early eighteenth century has drastically altered. The poet as an individual rather than a merely representative figure (and voice) increases in importance, and precisely because of the added weight of the burden (however self-imposed it might be), there is greater pressure to find the distinctively personal form that will embody the vision, and bear the responsibility. The heroic couplet (to restrict the argument momentarily to one dominant form) had served its particular purposes well, in that it had provided an appropriate vehicle for the sentiments it reflected – so that Keats's scorn was misdirected. The couplet had allowed for an astonishing range, for a versatility denied by its detractors. With such a weapon to hand, Dr Johnson felt justified in calling into question the apparently sprawling ethos (it was essentially a moral issue) of the blank verse poem. If Milton was open to censure on such grounds, then James Thomson could expect short shrift.

What Johnson could not grasp was that blank verse had its own organic and rhythmic structure; that Milton's 'deep organ tones' were matched by the scale and scope even of *The Seasons*. If the eighteenth century, as is so often asserted, wanted to write its own epic poem and yet failed, by the end of the century the Miltonic influence was still strong. Oddly enough it served equally those who were prepared to take themselves seriously, those who were deliberately not taking themselves seriously, and those in between, who were not sure how they should regard themselves in the mirror held up by art. This was the great advantage of the Miltonic tradition, however bastardised it had become: it was a medium fit for kings and clowns (the eighteenth century was the great age of burlesque), fit, too, for emperors surprised to find themselves in new clothes.[12]

James Thomson, in *The Seasons*, displays all the arrogance of the determined poet, aware of the problems he faces, but sublimely confident in his own abilities. The question of appropriateness raises itself early on, in 'Spring':

> Behold yon breathing prospect bids the Muse
> Throw all her beauty forth. But who can paint
> Like Nature? Can imagination boast,
> Amid its gay creation, hues like hers?
> Or can it mix them with that matchless skill,
> And lose them in each other, as appears
> In every bud that blows? If fancy then
> Unequal fails beneath the pleasing task,
> Ah, what shall language do? ah, where find words
> Tinged with so many colours and whose power,
> To life approaching, may perfume my lays
> With that fine oil, those aromatic gales
> That inexhaustive flow continual round?

But these are questions directed not against himself so much as against art; and they are easily shrugged off, not on the terms they themselves suggest, but by an airy appeal that seems to satisfy Thomson.

> Yet, though successless, will the toil delight.
> Come then, ye virgins and ye youths, whose hearts
> Have felt the raptures of refining love;
> And thou, Amanda, come, pride of my song!
> Formed by the Graces, loveliness itself!

If there is any sense of incongruity about a poem devoted to the seasons of the year, Thomson will not be perturbed for long. If his God has 'with a master-hand' 'the great whole into perfection touched', then it is only proper that he should reflect such wholeness and perfection in his poem. The appeal to a benign deity will excuse any amount of clumsy literalness:

At thy command the vernal sun awakes
The torpid sap, detruded to the root
By wintry winds, that now in fluent dance
And lively fermentation mounting spreads
All this innumerous-coloured scene of things.

God's command sanctions all. The opening lines of 'Spring' keep reverting to the possibility that poetry does not normally embrace such topics, but that is poetry's failing. Thomson himself is not in doubt; nor does he leave his reader in any doubt about the nature of a poem that is essentially and specifically religious. The poem may intermittently acknowledge its own adventurousness, but its gait never falters.

After Thomson, the deluge. In the flood of verse on nature, God got lost: he might merit a mention at the end, but Commerce would do just as well. If readers felt that some things should best be left out of poetry, their inclusion was sanctioned by the grand epic form, jovially inverted and gently mocked. Gay's *Trivia*, Swift's poetic satires, had hit hard and below the belt, combining vernacular verve with the formal propriety of the couplet. What Dyer and Jago, Hurdis and West (and numerous others) were offering was more leisurely, more genial, deliberately embracing the unpoetical in the arms of a tradition that bestowed its own glow of well-being and warmth on to the unlikeliest of suppliants. John Dyer can, in *The Fleece*, describe the growth of industrialisation, confident that Virgilian echoes save him from absurdity:

Thus all is here in motion, all is life:
The creaking wain brings copious store of corn:
The grazier's sleeky kine obstructs the roads;
The neat-dressed housewives, for the festal board
Crowned with full baskets, in the field-way paths
Come tripping on; th' echoing hills repeat
The stroke of axe and hammer; scaffolds rise,
And growing edifices; heaps of stones,
Beneath the chisel, beauteous shapes assume
Of frieze and column . . .
                              Industry,
Which dignifies the artist, lifts the swain,
And the straw cottage to a palace turns,
Over the work presides. Such was the scene

> Of hurrying Carthage, when the Trojan chief
> First viewed her growing turrets. So appear
> The increasing walls of busy Manchester,
> Sheffield, and Birmingham, whose reddening fields
> Rise and enlarge their suburbs.

Dyer's confidence extends to the handling, in poetry, of the ills of
sheep. His sheer nerve might cause us to exclaim, but he always has
Virgil's *Georgics* as a wry form of support. What Dyer is doing is not
remarkable: he is a representative figure, and important because of
that.

> Th' infectious scab arising from extremes
> Of want or surfeit, is by water cured
> Of lime, or sodden stave-acre, or oil
> Dispersive of Norwegian tar, renowned
> By virtuous Berkeley, whose benevolence
> Explored its powers, and easy medicine thence
> Sought for the poor: ye poor, with grateful voice,
> Invoke eternal blessings on his head.

It is a short step from this to William Whitehead's 'I sing of sweepers',
and countless other poems of the same ilk. Sometimes the intentions
may be honourable and philanthropic, but it needs a fine discrimination to distinguish between amusing mock-heroics (the Restoration had shown the effectiveness of literary scoffing)[13] and a
savage indignation clothed in the colours of the system under attack.
The drift tends to be away from social protest towards the sense of
self-congratulatory cleverness that such things can get into poetry at
all. The style so consciously adopted has its inherent ambiguities,
which few poets seem prepared, or able, to grasp.

William Cowper is the first poet to exploit this stylistic ambiguity for
his more personal ends. *The Task*, published in 1785, is an important
historical landmark. Its Advertisement is instructive, for it looks
ahead to the 'streamy associations' of Coleridge whilst at the same
time keeping itself firmly rooted in a particular time and place, where
it is legitimate to write poems on such things as sofas:

A lady, fond of blank verse, demanded a poem of that kind from
the author, and gave him the SOFA for a subject. He obeyed; and,

having much leisure, connected another subject with it; and, pursuing the train of thought to which his situation and turn of mind led him, brought forth at length, instead of the trifle which he at first intended, a serious affair — a Volume!

There would be little point in stressing the arch coyness of this preamble, the mock solemnity of that phrase, 'a serious affair' — if it were not for the tone of the poem itself. The epic echo is more revealing than we might suppose. The Virgilian '*arma virumque cano*' puts the proper emphasis on the objects of song; the uninflected English makes prominent the role of the singer, and Cowper is quick to develop the personal reference:

> I sing the SOFA. I, who lately sang
> Truth, Hope, and Charity, and touch'd with awe
> The solemn chords, and with a trembling hand,
> Escap'd with pain from that advent'rous flight,
> Now seek repose upon an humbler theme;
> The theme though humble, yet august and proud
> Th' occasion — for the Fair commands the song.
>
> (I, 1 – 7)

Cowper has almost covered his tracks in these few lines, almost retreated into the safety of stylised formality. He can proceed with his amusing, society game, playing it according to the rules. But not for long can he keep himself out of the game. This transition would take us by surprise, if Cowper had not by now established his particular mode of rambling discourse:

> Oh may I live exempted (while I live
> Guiltless of pamper'd appetite obscene)
> From pangs arthritic, that infest the toe
> Of libertine excess. The SOFA suits
> The gouty limb, 'tis true; but gouty limb,
> Though on a SOFA, may I never feel:
> For I have lov'd the rural walks through lanes
> Of grassy swarth, close cropt by nibbling sheep,
> And skirted thick with intertexture firm
> Of thorny boughs; have lov'd the rural walk
> O'er hills, through valleys, and by rivers' brink,

> E'er since a truant boy I pass'd my bounds
> T' enjoy a ramble on the banks of Thames . . .
>
> (I, 103–15)

Once back in childhood, Cowper finds it hard to drag himself away.
His interest in sofas becomes minimal as he focuses attention upon his
inner feelings, and their relationship with nature. His talk of 'fair
prospects' barely masks his particular love of favourite places.
Echoing through this poem is that remarkable opening stanza of
Gray's 'Elegy', where the relationship between poet, countryside and
reader is put in a new perspective:

> The curfew tolls the knell of parting day,
> The lowing herd wind slowly o'er the lea,
> The ploughman homeward plods his weary way,
> And leaves the world to darkness and to me.

As Wordsworth was to realise later, things please for what they are in
themselves, and for the associations that they have for particular
people. It is of some significance that when Cowper has reached this
point in his poem he makes one of his timid, shy little gestures to his
own possible absurdity. The exclamations serve their purpose more
directly than Colerdige's use of them in 'The Eolian Harp':

> Peace to the artist, whose ingenious thought
> Devis'd the weather-house, that useful toy!
> Fearless of humid air and gathering rains
> Forth steps the man – an emblem of myself!
> More delicate, his tim'rous mate retires.
>
> (I, 210–14)

That this is more than a passing fancy emerges in the second book,
where Cowper is torn between his desire for peace and security and
his sense of the world's stupidities. He begins to ponder his role as a
poet, aware for the first time that his audience is wider than the fair
woman who suggested the poem in the first place. The game has
become more serious:

> But is amusement all? Studious of song,
> And yet ambitious not to sing in vain,
> I would not trifle merely, though the world

Be loudest in their praise who do no more.
Yet what can satire, whether grave or gay?
(II, 311—15)

Cowper grows uneasy, as this passage shows. His hesitations derive,
not only from his anxieties over satire, but also from his need to justify
himself, to take himself seriously as a poet. The simile of the road at
the start of the third book is to become a powerful Wordsworthian
metaphor; Cowper invests it with sufficient importance for himself
for it to grow beyond the cliché it might initially appear. He emerges
from the thicket of the first two books, 'at large, / Courageous, and
refresh'd'; this hardwon freedom to explore inwards leads to a
directness his circuitous verse has not prepared us for, a devastating
openness that echoes the gulping final line of 'The Castaway'. The
desperation is held in check, but there is no doubt but that it is there.
Simile has become metaphor:

I was a stricken deer, that left the herd
Long since; with many an arrow deep infixt
My panting side was charg'd, when I withdrew
To seek a tranquil death in distant shades . . .
(III, 108—11)

But in an important sense this is not typical of Cowper. As he
proceeds through his poem he qualifies and emends, doing his best to
undercut the *gravitas* of this crucial passage. Necessary solitude, for
example, becomes shared and conscious domesticity:

The morning finds the self-sequester'd man
Fresh for his task, intend what task he may.
Whether inclement seasons recommend
His warm but simple home, where he enjoys,
With her who shares his pleasures and his heart,
Sweet converse, sipping calm the fragrant lymph
Which neatly she prepares; then to his book,
Well chosen; and not sullenly perus'd
In selfish silence, but imparted oft
As aught occurs that she may smile to hear,
Or turn to nourishment, digested well.
(III, 386—96)

The quiet benignity of the relationship is well caught here, as Cowper determinedly steers away from the melancholy solitariness he had been heading towards. His benevolent humour, once established, allows him to have fun at the cucumber's expense. Perhaps the difference between this famous passage and what we might consider similar attempts earlier in the century is that here the personal reference has already been effected. Cowper's account tells us a lot about himself:

> Pardon then,
> Ye sage dispensers of poetic fame,
> Th' ambition of one, meaner far, whose pow'rs,
> Presuming an attempt not less sublime,
> Pant for the praise of dressing to the taste
> Of critic appetite, no sordid fare,
> A cucumber, while costly yet and scarce.
> The stable yields a stercoraceous heap,
> Impregnated with quick fermenting salts,
> And potent to resist the freezing blast:
> For, ere the beech and elm have cast their leaf
> Deciduous, when now November dark
> Checks vegetation in the torpid plant
> Expos'd to his cold breath, the task begins . . .
>   (III, 456–69)

But even more revealing in its modulated combination of benevolent description and self-mockery is the opening of Book V, where once again the walk becomes a metaphor for the way Cowper sees himself.

This particular passage seems to me to have an historic significance. No one could possibly mistake this for Wordsworth, or for any other poet, and that is an index of its distinctive peculiarity. We are conscious of a particular voice speaking, the voice of the retiring countryman, the recluse of Olney: but in the very act of speaking, he is assuming an audience, and in that assumption becomes fairly confidently self-conscious. Cowper is combining a relatively conventional approach with one much more personal; he is also self-confessedly combining 'grave and gay'. It is an assured performance – and performance is the word, whatever the implied disclaimers – a demonstration of control, of seriousness of purpose and lightness of touch which is a measure of the distance between *The Seasons* and *The Task*. To begin with, Cowper is bald, relying on

unexceptionable language, as though some form of shorthand is
sufficient for his purposes:

> 'Tis morning; and the sun, with ruddy orb
> Ascending, fires th' horizon . . .

But even within the bounds of the opening sentence, Cowper
expands, as though his own horizons were widening. The stark
pronouncement of the morning's presence gives way to movement
and progression, to adventurousness of image, undercut by the
reminder that winter involves bleakness as well as fire:

> . . . while the clouds
> That crowd away before the driving wind,
> More ardent as the disk emerges more,
> Resemble most some city in a blaze,
> Seen through the leafless wood.

The sun's glory is all very well in its magnificence, but all it can do is
cast shadows on the snow.

> His slanting ray
> Slides ineffectual down the snowy vale,
> And, tinging all with his own rosy hue,
> From ev'ry herb and ev'ry spiry blade
> Stretches a length of shadow o'er the field.

Already, there have been shifts of tone, a gentle pricking of the
sun's bubble. The extension to the poet himself is easily made, and
Cowper seizes the chance to dwell on his own shadow – typical of
Cowper to introduce himself thus obliquely, still in control, but
wryly aware of the inherent humour of the shift of emphasis (and
perhaps meaning us to grasp an allusion to *Richard III*, and the
hunchback's obsession with his grotesque shadow in the sun). Talk of
the glorious sun has led quickly and apparently inevitably to talk of
shadows and shades – the implications are pointed but not stressed.
The self-mockery is echoed in the mock-epic diction:

> Mine, spindling into longitude immense,
> In spite of gravity, and sage remark
> That I myself am but a fleeting shade,

Provokes me to a smile. With eye askance
I view the muscular proportion'd limb
Transform'd to a lean shank. The shapeless pair
As they design'd to mock at me, at my side
Take step for step; and, as I near approach
The cottage, walk along the plaster'd wall,
Prepost'rous sight! the legs without the man.

That is the extent of it. Cowper reverts to the sights and sounds around him, almost like a man drawing himself up after a slight lapse. But it is hard not to let those opening lines work on us as we read the rest of this highly concentrated section. The winter morning walk impresses itself on us because it involves a particular man who is watching himself as he walks. And if, after this, we are still in any doubt about the central position of the poet in *The Task*, then the concluding lines, like the opening lines, should make us fully aware of what Cowper is doing:

'Tis not in artful measures, in the chime
And idle tinkling of a minstrel's lyre,
To charm his ear, whose eye is on the heart;
Whose frown can disappoint the proudest strain,
Whose approbation — prosper even mine.
(VI, 1020–5)

The final possessive pronoun emphasises the circularity of a poem which begins and ends with the self. It anticipates the more subtle movements to and from the self which characterise Coleridge's so-called 'conversation poems' and much of Wordsworth's most intimate (and public) poetry.

Robert Southey is an intriguing transitional figure in this particular line. Perhaps his best poems are not about himself at all, and it can be argued that much of his writing, especially the prose, is undertaken as an escape from the terrors of poetry, a stay against the confusions of personal emotion. He himself acknowledged that he was 'an unfit man to mingle with the world'.[14] His long epic poems were essentially escapist. But sooner or later Southey, like the other Romantic poets, felt the need to bring himself into his poems, and that is where they become moving, where the fear of involvement shows itself and is at least combatted. On one level this can be seen in the slight but effective poem, 'To a Spider' in which he plays with his theme engagingly:

> Spider! thou need'st not run in fear about
>   To shun my curious eyes;
> I won't humanely crush thy bowels out
>   Lest thou should'st eat the flies;
> Nor will I roast thee with a damn'd delight
> Thy strange instinctive fortitude to see,
>   For there is One who might
>   One day roast me.
>
> Thou art welcome to a Rhymer sore perplext,
>   The subject of his verse;
> There's many a one who on a better text
>   Perhaps might comment worse.
> Then shrink not, old Free-Mason, from my view,
> But quietly like me spin out the line;
>   Do thou thy work pursue
>   As I will mine.
>
>   . . .
>
>   . . . Spider, thou art like the Poet poor,
>   Whom thou hast help'd in song.
> Both busily our needful food to win,
>   We work, as Nature taught, with ceaseless pains:
>   Thy bowels thou dost spin,
>   I spin my brains.

This is neat and polished. It achieves its effects economically, and manages to keep something back for the final line. The rhyme is sufficient reminder of the pains Southey knows only too well. Southey has written a poem addressed to a spider, but it is really, and unselfconsciously, about himself. ('The Holly Tree' similarly says much about the poet, little about the tree.)

Occasionally, Southey addresses a poem to a person, and this calls for a peculiar tact. The poem 'To Margaret Hill', written in 1798, is one such. What is admirable here is the semi-colloquial tone, the evasiveness, the acknowledgement of his own limitations (elsewhere rather proudly discounted). In the larger context of Wordsworth's and Coleridge's attempts to capture a relaxed, conversational tone in poetry, this poem has its historical, as well as its obvious personal, interest:

> Margaret! my Cousin . . . nay, you must not smile,
> I love the homely and familiar phrase:
> And I will call thee Cousin Margaret,
> However quaint amid the measured line
> The good old term appears. Oh! it looks ill
> When delicate tongues disclaim old terms of kin,
> Sir-ing and Madam-ing as civilly
> As if the road between the heart and lips
> Were such a weary and Laplandish way,
> That the poor travellers came to the red gates
> Half frozen . . .
>   . . . Loth indeed were I
> That for a moment you should lay to me
> Unkind neglect; mine, Margaret, is a heart
> That smokes not, yet methinks there should be some
> Who know its genuine warmth . . .
>   . . . In a narrow sphere
> The little circle of domestic life,
> I would be known and loved: the world beyond
> Is not for me.

We can see what it costs Southey to write in this way, and the result is peculiarly moving in its refusal to make claims for itself. The same domestic tone characterises most of Coleridge's 'conversation poems', which elevate to a fine art this type of blank-verse rumination, and which provide a link between Cowper and Wordsworth. Cowper's 'divine chit-chat' had struck Coleridge for its combination of 'natural thoughts with natural diction', and he seems to be aiming at a similar effect in these poems.[15] It is interesting to see that Coleridge has problems similar to Cowper's in the way he tries to fit himself into these poems: the humour he resorts to is sometimes forced and self-conscious. It is not that these are the first poems in which Coleridge uses humour: he had written a number of poems which had been parodies of stylistic excesses, whether of the Romantic Della Cruscans or of the simplicities of Charles Lamb.[16] But the matter was complicated when the self was involved, and each of the 'conversation poems' grows out of an episode both occasional and intimate.

The right tone of voice is clearly not struck in 'The Eolian Harp', where there is a curious combination of cloying domesticity and complacent humour, which the exclamatory gestures emphasise excessively. As the poem develops, and we see that the 'pensive Sara' is a potential source of embarrassment to his central vision (and vice versa), then we can see, perhaps, some justification for what Coleridge is doing in these opening lines. But they are not redeemed.

> My pensive Sara! thy soft cheek reclined
> Thus on mine arm, most soothing sweet it is
> To sit beside our Cot, our Cot o'ergrown
> With white-flower'd Jasmin, and the broad-leav'd Myrtle,
> (Meet emblems they of Innocence and Love!)
> And watch the clouds, that late were rich with light,
> Slow saddening round, and mark the star of eve
> Serenely brilliant (such should Wisdom be)
> Shine opposite! How exquisite the scents
> Snatch'd from yon bean-field! and the world *so* hush'd!

Much more successful is 'This Lime-Tree Bower My Prison', where the slight initial humour at his own expense soon gives way to an imaginative recreation of the scene inhabited by his absent friends. The intimacy between poet and reader, essential to the poem's effect, is established in the opening lines:

> Well, they are gone, and here must I remain,
> This lime-tree bower my prison!

This naturalness of tone is crucial: we need to sense the poet's exasperated isolation, his forced imprisonment with his own self, before the poem expands outwards, and accounts for an increased awareness of himself by removing himself from the centre of his attention. The poem ebbs and flows in a series of gentle affirmative movements. A similar concentration of energies is to be found in 'Frost at Midnight', where Coleridge is sufficiently confident to begin with his majestic description of the world outside, and the world within. There is no faltering, no hesitation. But in the central part of the poem, where he remembers his schooldays, he allows himself a humorous touch: the domestic memory is a reflection of the present domestic setting, in which he sits by his sleeping infant, and it evokes the warm benevolence of a smile.

And so I brooded all the following morn,
Awed by the stern preceptor's face, mine eye
Fixed with mock study on my swimming book:
Save if the door half opened, and I snatched
A hasty glance, and still my heart leaped up,
For still I hoped to see the *stranger's* face,
Townsman, or aunt, or sister more beloved,
My playmate when we both were clothed alike!

These 'conversation poems' are elusive, their slightness deceptive. It is interesting that Southey, Coleridge and Wordsworth were all writing a similar type of poetry at the same time. Wordsworth certainly learnt from Coleridge. But in *The Prelude* he could only learn from himself.

Wordsworth had explored the possibilities of humour in the *Lyrical Ballads*; poems of a more personal cast, for all their implicit and explicit seriousness, had fallen back on at least a self-deprecating smile when the awkwardnesses of talking about himself pressed too heavily on the poet. When it came to writing a poem entirely about himself, Wordsworth again found that the problems of self-centredness could at least be eased by a variety of tones, including the self-mocking and self-deflating. It is here, in *The Prelude*, that we can most clearly see the continuation of the line developed by Cowper, whilst recognising the essential differences between the two poets. For Wordsworth is consciously adopting the apparatus and the style, in the first instance, of the Miltonic epic, for a poem which is to be devoted exclusively to his own growth as a poet. There is no need here to go into the various stages of the poem's composition: it is enough to make the point that *The Prelude*, in all its forms, is intended as no more than a testing-ground, somewhere for Wordsworth to prove to himself and to Coleridge that he is, after all, fitted to undertake the mammoth task of *The Recluse*. It becomes a poem of self-justification. In one of his brasher moments Wordsworth might have confided that it seemed perfectly natural to devote a poem of such length to self-justification; our answer to that could be that it would appear reasonable only to someone of Wordsworth's temperament and constitution. But a more complete answer would have to acknowledge that the perfect reasonableness of the enterprise was not always so apparent to Wordsworth, and that that is a very large part of the poem's *raison d'être*. One of the poem's larger ironies is that, in a work which is merely meant to be clearing the ground, Wordsworth finds it incredibly difficult to get going at all.

Whereas Cowper's leisurely rambles round about in *The Task* had been the occasion for some self-questioning as to the true direction of his poem, Wordsworth's floundering is more desperate, because his ambitions are higher. He can adopt the sacramental tone as he puts on his priestly robes, but his 'cheerful confidence in things to come' is misplaced. Blake had been able to don such robes and keep a straight face. Wordsworth finds it harder. His ready admittance of this constantly undercuts the 'high-astounding terms' he would like to cultivate:

> It was a splendid evening, and my soul
> Did once again make trial of the strength
> Restored to her afresh; nor did she want
> Aeolian visitations; but the harp
> Was soon defrauded, and the banded host
> Of harmony dispersed in straggling sounds
> And lastly utter silence!
>
> (I, 101−7)

Mention of the harp reminds us of Coleridge, and Sara's pooh-poohing of his lofty musings on the Eolian harp. But Wordsworth faces a more severe problem than domestic discord: the harmony is shattered from within. The vision is all the more tantalising because it appears to be so tenuous. Discouragement (Wordsworth's word) takes the form of mockery (another significant word in Wordsworth's vocabulary, as it is to be, later, in Byron's):

> gleams of light
> Flash often from the east, then disappear
> And mock me with a sky that ripens not
> Into a steady morning . . .
>
> (I, 134−7)

The confusions which arise from this uncertainty strike damagingly at the heart of Wordsworth's need for belief. For a poet whose prime concern is moral in the broadest sense, the greatest calamity is to be unable to make the necessary fine distinctions. Interestingly, Wordsworth sees his difficulties in terms of selfishness:

> Thus from day to day
> I live, a mockery of the brotherhood
> Of vice and virtue, with no skill to part
> Vague longing that is bred by want of power
> From paramount impulse not to be withstood,
> A timorous capacity from prudence,
> From circumspection, infinite delay.
> Humility and modest awe themselves
> Betray me, serving often for a cloak
> To a more subtle selfishness . . .
>
> (I, 238−47)

Soon after this passage Wordsworth finds the inspiration for which
he has been thrashing about. But the return to childhood heralded by
his invocation to the River Derwent does not automatically solve all
his problems. The doubts and uncertainties continue; in fact, they
broaden out from what had been a local difficulty − that of how
to start an epic poem of the self − into something even more
perplexing − how to sustain the momentum once started, how to
account for the peculiarities of the past rather than of the present.
Things removed by time to a fit distance are not necessarily any easier
to comprehend. One of the ways to confront these perplexities is to
exploit the implications of the formal perspective so self-consciously
adopted: the epic voice contains within itself the possibility of mock-
epic, and before the first book is over mock-epic begins to assert itself.
Wordsworth has already given us several of those superb moments
when his difference from his fellows is acknowledged, his sense of
isolation, of fear when confronted with nature's awesome beauty.
Significantly, these have all been episodes experienced at the
extreme − solitude, winter, night-time − all have conspired against
the young boy. Wordsworth then turns to some of the undeniable
pleasures of childhood, particularly those associated with long winter
evenings spent in the warmth of the home. He naturally falls into the
mock-heroic mood, readily admitting that this is material 'too
humble to be named in verse'. The very notion of epic suggests
particular limitations of propriety, and Wordsworth is conscious of
offending against these in two ways: either his concern with himself
cuts across the epic's usual dismissal of merely personal interests, or he
feels he is writing about things too trivial for the epic mode self-
consciously adopted. In the one case self-deflation is required; in the

other, elevation of lowly material. In both instances, mockery and humour play their part.

The point to note in the following passage is the way in which Wordsworth seems to hark back to something as central as Pope's *Rape of the Lock.* By comparison, of course, Wordsworth comes off very badly, if we are disposed to view both poets in the same light. But the comparison should indicate at once how different Wordsworth's purposes are: his lumbering epic engine has none of the point, wit or finesse of Pope. And yet it is precisely this rather heavy, awkward movement that enables Wordsworth to make the transition to the world outside, back, in fact, to the awesome presences he has momentarily escaped in the domestic fun and games indoors. The humour serves an important function in its own right, but also in the way it acts as a foil to the main point Wordsworth wants to make, the terror of that other world which he cannot really understand or explain. Wordsworth in this passage is rather like an engaging cuddly teddy bear who is suddenly alerted to the fact that such a guise does not prevent his being prey to the savageries of the real animal world.

> We schemed and puzzled, head opposed to head
> In strife too humble to be named in verse:
> Or round the naked table, snow-white deal,
> Cherry or maple, sate in close array,
> And to the combat, Loo or Whist, led on
> A thick-ribbed army; not, as in the world,
> Neglected and ungratefully thrown by
> Even for the very service they had wrought,
> But husbanded through many a long campaign.
> Uncouth assemblage was it, where no few
> Had changed their functions; some, plebeian cards
> Which Fate, beyond the promise of their birth,
> Had glorified, and called to represent
> The persons of departed potentates.
> Oh, with what echoes on the board they fell!
> Ironic diamonds, – clubs, hearts, diamonds, spades,
> A congregation piteously akin!
> Cheap matter did they give to boyish wit,
> Those sooty knaves, precipitated down
> With scoffs and taunts, like Vulcan out of heaven;
> The paramount ace, a moon in her eclipse,

Queens gleaming through their splendour's last decay,
And monarchs surly at the wrongs sustained
By royal visages. Meanwhile abroad
The heavy rain was falling, or the frost
Raged bitterly, with keen and silent tooth;
And, interrupting the impassioned game,
From Esthwaite's neighbouring lake the splitting ice,
While it sank down toward the water, sent,
Among the meadows and the hills, its long
And dismal yellings, like the noise of wolves
When they are howling round the Bothnic Main.
                                        (I, 539–70)

Wordsworth's debt to traditions of various kinds is clear enough; but
so too is his outstanding originality. His genius here is not simply a
matter of change of mood, the personal insight granted to him
alone – essential though that is; it is his admission of the full range of
experience into so compact a space, a combination of the apparently
trivial and the majestic central to his vision. One of the major
paradoxes of *The Prelude* is that the majesty can itself appear trivial,
and the trivial majestic.

Wordsworth is aware, then, of his own embarrassments as an epic
poet when epic poems are no longer really possible, and he is prepared
to exploit that embarrassment. He is also fully conscious of the
ridiculous figure he used to cut. The books on Cambridge are
particularly given to the sort of mockery he invites his readers to share
with him in the greater wisdom of his maturity. At one point he
expresses his amazement that he did not, then and there, write a satire
on himself, so ridiculous does he now seem in retrospect. The
alteration in the revision of this passage in Book IV is interesting for
Wordsworth explains why he could not do just that:

                   but the heart was full,
        Too full for the reproach.
                   (1850: IV, 64–5)

This is the great advantage of the distancing effect of recollection, that
the heart's fullness can, to some extent, be resisted. If satire is too
strong an impulse for Wordsworth (though we should not under-
estimate his satiric bent),[17] then at least humour is called for, whether
it be to describe childhood meals ('frugal, Sabine fare!' II, 82), the

pompous obscurity of life in Cambridge as a student at St John's, or the antics which included his getting drunk celebrating Milton's name and then charging like a bull into Chapel (III, 708). The humour, as applied to Cambridge, ranges from the mild to the vitriolic: this variety is necessary for a true reflection of his life there. It is a formative part of his life, if only negatively, and the memory of it is something that he can share with Coleridge.

Coleridge's place in the poem as Wordsworth's prime audience is important.

> Nor will it seem to thee, my Friend! so prompt
> In sympathy, that I have lengthened out
> With fond and feeble tongue a tedious tale.
>
> (I, 645 – 7)

This sense of an indulgent Coleridge hovers over much of the verse: but it is an indulgence anticipated and treasured only because there is, implicitly, a wider audience in mind. The checks to Wordsworth's self-importance act as safety valves, allowing for incredulous, confused responses. As he declares in Book V,

> My drift hath scarcely,
> I fear, been obvious;
>
> (V, 291 – 2)

and the revised version makes no effort to eradicate such obtuseness or its self-advertisement. In other words, the more than occasional coy glance in the mirror is not a temporising thing: it is built into the considered structure of the poem, part of the fabric of a work concerned with the self. Wordsworth has seen what others, from Cowper onwards, did in this particular line of self-communing that was nevertheless public; he has appropriated the technique and made it his own.

Coleridge in his 'conversation poems' had deliberately kept his sights fairly low; even then the awkwardness showed through from time to time. He had not attempted anything really ambitious in that intimate form, until he transformed it into the public statement of the 'Dejection Ode'. Southey had looked at himself coolly, with amusement, in those poems he allowed to be personal — rather like his beloved Cowper, he could only be personal when humour was there to hide behind (Cowper said that 'Self is a subject of inscrutable misery and mischief, and can never be studied to so much advantage as in the dark'; he went on to say that 'Despair made amusement necessary, and I found poetry the most agreeable amusement').[18] Wordsworth started out, in 'Tintern Abbey', with a similar premise. But in *The Prelude* he came to terms with the full complexities of the self, and of a poem devoted to them. He found that humour was still available to him, not merely as an antidote to his high seriousness of purpose, but as an integral part of his vision, which was a matter, amongst other things, of how he saw himself.

II

We tend not to associate Keats as poet with the comic. But the critical debate as to his true stature as either thinker or purely sensuous beast has obscured what is an extremely real preoccupation throughout his working life, a preoccupation with the possibilities of humour either inside, or just on the outside, of poetry. A glance at the letters is enough to tell us of Keats's warm-hearted, ebullient, sometimes outrageous sense of humour, but the temptation has been to draw a sharp line between the letter-writer and the poet. As with most arbitrary divisions, this is a complete falsification of what is staring at us in the poetry. After all, many of the poems begin as letters, even end as letters in some instances: a common enough early nineteenth century practice which necessarily reinforces the point that critical purism cannot simply chop things up into life and works. It should be no surprise to find the punning, witty temperament of the letter-writer occasionally seeking an outlet in the poetry (Flann O'Brien's hilarious *Keats and Chapman* episodes underline obliquely a central facet of Keats's mind). As an indication of Keats's interest in — indeed, his need for — the comic, we might bear in mind that after his second attempt at *Hyperion* had failed, he turned, after *King Stephen*, to 'The Cap and Bells', a Spenserian 'fairy poem' which is the closest Keats comes to sustained literary satire.

The letters provide ample, though contradictory, evidence of Keats's attitude to poetry, and to himself as a poet. It is these contradictions and confusions which need to be registered. His disarming honesty might not make for consistency, but it prevents him from settling into easy formulae. If at one stage he regards poetry as essential to his existence, that does not prevent his regarding it, at another stage, as all rather unimportant. The steady progression of thought, of seriousness, that so many readers eagerly chart through his work tends merely to be the reflection of our own dull and simplistic need to impose a pattern on the corpus.

Henry Stephen, a student contemporary of Keats, provided G. F. Mathew with some recollections of the poet in 1847. What he said echoed Keats's own uneasiness beneath the proud exterior:

> Poetry was to his mind the zenith of all his Aspirations — The only thing worthy the attention of superior minds — So he thought, All other pursuits were mean and tame, He had no idea of Fame, or Greatness, but as it was connected with the pursuits of Poetry, or the Attainment of Poetical excellence, The greatest men in the world were the Poets, and to rank among them was the chief object of his ambition. — It may readily be imagined that this feeling was accompanied with a good deal of Pride and some conceit, and that amongst mere Medical students, he would walk, & talk as one of the Gods might be supposed to do, when mingling with mortals. This pride had exposed him, as may be readily imagined, to occasional ridicule, & some mortification. [19]

Keats could certainly be proud (especially when bolstered by Leigh Hunt's enthusiasm), and he acknowledged the risks involved. When he wrote the preface to *Endymion*, a poem he knew was not a total success, his scorn of the public ('a thing I cannot help looking upon as an Enemy, and which I cannot address without feelings of Hostility') led to a complete refusal to stoop to humility, to give up his independence. [20] His belief in the individual creative processes, however imperfect they might be, necessitated pride, ambition, risk, and wry self-deflation:

> The Genius of Poetry must work out its own salvation in a man: It cannot be matured by law and precept, but by sensation & watchfulness in itself. That which is creative must create itself — In Endymion, I leaped headlong into the Sea, and thereby have become better acquainted with the Soundings, the quicksands, & the rocks, than if I had stayed upon the green shore, and piped a silly pipe, and took tea & comfortable advice. — I was never afraid of failure; for I would sooner fail than not be among the greatest. But I am nigh getting into a rant. [21]

This is almost Byronic in its determination to see things in terms of physical challenge (the heroic counterpart of the sensuousness of so much of the poetry); Byronic, too, in its readiness to see the absurdity of such an attitude if carried to its limits. It is as though the necessity to believe in such postures carries with it the necessity to see through them. As Byron had protested about one of his worst fits of despondency, 'I should, many a good day, have blown my brains out, but for the recollection that it would have given pleasure to my mother-in-law.'[22] Keats does not display quite the same histrionic temperament; but there is a similar rationale whereby he takes himself seriously by appearing not to do so. To some extent this is one of the manifestations of the developing poet: it was barely eighteen months before his outburst over *Endymion* that Keats had drawn the contrast between himself and his mentor Leigh Hunt, whose 'self-delusions' seemed to Keats excessive. Typically, Keats sees the potential paradox in his rejection of Hunt's ambitions:

> Perhaps it is a self delusion to say so – but I think I could not be deceived in the Manner that Hunt is – may I die tomorrow if I am to be. There is no greater Sin after the 7 deadly than to flatter oneself into an idea of being a great Poet – or one of those beings who are privileged to wear out their Lives in the pursuit of Honor.[23]

In a letter to Benjamin Bailey of March 1818 Keats comments, more or less in passing, 'I am sometimes so very sceptical as to think Poetry itself a mere Jack a lanthern to amuse whoever may chance to be struck with its brilliance'.[24] This scepticism haunts him. At the same time, if poetry has value, it derives it from the poet's sense of his own importance – 'every mental pursuit takes its reality and worth from the ardour of the pursuer – being in itself a nothing – '.[25] This perception explains Keats's insistence on the poet's role, and also explains his perplexity: he keeps returning to himself, to the fact that it is he who is trying to be the poet. He might be upset when an acquaintance says of him, 'O, he is quite the little Poet';[26] and yet a year beforehand he laments the impression Wordsworth made in town 'by his egotism, Vanity, and bigotry'.[27] The distinction is between Wordsworth's 'egotistical sublime' and Keats's need to annihilate self in the 'negative capability' that he admires in Shakespeare. In November 1817, he observes that men of genius 'have not any individuality, any determined Character'[28] and nine months after this regrets his own lack of magnanimity which would enable him to 'annihilate self'.[29] Self-forgetfulness, of course, as the Romantic poets find, is an ambiguous and precarious process: Keats in October 1818 exults in his own solitude as the true sublime, with the recognition that he is most truly himself when he most voluptuously loses himself.[30]

Such affirmations are rare. For a poet who spends so much of his time writing poems about poetry, the doubts that dog him are not merely passing irritations on the way to maturity — they are essential elements in his integrity, which is itself a paradoxical concept for a poet who talks of the ideal poet as a chameleon, constantly changing his colours. The image is appropriate, though; for Keats eludes our grasp as he slips through his letters, jumping from mood to mood. He is only too aware of this, and exploits the propensity, declaring it a weakness but knowing it to be a strength. Many of his letters span days, even weeks and months, so that they become journal-letters, diaries for semi-public perusal, works of unpremeditated artlessness in which he runs the whole gamut of emotions, rejoicing in the freedom, the lack of constraining formal pressures.

A typical instance is the long letter to George and Georgiana Keats, written between 14 February and 3 May 1819.[31] The range of topics discussed is enormous: it is perhaps significant that one of the things he mentions in passing is meeting Coleridge ('In those two Miles he broached a thousand things'). On 19 March Keats ponders his rather curious attitude to life, his indolence and 'supreme careless[ness]'; it is out of discussion in this context of his friend Haslam's concern over his dying father that he talks of the various purposes in life, the conflicts that send most things, especially pleasures, awry:

While we are laughing the seed of some trouble is put into the wide arable land of events — while we are laughing it sprouts [it] grows and suddenly bears a poison fruit which we must pluck.

This leads into a complex passage in which he tries to argue for the maturity of his own view of the world's cruelty and incongruity. He then includes a sonnet, an attempt to express the mood that has arisen in response to his thoughts on death.

Why did I laugh tonight? No voice will tell;
No God, no Demon of severe response,
Deigns to reply from Heaven or from Hell.

> Then to my human heart I turn at once —
> Heart, thou and I are here sad and alone;
>   Say, wherefore did I laugh? Oh, mortal pain!

The poem ends with his familiar death-wish:

> Verse, fame and beauty are intense indeed,
> But Death's intenser — Death is Life's high meed.

A few days later Haslam's father (who might have disagreed with
Keats) is dead. Keats continues the letter a month after this, and is full
of *Peter Bell* and the accompanying furore, full of wit and puns. He
launches into some extempore nonsensical rhyming, laments a want
of wit his sister could remedy, and provides a mock review of
Reynolds's *Peter Bell*. The point about this letter is that the sonnet
'Why did I laugh tonight?' seems to derive a new significance from its
bizarre context. It is representative of one aspect of Keats's character,
the solemnly romantic aspect that sees only too well the risk in
laughter. But at the same time the insistent question reminds us
emphatically that the poem is by a laugher, and that if he concludes
'Death is Life's high meed', a good night's sleep is going to put that
right: 'I went to bed, and enjoyed an uninterrupted sleep — sane I
went to bed & sane I arose'.

This sort of epistolary context cannot always explain the mysteries
of Keats's creative processes; it certainly underlines the mysteries. On
3 May 1818 Keats writes to John Hamilton Reynolds about the
problem of suffering, in relation to Wordsworth and Milton.[32] He
throws the issue aside carelessly — 'for aught we can know for
certainty "Wisdom is folly!"' — and turns to consideration of his own
letters:

> If I scribble long letters I must play my vagaries. I must be too
> heavy, or too light, for whole pages . . . I must play my draughts
> as I please . . . I must go from Hazlitt to Patmore, and make
> Wordsworth and Coleman play at leap-frog — or keep one of
> them down a whole half-holiday at fly the garter — 'from Gray to
> Gay, from Little to Shakespeare' —.

The Popean quotation does not deter Keats from getting back, by a
process of crazy association, to Wordsworth, 'Tintern Abbey', and
the 'Mansion of Many Apartments'. Now these extraordinary

imaginative leaps (a summary fails to give the feel of excitement and bewilderment) reflect what Keats had three months previously tried to do in verse, in a letter to the same Reynolds. This so-called 'Epistle', in which Keats agonises as he had never done before on the direction his poetry might take, has received recent critical attention, but it merits some discussion here.[33]

The poem epitomises primarily – and in a way the earlier 'Sleep and Poetry' does not – the confusions within Keats's mind as to poetry and its possibilities. It inhabits the border country between poetry and prose, where Keats can most appropriately question the very nature of poetry and his suitability as a poet. The opening lines look ahead to that same jumble of absurdities catalogued by Keats as typical of his letters when he writes to Reynolds in May:

> Dear Reynolds, as last night I lay in bed,
> There came before my eyes that wonted thread
> Of shapes, and shadows, and remembrances,
> That every other minute vex and please.
> Things all disjointed come from north and south,
> Two witch's eyes above a cherub's mouth,
> Voltaire with casque and shield and habergeon,
> And Alexander with his night-cap on,
> Old Socrates a-tying his cravat,
> And Hazlitt playing with Miss Edgeworth's cat,
> And Junius Brutus pretty well so so,
> Making the best of his way towards Soho.

Vexation, as *Hyperion* suggests, is a Keatsian preoccupation, even if only as something ideally to be avoided. What is remarkable about these fragmentary lines is their candour and honesty. The dream vision, so crucial for Keats in so many poems, becomes a shambolic nightmare. The reconciliation of opposites urged by Coleridge, and by Keats in his remarks on the 'necessary evaporation of disagreeables', is here apparently impossible. The world's, and the imagination's, incongruities are too pressing on the inward eye. What we have here is the jumble of undigested experience that the poet cannot comprehend (in the genuine Biblical sense). The great and the clever are merely absurd and grotesque; the critic no better than his target, the actor (or the noble Roman?) a pathetic drunkard. This is not great poetry, nor even fine humour. What the lines represent is an acute awareness of absurdities directly related to the visionary experience in its unmediated, naked form. Keats is playing here, clearly, and Reynolds, ill in bed, must wonder what is going on.

The playfulness has an edge to it, in that it leads Keats to consider what is possible in poetry, and he draws a clear distinction between himself and that not necessarily select few 'who escape these visitings': if there is grotesqueness in the 'wild boar tushes' and the 'mermaid's toes' of his own fevered mind, there is an element of scorn directed at the 'flowers bursting out with lusty pride' and the 'young Aeolian harps personified'. Less risible seems to be the kind of art typified by Titian (Keats has learnt from Hazlitt's comments on Titian and Claude):

> Few are there who escape these visitings —
> Perhaps one or two, whose lives have patient wings,
> And through whose curtains peeps no hellish nose,
> No wild boar tushes, and no mermaid's toes;
> But flowers bursting out with lusty pride,
> And young Aeolian harps personified;
> Some, Titian colours touched into real life.
> The sacrifice goes on; . . .

But even the vision which is elaborated at this point is open to question: it suggest an alertness to the opposite poles of 'love and hate', 'smiles and frowns', but it suggests, too, something portentous, minatory ('some giant, pulsing underground') and rather laughable. Claude's 'Enchanted Castle' is an architectural monstrosity that tells its own tale:

> Part of the building was a chosen see
> Built by a banished Santon of Chaldee;
> The other part two thousand years from him
> Was built by Cuthbert de Saint Aldebrim;
> Then there's a little wing, far from the sun,
> Built by a Lapland witch turned maudlin nun —
> And many other juts of agèd stone
> Founded with many a mason-devil's groan . . .

It is a world of distortion and madness. Even the 'echo of sweet music' is cause for fear to the innocent shepherd bringing his sheep to the 'enchanted spring'. The two worlds are a 'trouble' to each other; it is no surprise that the shepherd's friends do not want to hear his story.

Here the poem shifts direction. The fanciful imaginings, characteristically centring on a work of art with its own curious distortions,
give way to the harshness of reality. Keats makes the specific point
that his visions reflect only too well the chaos of the world he lives in
day by day: the perturbations are not ironed out by art, nor are they
invented by it. What began as apparently idle chit-chat has become a
devastating announcement of art's limitations, and of the poet's
personal deficiencies:

> Oh, that our dreamings all of sleep or wake
> Would all their colours from the sunset take,
> From something of material sublime,
> Rather than shadow our own soul's daytime
> In the dark void of night. For in the world
> We jostle . . . but my flag is not unfurled
> On the admiral staff — and to philosophize
> I dare not yet . . .

His state of what he calls 'Purgatory blind' reflects his own
immaturity, his lack of worldly knowledge; it reflects, too, his doubts
as to poetry's capacity for the world's harsh truths. And those truths
forbid any easy sentimentalism about nature as a means of escape. It is
all very well for Keats to dismiss all this as so many 'horrid
moods . . . of one's mind', but the tenor of the poem has darkened
progressively, and the final throwaway lines are a sign of desperation
rather than resolve:

> Do you get health — and Tom the same — I'll dance,
> And from detested moods in new romance
> Take refuge. . . .

'Isabella' is to be that 'new romance', and it has little of comfort to
offer the dreamer in a savage world. 'Romance' is not necessarily the
answer. What matters in the 'Epistle', as so often with Keats, is the
questions. We can hear the sound of rather desperate laughter behind
this poem, as the questions bounce back at the questioner.

Of the three narrative poems that announce Keats's concerns so
bravely at the front of the 1820 volume, 'Isabella' is the least
satisfactory, and Keats realised this. He and Reynolds were to have
collaborated on a volume of 'versions' from Boccaccio, but Reynolds
soon decided to give Keats his head, once 'Isabella' was written. Keats

saw the poem's drift into sentimentality and 'mawkishness', attribu-
table to his 'inexperience of life'; if he had been a reviewer, he said he
would have called it 'A weak-sided Poem with an amusing sober-
sadness about it'.[34] The consciously struck pose was something that
he saw through, when he could contemplate the poem objectively.
One of the unconscious ironies of the poem is that its *ottava rima* form
was in the same year adopted by several specifically satirical or
burlesque works, notably Byron's *Beppo*. This irony is underscored
by Keats's attempt to introduce an overtly satirical tone into his
account of the wicked (absurdly so) brothers after stanza XVII in the
fair copy. Coming after the empty rhetoric of stanza XVI, this
incongruity, although it never gets into print, shows Keats's juggling
act at its most risky. Well might he invoke Boccaccio's forgiveness for
the introduction of such 'ill-beseeming' syllables. What is of interest
here, in view of the debate that consumes poets later in the century, is
the consciousness of the attempt to turn 'old prose' into 'modern
rhyme'. The attempt at 'social realism' is awkward and self-
conscious; the rhetoric is similarly clumsy; beneath it all lies the
possibility of a satirical attack, from which Keats gingerly withdraws.
Even without the satire, Keats in retrospect finds the poem amusing
because of its excesses in the other direction. It is as though 'Isabella'
represents a papering-over of the cracks acknowledged in the 'Epistle
to J. H. Reynolds'; a year later Keats can see that the cracks are part of
his experience of the world, and cannot be ignored.

The difficulties appear starkly in Keats's reactions to what is
perhaps the most optimistic, the most open, of these narrative poems,
'The Eve of St Agnes'. Keats had his doubts about this, too,
bracketing it with 'Isabella' as too sentimental: but at one stage he
suggested it took pride of place in the 1820 volume, rather than
'Lamia'. This is interesting, because later in the poem's history he
introduced, as in 'Isabella', a variant reading, this time of the final
stanza, which completely altered the tenor of the poem; his despairing
vision required emphasis in the teeth of the poem's prevailing
optimism. In the end the ambiguities of 'Lamia', ironic rather than
satiric, served his purposes better. But it is too tempting to dismiss the
alterations to 'The Eve of St Agnes' as further instances, merely, of
Keats's moodiness. The original version of the poem had suggested
the importance of the dream world, the necessity for wish-fulfilment,
whilst at the same time acknowledging the pressures from without,
and the need to confront them at some stage. The lovers have to go
out into the storm. Keats knew that the tradition of St Agnes Eve was

in itself open to satire. John Brand's *Popular Antiquities*, which he knew, gave a satirical verse account, dating from 1794, of the church festivities. But in the bulk of Keats's poem the beautifully controlled Spenserian stanza holds such potential satire well in check, without preventing questions being raised. Yet in September 1819, Woodhouse reported a visit from Keats with a fair copy of the poem. The final stanza had been altered:

> Angela went off
> Twitch'd with the Palsy; and with face deform
> The beadsman stiffen'd, 'twixt a sigh and laugh
> Ta'en sudden from his beads by one weak little cough.

Woodhouse went on to explain this strange development:

> . . . [he] has altered the last 3 lines to leave on the reader a sense of pettish disgust by bringing old Angela in (only) dead stiff & ugly. He says he likes that the poem should leave off with this change of sentiment – it was what he aimed at, & was glad to find from my objections to it that he had succeeded. – I apprehend he had a fancy for trying his hand at an attempt to play with his reader, and fling him off at last – I sh'd have thought he affected the 'Don Juan' style of mingling up sentiment and sneering: but that he had before asked Hessey if he co'd procure him a sight of that work, as he had not met with it, and if the E. of St. A. had not in all probability been altered before his Lordship had thus flown in the face of the public.[35]

Keats's later moral objections to *Don Juan* make the implication of similarity surprising:[36] and it seems fair to say that Keats's intended overall effect is unByronic. Clearly three lines cannot alter the complexion of a whole poem, but they certainly change its tone in retrospect. This gesture of world-weariness on Keats's part is also a gesture against the balance he had been fighting to maintain in the bulk of the poem. For that reason alone it is an important fact to note, especially when put next to the stylistic variety of 'Lamia', which reflects the greater uncertainty that beset Keats towards September 1819. For all its richness and magnificence, 'Lamia' contains a world that is ripe to the point of rottenness, and if sympathy cannot be withheld from Lycius and Lamia in their tragedy, the 'sage Apollonius' is essentially right in his cruelly honest diagnosis. It should be no surprise to find Keats indulging here not in 'pettish disgust' but in something more extensively ironical.

A number of recent critics have argued for a view of 'Lamia' as a humorous, satiric poem, even mocking the idealism of *Endymion*.[37] This seems to me to be taking too far hints that occur both in the finished version, and more especially in drafts, of something deeply ironic and subversive. For a writer so concerned with loading every rift with ore, Keats can at times be a disarmingly chaotic poet, holding in his head, simultaneously, contradictory notions of the same poem: so anxious is he not to have designs upon us that he positively relishes the opportunities his vision offers him for puzzlement and obfuscation. This is why it is both so tempting, and so dangerous, to try to reduce his poems to narrative structures with explicit meanings: the ambiguities of the Odes, with their teasing 'poise and retention' (a phrase of significance for Clough later in the century) are sufficient warning against easy 'readings'. 'Lamia' is the most complicated of the narrative poems: the very division into two parts invites us to think in terms of contrasts and oppositions which by their nature cannot be resolved. The framing device, whereby we are introduced to Lamia through the story of Hermes' love for a nymph, might seem to serve an obvious purpose, a strategically placed warning to mortal lovers:

> It was no dream; or say a dream it was,
> Real are the dreams of Gods, and smoothly pass
> Their pleasures in a long immortal dream.
> . . .
> Into the green-recessèd woods they flew;
> Nor grew they pale, as mortal lovers do.
>   (I, 126–8; 144–5)

But there is something slightly ridiculous about the 'ever-smitten Hermes', just as there is later about the relationship between 'happy Lycius' and the transformed Lamia –

> As though in Cupid's college she had spent
> Sweet days a lovely graduate, still unshent,
> And kept his rosy terms in idle languishment.
>   (I, 197–9)

The conclusion of the first part reminds us of the busy world's haunting shadow, whilst acknowledging that "Twould humour many a heart to leave them thus.' He characterises his verse at this point as 'flitter-wingèd', which is itself an ambiguous attribute, suggesting amongst other things, volatility; yet his verse is driven by a need to tell 'for truth's sake, what woe afterwards befell'.

Keats is fascinated by definitions of truth, beauty and such like; he knows that he can, momentarily, make almost anything seem true. I do not think we can say, as one critic does, that the first part of the poem is nothing more than finely spun sugar:[38] Keats is not the sort of poet to expend four hundred carefully wrought lines in the elaborate erection of an Aunt Sally. For the poem's harsh morality to be effective (it is no disservice to Keats to think of morality as effective) we need to believe in the various realities that are offered: the love between Lycius and Lamia is one of these, whatever its shortcomings. Keats displays in the second part his sympathies for Lycius even as he despairs at his folly:

> O senseless Lycius! Madman! Wherefore flout
> The silent-blessing fate, warm cloistered hours,
> And show to common eyes these secret bowers?
>
> (II, 147−9)

The philosopher Apollonius laughs as he enters, but Keats cannot laugh with him.

As the fateful party develops, we have an interesting glimpse of Keats's workings in the draft: after a marvellously rich account of the banquet, which in its context is dramatically powerful, convincing whilst it is ironic, Keats had originally (and seemingly until just before publication) allowed himself the satirical view that had obviously been lurking in his mind:

> Swift bustled by the servants: − here's a health
> Cries one − another − then, as if by stealth,
> A Glutton drains a cup of Helicon,
> Too fast down, down his throat the brief delight is gone.
> 'Where is that Music?' cries a Lady fair.
> 'Aye, where is it my dear? Up in the air?'
> Another whispers 'Poo!' saith Glutton 'Mum!'
> Then makes his shiny mouth a napkin for his thumb.[39]

This belongs clearly to a different sort of poem − or rather to a completely different concept of the poem – and yet there is Keats sending it off in a letter in September 1819, and Woodhouse copying the version on to the proof sheets. We can sense, now, that Keats's instincts were right, that 'Lamia' could not embrace such potential disparities of tone within its essentially tragic compass. But it is a close thing: as with the revised ending to 'The Eve of St Agnes', Keats very nearly throws us. What we have in any case is a poem of great irony and subtlety about the claims of the imagination, of beauty, of truth – all of which seem relative; underneath that, though, in the substructure of the poem, is something much more anarchic, something very reminiscent of that strain of wild misrule caught in the 'Epistle to J. H. Reynolds'.

Keats, as we know him in his letters, is testing his readers; he is also testing himself, seeing how far he can go. In the end he draws back, in the poetry, from chaos. But his two attempts at *Hyperion*, where he is most seriously and sustainedly the heir to the Miltonic, bardic tradition, are left unfinished; it is also true that 'The Cap and Bells', his final long poem, is hardly successful as satire.[40] Where Keats is most interesting, most valuable, is where he manages, but only just, to contain within one poem these conflicting impulses, where he is most fully aware of how close he is to the rawness of experience, at the point where he no longer knows whether to laugh or to cry.

4 'The Eloquence of Indifference': Byron

Byron is often seen as a figure apart from the other Romantic poets: it was an image he carefully cultivated. But that careful cultivation was necessary because he knew how little apart, in many ways, he was, either from the Keatsian or the Wordsworthian tradition. The irrational animosity between Keats and Byron is explicable only when we acknowledge what they have in common: each in his own way is obsessed with the problems of writing about the self, and the self's perplexities. As for Wordsworth and Byron, the differences are obvious. Perhaps the surest indication of their dissimilarity is to register Byron's famous *mobilité* against Wordsworth's stolid consistency. It is, at its simplest, a question of gait, and paradoxically the poetry is a mirror-image of what we know from life — Wordsworth's gigantic strides across the moors are transformed in the poetry into something much more sedate and sober; Byron's limp becomes the heroic swagger of his *ottava rima*. But the polarities are too easy, too tempting: Byron has to face the same problems of self and subject-matter, and how these are to be accommodated in a poetry that speaks to and for the age. Byron's aristocratic *hauteur* and Wordsworth's 'egotistical sublime' have points in common. It should not surprise us that *Childe Harold* has its Wordsworthian echoes; nor should it to see both poets caught in that quagmire where the conflicting tugs of genre, decorum and the pressures of the world's bafflements, leave the writer struggling for the appropriate form, and turning not to the tragic, but to the comic. It is salutary to be reminded that behind the chaos of *Don Juan* lies that most disruptive of works, *Tristram Shandy*; and that the same is true of a poem that is in other respects from a different world, 'The Idiot Boy'.

Byron's *Complete Works* are daunting in scope and variety. Divisions into early and late, classic and romantic, are false, because they blur the poetry at those very points where what matters is the confusion, the conflation, the hectic marriage of genres. If it is comforting to regard the mature satires as the triumph of Byron's achievement, there is the rebuff given by *The Island*, and other later dramatic works; there is, too, the more important rebuff within *Don Juan* itself, which effectively challenges most of our assumptions about literature and life and the cosy categories we devise to make them tolerable. If we look closely at a supposedly Romantic narrative poem such as *Childe Harold*, it is not simply its piecemeal composition that raises questions about genre: even within the loose boundaries of the finished poem, the territory of traditional kinds suddenly appears deceptive and treacherous. Going back to the first volume, *Hours of Idleness* (the title announcing its carelessness so pointedly, apologetically, proudly and defiantly) what we engage with is certainly not merely the effete rhapsodisings of an aristocratic amateur. Already the categories crumble.

In the Preface to the first edition (1807) of *Hours of Idleness*, Byron characteristically undercuts any pretensions he might be thought to be entertaining: essentially – and the same point is made years later in *Don Juan* – he is staving off boredom. All he expects is a place amongst 'the mob of gentlemen who write.' But the tone is deceptive, as so often with Byron's disclaimers: it suggests much more than it is claiming, just as the epigraph from Dryden ('He whistled as he went, for want of thought') does not entirely eliminate the sense of a man very cautiously gauging the impression he is about to make. If Hobhouse was right in saying that Byron very nearly killed himself because of hostile Scotch reviews, then we have to be careful before we accept the Preface on its own terms.[1] Jerome J. McGann has shown well the extent to which Byron is concerned with presenting a particular image of himself in these early lyrics, and the extent to which he is indebted to that affable, urbane tradition of light society verse represented most compellingly for Byron by Thomas Moore's adopted persona, Thomas Little.[2] The impulse behind the poetry is simple: to convey the notion of someone 'feeling as he writes'. But Byron is not merely baring his soul. He assumes a limited range of guises, masks, behind which he can hide, concealing or escaping from his own feelings, taking them by turns seriously and lightly, but ultimately not daring to make too many claims for them, either as feelings or as poetry. The languid posture is balanced by the aristocratic contempt for anything that is *de trop*.

There are, certainly, poems which belong to a tradition of

seriousness, and which demand to be read in the light of that — poems
such as 'On the Death of a Young Lady', for example, or the 'Epitaph
on a Beloved Friend'. Quite often, the notion of tradition is itself
important, because it provides sanction and guidance. In his Preface
Byron had denied any aim at 'exclusive originality' because 'every
subject has already been treated to its utmost extent.' No serious poet
can seriously believe that; but it is a problem that vexes Byron as he
begins to take himself more and more seriously as a poet. Byron learns
to make use of the burden of the past, to exploit the decorum he so
often seems to deny: his careless posturing conceals a real concern for
the appropriate. In his maturity Byron makes nonsense of the concept
of decorum by his constant appeals to it; in his early years, it serves a
more limited purpose (it is in fact an acknowledgement of limitations), but is nevertheless important. In his notes to one poem ('To
a Lady') Byron plays on the notion of decorum as not simply a
literary quality, but as something with crucial reference to living;
ironically, he inverts the conventional account of 'indecorous'
behaviour, announcing as he does so the first blast in his lifelong war
against hypocrisy. As he says in another poem:

> The artless Helicon I boast is youth; —
> My lyre, the heart; my muse, the simple truth.

(Things, of course, are not that simple: 'To Romance' contains a
determined farewell to the pleasurable fancies of youth in order to
enter the realms of 'Truth', but the determination is less than
convincing, especially when it was in that very world of Romance
that 'even woman's smiles are true.' The accent of the poem is on the
loss.)

'Simple truth', initially equated with frank emotion, with sincerity
of feeling, gradually becomes something more equivocal. As Byron's
lighter side asserts itself, these equivocations are often related to his
own self-deprecation. 'Granta, a medley' is openly amusing, not
sparkling with wit, but enjoying its own bantering tone. It is an
undergraduate squib, and Byron is anxious that we take it as no more:

> No more thy theme my muse inspires;
> The reader's tired, and so am I.

The effect of this is that we leave the poem conscious above all of the
weary poet. In 'On a Distant View . . .' the effect is rather more

complex, with the lilting rhythmic flow doing its best to evoke the memory of childhood, whilst at the same time giving to that recollection a lightness that enables the central remembered fact to be laughed off. Typically, Byron remembers himself as an actor (that is how Keats saw the grown man):[3]

> Or, as Lear, I pour'd forth the deep imprecation,
>   By my daughters of kingdom and reason deprived;
> Till, fired by loud plaudits and self-adulation,
>   I regarded myself as a Garrick revived.

Byron reveals perhaps more than he means to of his temperament here: he hardly loses himself in the role of Lear.

These poems, and others like them, seem to be attempts to establish different kinds of truth. The inherent mockery implies a standard, a norm from which the inhabitants of the poem have deviated; but that is complicated by his wry looks at himself in the pursuit of such truths. That self, externalised, appears in 'To the Sighing Strephon' as the roué who refuses to tie himself to the charms of one woman ('What an insult .'twould be to the rest!'). The poem ends:

> Now, Strephon, goodbye, I cannot deny
>   Your passion appears most absurd;
> Such love as you plead is pure love indeed,
>   For it only consists in the word.

The worldly cynic refuses to accept the value, or the declaration, of a lasting relationship. But behind this apparently easy dramatisation, so easy that we are aware of no conflict (except in the larger context of the volume as a whole, where such declarations have, after all, a place), there is the more personal, more pressing, awareness of division, which centres on Byron's own experience and his response to it.

As he moves away from *Hours of Idleness*, Byron begins to face more squarely this problem of accounting for his own life, his own deeply felt experiences, in poetry (as opposed to the more stereotyped incidents of that volume). The occasional pieces, and *Childe Harold*, grow out of a developing personality: that growth can be charted in the letters and journals of the time, and it is instructive to see in what ways the poetry reflects the personality of the letters, and in what ways it differs. Byron's self-regarding eye is a well-attested fact amongst readers of his correspondence. With his *mobilité*, he displays the Keatsian qualities of the chameleon-poet-cum-letter-writer. There is one particular episode that is of special point here. In 1810 Byron achieves what seems to matter more than anything else — he swims the Hellespont, from Sestos to Abydos. It is one of those supreme instances of triumph over physical disability, and Byron makes the most of it.

Byron had bragged in August 1807 that he had swum the Thames — '3 miles!!' — 'you see I am in excellent training in case of a *squall* at Sea.'[4] Two years later in Lisbon he had been pleased with himself for swimming the Tagus 'all across at once', and it was characteristic that his account of that should be incorporated in a pell-mell, helter-skelter narrative of his doings: 'and I rides on an ass or a mule, and swears Portuguese, and have got a diarrhoea and bites from the mosquitoes.'[5] He is anxious that he does not allow his pride in his achievement too much purchase. In 1810 he makes two attempts to swim the Hellespont. The first is thwarted, but on 3 May he can write to Henry Drury:

> This morning I *swam* from *Sestos* to *Abydos*, the immediate distance is not above a mile but the current renders it hazardous, so much so, that I doubt whether Leander's conjugal powers must not have been exhausted in his passage to Paradise.[6]

In his letters of the following few days there is a barrage of recitations of this event, usually in the same terms, with the myth evoked, the parallel made and then laughed off.

Six days after this exploit (his 'only remarkable personal achieve-ment'),[7] Byron wrote a poem about it. Byron captures in his verse that same tone of dismissive self-deprecation, but he expands it, minimising his own sense of achievement in a way the letters, for all their braggadocio, cannot apparently do. He casts himself in the role of modern degenerate (an irrelevant point in the context), and decries even his own claims to have done anything unusual. What none of the letters prepares us for, beyond the obvious comparison with Leander, is the conclusion that the poem moves, surprisingly, towards: the whole episode, and the classical parallel, is reduced, in the face of inhospitable deities. Such exploits merely serve to diminish us, and our only hope is to anticipate that diminishment, to get in first, and so have the last laugh.

If, in the month of dark December,
   Leander, who was nightly wont
(What maid will not the tale remember?)
   To cross thy stream, broad Hellespont!

If, when the wintry tempest roar'd,
   He sped to Hero, nothing loth,
And thus of old thy current pour'd,
   Fair Venus! How I pity both!

For *me*, degenerate modern wretch,
   Though in the genial month of May,
My dripping limbs I faintly stretch,
   And think I've done a feat today.

But since he cross'd the rapid tide,
   According to the doubtful story,
To woo, – and – Lord knows what beside,
   And swam for Love, as I for Glory;

'Twere hard to say who fared the best:
   Sad mortals! thus the gods still plague you!
He lost his labour, I my jest;
   For he was drown'd, and I've the ague.

Clearly, this is a light-hearted poem: but its reverberations extend
beyond its own limited confines to the poems of Byron's maturity.
Within its compass it contains, hints at, the crucial problem that
wracks Byron in his major work – how seriously dare he take
himself, or, for that matter, the world of which he is a part. There
comes a point when the tidiness and neatness of this paradoxical
wryness is insufficient. As it happens, the events of the separation
force Byron into a painful acknowledgement of this fact. Once again,
it is impossible to separate biographical from literary concerns.

II

Childe Harold is crucial both for Byron, and for our understanding of
him. It has that opacity which can so easily give the Romantic poets a
bad name, that murkiness of theme and image which seems to deny

the claims of clarity and insight they themselves urge. Some of the critical problems stem from the poem's piecemeal composition — the separation drama occurs after the publication of the first two cantos, and inevitably affects the subsequent course of the poem. But what is especially interesting here is the way the poem anticipates, whilst in the end steering clear from, the culmination of his satiric vein in *Don Juan*. The anticipations do not come solely, as Andrew Rutherford seems to suggest, in the final canto; they are to be found in the first canto, and even more so in the first version of that canto, when Byron seems to have been thinking of a poem much more in the 'medley' manner. [8] As he works over the poem, Byron tones down the overtly satiric elements, to bring the poem more into line with an over-riding concept of decorum. But the nature of the poem challenges decorum at every turn; its direction is away from strict categories towards a more liberated idea of form and form's possibilities. [9] The poem, in any of its stages, does not seem to me a complete success: that is hardly surprising, and perhaps irrelevant. It is an amazingly ambitious poem in its attempt to make sense of personal, individual experience within the context of the general and universal. Byron had no reliable precedents: it is something of a quirk that he should turn to James Beattie's poem, *The Minstrel*, for sanction.

That form, content and language were not entirely separable concerns struck Byron when he read Beattie and the other eighteenth century Spenserians. The Preface to Cantos I and II of *Childe Harold* makes this point:

> The stanza of Spenser, according to one of our most successful poets, admits of every variety. Dr Beattie makes the following observation:—'Not long ago, I began a poem in the style and stanza of Spenser, in which I propose to give full scope to my inclination, and be either droll or pathetic, descriptive or sentimental, tender or satirical, as the humour strikes me; for, if I mistake not, the measure which I have adopted admits equally of all these kinds of composition.' Strengthened in my opinion by such authority, and by the example of some in the highest order of Italian poets, I shall make no apology for attempts at similar variations in the following composition; satisfied that if they are unsuccessful, their failure must be in the execution, rather than in the design, sanctioned by the practice of Ariosto, Thomson and Beattie.

Sanction is important for Byron, and it is typical of him that he should resort to the European, in particular the Italian, tradition.[10] But his use of the word 'design' is misleading, because as he has already admitted earlier in the Preface, these first two cantos are 'merely experimental' – in other words, he is already anticipating (with his reference to Ariosto especially) the notion of design that predominates in *Don Juan*, a design that denies itself as it unfolds. Nonetheless the concern with form is instructive. We may feel, as does Paul West, that the choice of stanza is totally misguided, that his sensitivity to form shows itself in *Childe Harold* only in the 'variety of Byron's efforts to evade the dangers of the stanza';[11] but the concern is there, as is the concern for language. Ultimately the two are inseparable.

One of T. S. Eliot's odder judgements is that Byron adds nothing to the language, that he has no sense of words, and that this betokens a defective sensibility ('I cannot think of any other poet of his distinction who might so easily have been an accomplished foreigner writing English').[12] Byron's contemporary reviewers could see that, even in *Childe Harold*, Byron was doing something new with language. Whilst Scott thought there was some 'affected ambiguity of the stile in some parts', and Wordsworth 'denied his style to be English', Jeffrey saw the originality: 'the diction, though unequal and frequently faulty, has on the whole a freedom, copiousness and vigour, which we are not sure we could match in any cotemporary poet.'[13] He made the connections that still seem to matter:

> Lord Byron's [language] has often a nervous simplicity and manly freshness which reminds us of Dryden, and an occasional force and compression, in some of the smaller pieces especially, which afford no unfavourable resemblance to Crabbe.

Even the objections are germane, in that they focus on qualities that we might regard as valuable: George Ellis, the satirist, in the *Quarterly Review*, referred to 'that motley mixture of obsolete and modern phraseology by which the ease and elegance of his verses are often injured.'[14] Byron's interests extended far beyond 'ease and elegance', far beyond the easy decorums of personal behaviour and literary fashion: he was deliberately brewing a heady, motley mixture, deliberately playing with his readers and what they might expect. If *Childe Harold* starts out as some sort of 'quest' poem (Byron calls it a 'romaunt'), with at least a nominal figure to give 'some connexion to the piece', it ends up as something much more ambitious and exciting — it becomes an exploration of poetry's possibilities, of what can be contained within the confines of a given form, of what language can achieve.[15] It is a poem, too, about personality (Byron eventually gives up, rather resignedly, the distinction he makes at first between himself and the Childe), and about how to view your own self in a way that is dispassionate, honest, and open to change. Behind the Pilgrimage (the initial version called the hero Childe Burun) lies Byron's journey across Europe: that biographical fact, the experience it represents, has to be accounted for, absorbed into the poem's structure. The dandy's Grand Tour becomes a spiritual journey of self-knowledge: and that knowledge is essentially changing, shifting, just as the self observed shifts and changes. There is no one truth to be discovered — the final image is of the ever-rolling, ever-changing ocean.

That all-embracing image of the ocean, with which the poem so movingly ends, is anticipated at the start, with the disgraced hero setting off on his travels. The sea's alternate turbulence and placidity encompasses the movement of the poem, and of the poem's ostensible hero, the restless Harold. It is this restlessness that receives the initial emphasis, set off against a scene he contemplates but whose opposing peace he cannot really grasp: 'more restless than the swallow in the skies', he cannot at this stage confront the truths urged by 'conscious Reason'. His need to move — it does not matter where — predominates:

> Onward he flies, nor fix'd as yet the goal
> Where he shall rest him on his pilgrimage;
> And o'er him many changing scenes must roll
> Ere toil his thirst for travel can assuage,
> Or he shall calm his breast, or learn experience sage.
>
> (I, 28)

By the time Byron begins the third canto, he is openly making the extension to himself. But at the start of the poem, he can see detachedly, or at least sufficiently so to invest the Ancient Mariner parallel with a sardonic undertow of wry mockery (John Galt actually commented on Byron's likeness to Coleridge's hero when they set sail).[16] Byron expostulates in his Preface (and elsewhere) that he would not in any case want to be mistaken for Harold, and the reasons are clear when we see the depths of depravity to which he has sunk in 'Sin's long labrynth'.

> Childe Harold was he hight: — but whence his name
> And lineage long, it suits me not to say;
> Suffice it, that perchance they were of fame,
> And had been glorious in another day:
> But one sad losel soils a name for aye,
> However mighty in the olden time;
> Nor all that heralds rake from coffin'd clay,
> Nor florid prose, nor honeyed lies of rhyme,
> Can blazon evil deeds, or consecrate a crime.
>
> (I, 3)

But as we read through these opening stanzas, it becomes apparent that this wastrel has some redeeming features: we end up being baffled as the focus and perspective shift, as curiously contradictory images cancel each other out. Just as his father's 'venerable pile' seems both insecure and strong, so strength and frailty characterise the poem and its movements, and those of the hero, too. The Childe is isolated, misunderstood; already described as stalking apart 'in joyless reverie' (I, 6), he is now shown, paradoxically, in 'maddest mirthful mood' which is itself deceptive.[17] We get a glimpse here of the satanic figure turning into something much more like the Byron we know in *Don Juan*:

> For his was not that open, artless soul
> That feels relief by bidding sorrow flow,
> Nor sought he friend to counsel or condole,
> What'er this grief mote be, which he could not control.

> And none did love him: though to hall and bower
> He gather'd revellers from far and near,
> He knew them flatt'rers of the festal hour;
> The heartless parasites of present cheer.
>
> (I, 8—9)

Our sympathies sway with the verse. Harold's conflicting emotions, his hysterical moodiness, seem to reflect his surroundings, which are themselves ambiguous. But it is not merely a matter of ensuring our sympathy in the face of the Childe's obvious shortcomings. The diction of these opening stanzas should be enough to put us on our guard. The imagery of contradiction and opposition is matched by a language, a style of conflicting impulse. If Childe Harold is 'restless',

then so too is the poet in his attitudes: Spenserianisms, archaisms
jostle uneasily with directness and simplicity. This is not quite the
mixture heralded by the prefatory appeal to Beattie. Going back to
the second stanza of the poem, we realise that uneasiness is the right
response, for what these lines announce is neither plain seriousness,
recreation of past heroics, nor simple mockery of that ethos. We are
disorientated by a language that misleads (even 'whilome' does not
absolutely give the game away, as its use elsewhere in the poem can be
ambiguous):

> Whilome in Albion's isle there dwelt a youth,
> Who ne in virtue's ways did take delight;
> But spent his days in riot most uncouth,
> And vex'd with mirth the drowsy ear of Night.
> Ah me! in sooth he was a shameless wight,
> Sore given to revel and ungodly glee;
> Few earthly things found favour in his sight,
> Save concubines and carnal companie,
> And flaunting wassailers of high and low degree.
>
> (I, 2)

It might seem perverse to be reading the poem backwards in this way.
But in practice this is what happens — we need to keep checking our
bearings in a continuing process that is unnerving. In any case, Byron
approached the poem himself, in its final version, in this way. For, if
he toned down some of the original burlesque passages, he added a
first stanza which puts his own poetic self firmly in place, and which
further undermines whatever confidence we might like to have in the
way we read the poem. The appeal to Parnassus later on in the first
canto is all the more effective because of the almost offhand address to
the muse with which the poem starts. The Childe might seem an
unworthy hero, but the poet's credentials are not too impressive
either:

> Oh, thou! in Hellas deem'd of heavenly birth,
> Muse! form'd or fabled at the minstrel's will!
> Since shamed full oft by later lyres on earth,
> Mine dares not call thee from thy sacred hill:
> Yet there I've wander'd by thy vaunted rill;
> Yes! sigh'd o'er Delphi's long deserted shrine,
> Where, save that feeble fountain, all is still;

> Nor mote my shell awake the weary Nine
> To grace so plain a tale – this lowly lay of mine.
>
> (I, 1)

This might seem reminiscent of Wordsworth's debunking technique in some of his *Lyrical Ballads*: the difference is that Byron is not entirely relinquishing a belief in the Muses. We are conscious of their presence, and of the demands they make, increasingly throughout the poem; and we are the more conscious of the precariousness of the relationship between Muse and poet by virtue of the deliberate blurring that Byron indulges in these opening stanzas. It is as though decorum is there somewhere, an ideal hovering in the background, but virtually unattainable in a world that is so unpredictable, so composed of contrary elements. Byron has not, at this stage, the confidence with which Wordsworth can use humour to redirect our emotions, our responses along channels hitherto unexplored; rather, this resort to humour is an index of his desperation, of his not knowing himself quite how seriously to take Childe Harold, quite how much weight to give to the romantic trappings of his tale.

The degree of disorientation involved (it affects Childe, poet, reader) can be gauged by looking at the song Childe Harold sings on his departure. There are very clear Coleridgean echoes:

> And now I'm in the world alone,
> Upon the wide, wide sea:

But the defiance of the next lines is typically Byronic:

> But why should I for others groan,
> When none will sigh for me?
> Perchance my dog will whine in vain,
> Till fed by stranger hands;
> But long ere I come back again
> He'd tear me where he stands.
>
> (I, 13, 9)

This allusion to the *Odyssey*, and the hero's return, foreshadows a similar allusion in *Don Juan*, when Lambro returns unexpectedly to his island home. Behind the self-pity lies a serious point that Byron insists on repeatedly – that is, the fragility of the heroic ideal. He knows, realistically, that the faithful Penelope was an exception, rather than the rule; he knows, too, that Odysseus is himself an ambiguous, even comic, figure in the heroic pantheon. But this song is riddled with more than Byronic cynicism: running through it is something not fully explained, something near to schizophrenia in its awareness of division. The Childe has a counterpart in the song:

> 'Come hither, hither, my little page!
>   Why dost thou weep and wail?
> . . .
> But dash the tear-drop from thine eye;
>   Our ship is swift and strong:
> Our fleetest falcon scarce can fly
>   More merrily along.'
>   (I, 13, 3)

And again:

> 'Enough, enough, my yeoman good,
>   Thy grief let none gainsay;
> But I, who am of lighter mood,
>   Will laugh to flee away.'
>   (I, 13, 7)

The journey is welcomed, embraced, and it is so in terms of laughter.
    That laughter does not, admittedly, ring throughout the poem. But it is an essential part of the opening canto in particular, part of the realisation that the world in which oppositions prevail can be met only by laughter, by detachment, by satire. This combination is seen at work in the stanzas which prepare for the description of Cintra and its notorious convention. Byron wonders how any pen can capture the scene, and at first reading this might seem like the conventional 'if only I could . . .' type of expostulation:

> . . . views more dazzling unto mortal ken
> Than those whereof such things the bard relates,
> Who to the awe-struck world unlock'd Elysium's gates?
>   (I, 18)

But the Childe's later scorn at the convention's outcome is bound to make us revise our judgement of this earlier passage: the appeal to precedent assumes a sour taste in retrospect. Furthermore, the two

stanzas that follow are a curious combination of grotesque description
(recalling Keats's 'Epistle to J. H. Reynolds') and open satire that
owes its strengths to a much earlier tradition:

> The horrid crags, by toppling convent crown'd,
> The cork-trees hoar that clothe the shaggy steep,
> The mountain-moss by scorching skies imbrown'd,
> The sunken glen, whose sunless shrubs must weep,
> The tender azure of the unruffled deep,
> The orange tints that gild the greenest bough,
> The torrents that from cliff to valley leap,
> The vine on high, the willow branch below,
> Mix'd in one mighty scene, with varied beauty glow.
>
> Then slowly climb the many-winding way,
> And frequent turn to linger as you go,
> From loftier rocks new loveliness survey,
> And rest ye at 'Our Lady's house of woe;'
> Where frugal monks their little relics show,
> And sundry legends to the stranger tell:
> Here impious men have punish'd been, and lo!
> Deep in yon cave Honorius long did dwell,
> In hope to merit Heaven by making earth a Hell.
>
> (I, 19–20)

The satire blossoms from this point onwards: though it soon becomes
clear that, for all the occasional felicity, for all the informing anger,
the Spenserian stanza as Byron uses it is not the ideal vehicle for
sustained satire; and the poem as a whole does not attempt it. It serves
Byron's purposes at this juncture partly because of its place in the
structure – to have the apparently indolent hero indulging in a
satirical attack on the British is to make us wonder about his identity,
and about the poet's purpose; partly because it is a more extreme
version of the romantic-ironic stance that characterises the poem
generally, typified by this couplet that comes just before the
convention passage:

> . . . how
> Vain are the pleasaunces on earth supplied;
> Swept into wrecks anon by Time's ungentle tide!
>
> (I, 23)

Nothing established in the course of the poem alters the conviction behind those lines. And just as Byron's awareness of irony impresses itself here on verse that still has its Spenserian ring, so that awareness informs the more powerful stanzas on the war in Spain (heralding the bitter third canto on Waterloo), where the poet's own voice assumes an authority that was missing in the Childe's more halting observations. Byron warms to his theme, and his personification of Death and Destruction is grimly precise, powerful in its foreshadowing of the culminating scene in the bullring — already Byron knows how to use imagery and metaphor to lend his verse reverberation in a way that is both telling and humorous in the direst sense:

> Death rides upon the sulphury Siroc,
> Red Battle stamps his foot, and nations feel the shock.

> Lo! where the Giant on the mountain stands,
> His blood-red tresses deep'ning in the sun,
> With death-shot glowing in his fiery hands,
> And eye that scorcheth all it glares upon;
> Restless it rolls, now fix'd, and now anon
> Flashing afar, — and at his iron feet
> Destruction cowers, to mark what deeds are done;
> For on this morn three potent nations meet,
> To shed before his shrine the blood he deems most sweet.

> By Heaven! it is a splendid sight to see
> [and the mind immediately picks up the earlier cry —
> 'Oh Christ! it is a goodly sight to see
> What Heaven hath done for this delicious land:']
> (For one who hath no friend, no brother there)
> Their rival scarfs of mix'd embroidery,
> Their various arms that glitter in the air!
> What gallant war-hounds rouse them from their lair,
> And gnash their fangs, loud yelling for the prey!
> All join the chase, but few the triumph share;
> The Grave shall bear the chiefest prize away,
> And Havoc scarce for joy can number their array.
>   (I, 38—40)

The command of voice and tone is impressive — and needs much fuller quotation to do it justice.[18] Passion, anger and despair seem to require from Byron — they certainly elicit — a combination of directness, sobriety and a sense of folly that verges on the riotously comic because that is the only possible view of things. The simple, mirthful pleasures of life have been replaced by the manic, mocking laughter that accompanies an open-eyed refusal to accept the truth and leave it at that.

From here onwards images of mockery pervade the poem, whether it be the Spanish girl's 'black eye that mocks her coal-black veil', the broken mirror that sends back an apparently false reflection, or, most crucially, 'Despair' that has to perforce 'a smilingness assume'. It is typical of Byron that he should exploit the image of the crazed, destructive animal, make it serve so many purposes, in the later stanzas of this canto. Against the tiredly conventional, smugly superior sabbath of London (evoked with suitable mockery and burlesque, reminding us of the Swiftian heritage behind *Don Juan* especially), Byron sets the sabbath of Cadiz, which has an unholy gusto about it — but a gusto that is disturbingly equivocal, and made the more so by some giddy shifts in diction. The knowing smirk here (vaguely reminiscent of the coy Milton enjoying a joke in *Il Penseroso* at the pensive nun's expense):

> Much is the VIRGIN teased to shrive them free
> (Well do I ween the only virgin there)
> From crimes as numerous as her beadsmen be —
>
> (I, 71)

— the knowing smirk gives way in the next stanza to something more complicated, where even the detail — so important an element in Byron's vision — is denied its own complete validity, by the consciously Spenserian self-mockery (and that in itself turns out to be a crucial point, for by pinpointing the element of play here, Byron is exposing the playfulness for what it is, a callous disregard for others, for others' wounds):

> The lists are oped, the spacious area clear'd,
> Thousands on thousands piled are seated round;
> Long ere the first loud trumpet's note is heard,
> Ne vacant space for lated wight is found:
> Here dons, grandees, but chiefly dames abound,
> Skill'd in the ogle of a roguish eye,
> Yet ever well inclined to heal the wound;

None through their cold disdain are doom'd to die,
    As moon-struck bards complain, by Love's sad archery.

(I, 72)

That 'cold disdain' is, we sense, a bit too glib (and a comment on the Childe's own aloofness), that 'roguish eye' a chilling reminder of Destruction's red-shot eyes of the earlier passage and a foretaste of the bull — 'red rolls his eye's dilated glow' (I, 75). And the 'moonstruck bard', whilst mocked, is, in this company, this context, not so despicable, vindicated as he is by that marvellous phrase, 'Love's sad archery'. This section, in its sustained and varied power, is an indication of the integrity that increasingly stamps the poem's progress. This particular scene, with its savagery and ceremony, its bantering sexuality, its playing of one mood against another, can be taken as an emblem of the larger movement of the poem as a whole.

After the variety, the kaleidoscopic shifts, the hesitations and uncertainties of Canto I (and the final stanza with its address to reader and critic underlines Byron's lack of total ease), the poem assumes a gravity not hitherto achieved, with the Childe's arrival in Greece at the start of Canto II. This is writing with its own very measured decorum, all the more powerful because of what has preceded it: the shuffling feet have at last found, even if momentarily, the right posture. Just as importantly, Harold is unable to appreciate the significance of what he sees: increasingly, we realise that it is the poet who matters in this pilgrimage. Harold, it turns out, is — as Don Juan will be — a puppet in his master's hands. The full implications of that have yet to be worked out — at this stage, Byron does little more than draw it to our attention, so that we are, in terms of decorum, unduly conscious of it, and him, as though he has to kick himself as a reminder of what the poem is ostensibly about. But if Byron does not make a structural or stylistic virtue out of this tension between himself and his hero, the poem nonetheless shows a convergence of the twain. We get sucked into a spiral of introversion, often wondering (as in II, 2 or 31) just how much interior monologue is the poet's, how much Harold's, and accordingly attributing bafflement to both poet and hero, and by extension to ourselves.

The desperation that recurs in Canto II has, really, little to do with Harold, all to do with Byron, the Byron who at the end of this canto mourns the loss of his friend Edleston, the being on whom his own being depended. With Edleston's death he has lost a vital part of himself, and all that is left him is a recklessness, to 'plunge again into the crowd/And follow all that Peace disdains to seek': a conscious mask has to be assumed, a distasteful one, but all too necessary. There is a terrible, piercing honesty in this self-portrait:

> Where Revel calls, and Laughter, vainly loud,
> False to the heart, distorts the hollow cheek,
> To leave the flagging spirit doubly weak;
> Still o'er the features, which perforce they cheer,
> To feign the pleasure or conceal the pique;
> Smiles form the channel of a future tear,
> Or raise the writhing lip with ill-dissembled sneer.
>
> (II, 97)

Byron has come a long way in his search for himself, when he can so clearly see what is happening: he realises that the gap between himself and his hero has narrowed alarmingly. All is dissembling: it is no accident that even here we get at least a smidgeon of the Hamletesque flavour that is to be a major part of the relish, the paradoxical gusto, of *Don Juan.*

The development of *Childe Harold* from this point onwards owes much to biographical circumstances not directly reflected in the poem, even if referred to obliquely with the address to his daughter Ada in the first stanza of Canto III. The poems written at the time of the separation have been brilliantly discussed by W. W. Robson, and it would be impossible to rehearse here the delicacy of his argument. Patricia Ball has written about some of these poems as forerunners of the Victorian poetry of relationships.[19] I simply want to point to the importance of the 'Epistle to Augusta'.

Byron copes with the various characters in the drama in different ways: to his wife he addresses the extraordinarily self-pitying, maudlin 'Fare thee well!', a poem rightly castigated by Wordsworth. To Mrs Clermont he writes 'A Sketch', in which his venom is brilliantly encapsulated in Popean couplets. It is hard to imagine anything more cruel, more withering, where all personal feeling is concentrated exclusively in hate. This is a tone of voice we need to register, because it reappears elsewhere, if less hysterically, less histrionically —

> Oh, may thy grave be sleepless as the bed,
> The widow'd couch of fire, that thou hast spread!

Then, when thou fain wouldst weary Heaven with prayer,
Look on thine earthly victims — and despair!
Down to the dust! — and, as thou rott'st away,
Even worms shall perish on thy poisonous clay.
But for the love I bore, and still must bear,
To her thy malice from all ties would tear —
Thy name — thy human name — to every eye
The climax of all scorn should hang on high,
Exalted o'er thy less abhorr'd compeers —
And festering in the infamy of years.

More subtle in its effects, more ambivalent in its attitudes to his wife and to his suffering, are the 'Lines on Hearing that Lady Byron was Ill'. Here, Byron ends by resorting to extravagance and self-justification; but he begins more moderately, more considerately, more conscious of another person's woes, of the waste involved. Formally the poem is interesting in that by moving away from the couplet Byron has released himself from its restrictions, enabling himself to follow the shifts of his own thoughts.

And is it thus? — it is as I foretold,
    And shall be more so; for the mind recoils
Upon itself, and the wreck'd heart lies cold,
    While heaviness collects the shatter'd spoils.
It is not in the storm nor in the strife
    We feel benumb'd, and wish to be no more,
    But in the after-silence on the shore,
When all is lost, except a little life.
I am too well avenged! —

It is, however, in the 'Epistle to Augusta' that Byron achieves a fully-felt, fully worked-out poem, crucial in its use of the stanzaic form that is to emerge triumphantly in *Beppo*, *The Vision of Judgement*, and *Don Juan*, but here applied to a theme of the utmost personal import, his feelings for his half-sister as he is on the verge of departure. It is a poem of quiet acceptance, built on the acknowledgement of a particularly wretched fate:

There yet are two things in my destiny, —
A world to roam through, and a home with thee.

Again Byron uses the imagery of sea and storm, but projects it inwards, into the strange terrain of his own mind, just at the moment when he is about, literally, to set out on a voyage that is away from himself, from what matters. Eliot's talk of Byron's ineptitude with language is itself shown to be inept, when we see Byron so acutely conscious of the weight and significance of words, of their connotations as well as their denotations:

> If my inheritance of storms hath been
> In other elements, and on the rocks
> Of perils, overlook'd or unforeseen,
> I have sustain'd my share of worldly shocks,
> The fault was mine; nor do I seek to screen
> My errors with defensive paradox;
> I have been cunning in mine overthrow,
> The careful pilot of my proper woe.

The honesty is firmly controlled, no tremor of self-pity gets in the way; that phrase 'defensive paradox' is itself paradoxical, because it is a quality that we come to associate with the mature Byron. He can combine what Robson calls 'sincerity' with 'paradox'. Even at this point in his life, he can say, buoyantly, amusedly:

> But now I fain would for a time survive,
> If but to see what next can well arrive.

He has, rather to his surprise, attained a quiet wisdom he had thought beyond him: he can make connections with the past, and with the future, which carry conviction because they are weighted with a due sense of life's sorrow, and of his own stupidity. His grand gesture to Miltonic precedent ('The world is all before me' – to be echoed in *Don Juan*) cannot, alas! be related directly to Wordsworth's similar appeal at the start of *The Prelude*: independently they each look back to that expulsion from Eden, anxious to derive hope from it. For Byron, it is a muffled, muted hope that emerges, tinged with regret. He shares the bafflement of Harold, the more deeply felt in that it is not factitious:

> With false Ambition what had I to do?
> Little with Love, and least of all with Fame;
> And yet they came unsought, and with me grew,

And made me all which they can make – a name.
Yet this was not the end I did pursue;
Surely I once beheld a nobler aim.
But all is over – I am one the more
To baffled millions which have gone before.

Whereas the other poems generated by the separation play, for the most part, on one note, reluctant to move beyond self-imposed confines, the 'Epistle' has that element of freedom within a strict form that is to become the hallmark of the satires. In it, we can see Byron laying himself bare, exposing himself in the most necessary way; in so doing he creates a poem that is like himself, unpredictable and unfixed, feeling its way forward, combining the tenderness of feeling for Augusta with open-eyed acknowledgement of himself and his own failings. It is a remarkable fusion of insight and technically accomplished distancing – as though Byron has suddenly, even for the first time, grasped the truth that it is in that very act of distancing that he can see himself most clearly, most truly.

This truth permeates the rest of *Childe Harold*, giving it a weight and poignancy that can now act as a counterbalance to the shifting moods of the first two cantos. Byron can now be more open about his own part in the poem: it is he who is tossed along, who both revels in and stands aghast at this fact –

> – for I am as a weed
> Flung from the rock, on Ocean's foam to sail
> Where'er the surge may sweep, the tempest's breath prevail.
>   (III, 2)

From this point onwards the poem is to be an exercise in self-forgetfulness: what matters now is the elimination of self in favour of the creative act, the 'soul of thought'. But it proves to be elimination of a curious kind: certainly the Childe's 'guarded coldness' (III, 10), as though he 'deem' his spirit now so firmly fix'd /And sheath'd with an invulnerable mind,/That, if no joy, no sorrow lurk'd behind', does not appear to be the ideally honest solution, however inevitable. In fact, the Childe's solution is to lie, not in such coldness, but in engagement, his restlessness is a virtue in that it urges him across the world: as his lassitude disperses and diminishes, so the poet's spirit engages with issues of high moment. The personal loss he himself had suffered is now placed in a broad European context: the savage ironies of Waterloo epitomise and put into perspective his own sad failures, his own desperate losses — the canto ends, as it begins, with an address to his daughter. This is all the more moving because Byron has expressed such doubts about his poem, aware as he is of the need, still, to conceal; the open communion with nature which early in this canto is seen as the creative ideal is, perhaps, impossible. The poem is becoming an act of immense self-discipline —

> Thus far have I proceeded in a theme
> Renew'd with no kind auspices: — to feel
> We are not what we have been, and to deem
> We are not what we should be, and to steel
> The heart against itself; and to conceal,
> With a proud caution, love, or hate, or aught, —
> Passion or feeling, purpose, grief or zeal, —
> Which is the Tyrant spirit of our thought,
> Is a stern task of soul:— No matter, — it is taught.
>
> (III, 111)

This directness is devastating.

The final canto demonstrates Byron's concern for language, at the very moment when he doubts his achievement — 'I twine /My hopes of being remember'd in my line /With my land's language'. He sets himself, therefore, in a parallel tradition to that of Dante, who 'arose /To raise a language, and his land reclaim /From the dull yoke of the barbaric foes' (IV, 30). But the whole canto oozes with the despair that the 'ruins of paradise' invite. Eloquence is contained, not in words, but in the 'nameless column with the buried base' (IV, 110). Again and again, Byron confronts the problem of expression, of poetry's justification. In the third canto, he had thought that perhaps he could put his belief in the notion of 'words as things'; but there seems to be nothing so definite here, we cannot grasp external realities. Typically, Byron reverts to the idea of mockery:

> Our outward sense
> Is but of gradual grasp — and as it is
> That what we have of feeling most intense
> Outstrips our faint expression; even so this
> Outshining and o'erwhelming edifice
> Fools our fond gaze, and greatest of the great

Defies at first our Nature's littleness,
Till, growing with its growth, we thus dilate
Our spirits to the size of that they contemplate.

(IV, 158)

It is the poem's triumph that the answer to mockery is this expansion
of spirit, a triumph, too, that the reflective sea imagery of the final
stanzas picks up the notion of Venice as a city of reflections, of dreams.

In Rome, Byron had felt 'the moral of all human tales' (IV, 108),
and he had declared 'Away with words!' In a sense, the poem is an
anti-poem, in its frequent urging of the contradictory impulse away
from words, to naked feeling, its increasing concern with the nature
of the poetic dream. This is not fully worked out in *Childe Harold*: but
if we sense the stirrings of something significantly different in
emphasis, then this is right. There certainly are stanzas which seem to
be reaching for the pithy epigrammaticism of *Don Juan*, and we are
bound to notice these, and their effect on the culminating movement
of the poem, on the carefully worked climax; just as in the earlier
cantos there is sufficient mixing of tones for us to be made conscious
of changing patterns and moods. But one stanza in particular sums up
the way Byron is moving, and it comes after that injunction 'Away
with words' as Byron surveys the Roman scene. In these lines Byron
captures, with proper solemnity, the tragedy and comedy of man's
being:

Admire, exult, despise, laugh, weep, – for here
There is such matter for all feeling: — Man!
Thou pendulum betwixt a smile and tear,
Ages and realms are crowded in this span,
This mountain, whose obliterated plan
The pyramid of empires pinnacled,
Of Glory's gewgaws shining in the van
Till the sun's rays with added flame were fill'd!
Where are its golden roofs? where those who dared to build?

(IV, 109)

It may well be that Byron was right, that expression as normally
understood was insufficient to the task he was setting himself, that the
dream was indeed too fragile, only sustainable in a mirror 'unruffled'
by the artist's hand (IV, 53). But even as he expressed his despair at
art's capabilities, Byron was growing conscious of another way of

handling the components of the dream. The grotesque incongruities of life could perhaps be met on their own terms. The major satires represent the solidifying of those mirror images that lurk throughout *Childe Harold*.

III

Byron's sense of poetic failure, as we see it in *Childe Harold*, derived as much as anything from the realisation of his true lineage. His satires acknowledge what we might have expected from a careful reading of the disillusionment of *Childe Harold*, that his real forebears are Pope and Dryden and Swift. In September 1817 he writes:

> I am convinced . . . that . . . *all* of us — Scott, Southey, Words-worth, Moore, Campbell, I, — are all in the wrong, one as much as another, that we are upon a wrong revolutionary poetical system, or systems, not worth a damn in itself, and from which none but Rogers and Crabbe are free; and that the present and next generations will finally be of this opinion.[20]

This was too sanguine an expectation. But Byron, unlike many of his contemporaries, saw the value of continuity — a continuity repre-sented, perhaps imperfectly, by Crabbe — and he could do so the more readily and convincingly because he was one of the worst offenders against it. This he admitted: 'no one has done more through negligence to corrupt the language' and to 'produce that exaggerated and false taste'.[21]

Byron revives the idea of the virtuoso, and combines it with his maturing nonchalance to create a poetry of bangs and flashes, a poetry coruscating in its brilliance (as he saw it himself, a 'versified aurora borealis').[22] What is so typically brazen of Byron is that along with this virtuosity he revives that very notion of taste that was so crucial in the eighteenth-century poetic tradition. And he does so wickedly, in the full knowledge that taste was just the word that Warton had appropriated to himself and to his own ideas of what poetry should be, against Pope and the Augustans. So Byron entered the Pope controversy not simply as an antiquarian, but as someone who passionately believed that his own age could still learn from Pope. It was not, either, merely an acid wit that he admired in the 'little Queen Anne's man'[23] — it was the invention, the imagination, the living quality of a language engaged with its appropriate materials. Wordsworth had decried the idea of taste that implied little more than a 'taste for sherry or rope-dancing', the taste invoked by Southey, but his arrogance had nothing theoretical to put in its place. Byron saw that much of modern literary life was a mixture of 'cursed humbug and bad taste';[24] his crusade was both literary and moral.

Byron is too astute to revamp Pope for a nineteenth-century audience: he effects one of the most curious marriages in the history of poetry. The relatively insignificant John Hookham Frere becomes, through his *Whistlecraft*, Byron's way into the colloquial verve of the Italian poets he had heard of, but scarcely read, Pulci and Casti, and their sustained and brilliant use of the *ottava rima*. But the sense of decorum is derived from the Augustan tradition that Byron increasingly felt was what mattered. With this goes an alertness to the different possibilities inherent in the resort to the speaking voice: Byron knows well the advantages of his place in society. Much of what he says on this subject might seem merely the snobbery of an aristocrat, of one who had every reason to scorn both the 'democratic' Lake poets and the Cockneyisms of Leigh Hunt and Keats: but his pinpointing of 'vulgarity' as the besetting sin of modern poetry gives an important hint as to the tone he is aiming at. Vulgarity for Byron is not coarseness:

> Far be it from me to presume that there ever was, or can be, such a thing as an *aristocracy* of *poets*; but there *is* a nobility of thought and of style, open to all stations, and derived partly from talent, and partly from education, – which is to be found in Shakespeare, and Pope, and Burns, no less than in Dante and Alfieri, but which is nowhere to be perceived in the mock birds and bards of Mr Hunt's little chorus.[25]

When it comes to precise definitions, Byron can do little more than give examples of what he means by a gentleman. This is the argument we would expect: after all, it is a social point he is making, and it is a characteristic of social groups that each knows its own place and potentialities. We do not have to believe Byron to be Fielding's successor to take the point he makes about Fielding's essential lack of vulgarity. 'You see the man of education, the gentleman, and the scholar, sporting with his subject – its master, not its slave.'[26] That sporting metaphor is perhaps the crucial one.

Both *Beppo* and *The Vision of Judgement* exemplify the new style –

it is nothing less than that, for all the hints and nudges towards it; but it is in *Don Juan* that Byron achieves his masterpiece. Not all commentators have agreed: if few have concurred with Bernard Blackstone's rather dismissive attitude to the 'cult' of *Don Juan*, several have thought, with Andrew Rutherford, that the long poem is too long, too uncoordinated, and that the brevity of *The Vision of Judgement* forces Byron to compress and condense, to distil the essence of his comic vision.[27] There can be no disputing the overall accomplishment of all three poems: but it seems to me that whereas *Don Juan* combines the virtues of each of the two shorter poems, neither of these has that scope and range that are the hallmarks of the true masterpiece.

Beppo is essentially a light poem, a satire with definite limits. It provides Byron with the ideal opportunity to try out his new mode, and it is as an experiment that we can most usefully see it. In *Childe Harold* Byron had frequently had to bring himself to heel, to remind himself that somewhere in the poem there was a hero with a tale of his own; in *Beppo* Byron makes a virtue out of this digressive habit, and elevates his self-consciousness to a new pitch. Far from indulging in the self-forgetfulness advocated in *Childe Harold*, Byron actively exploits his sense of himself as raconteur, his sense of an audience waiting to be told things by someone who appears not to be in control.

> To turn, – and to return; – the devil take it!
>   This story slips for ever through my fingers,
> Because, just as the stanza likes to make it,
>   It needs must be, and so it rather lingers:
> This form of verse began, I can't well break it,
>   But must keep time and tune like public singers;
> But if I once get through my present measure,
> I'll take another when I'm next at leisure.
>
>   (63)

The studied carelessness and indifference inevitably draws our gaze towards the poet, towards his technique – even as he disclaims it. This indeed is the manner of the gentleman. He confesses that 'digression is a sin', aware as he is of 'the gentle reader' and his expectations. But that 'gentle reader' is an Aunt Sally:

Oh that I had the art of easy writing
   What should be easy reading! could I scale
Parnassus, where the Muses sit inditing
   Those pretty poems never known to fail,
How quickly would I print (the world delighting)
   A Grecian, Syrian, or Assyrian tale;
And sell you, mix'd with western sentimentalism,
Some samples of the finest Orientalism!

(51)

And the next stanza announces the role he has adopted, the
anonymous mask which particularises him so clearly:

But I am a nameless sort of person
   (A broken Dandy lately on my travels) . . .

Byron insists on this quality: this poem, he is saying, is not really a
poem at all, any more than he is your 'all or nothing' author. Writing
is a gentlemanly accomplishment, a sport, in which the poet can be as
self-conscious and as gauche as he chooses ('And so we'll call her
Laura, if you please /Because it slips into my verse with ease' — this is
not mere knowingness, it is the throwing to the winds of pretence,
and simultaneously a reminder of the pretence of art). *Beppo's*
rollicking narrative could not, we feel, have continued much further
than it does: there are occasional patches of concentrated poetry
which still have the power to startle and amaze, but Byron's insistence
on his own amateurishness allows for a laxity that gives diminishing
returns. The central lines, from the point of view of Byron's attitude
to his art and his development, are these:

I fear I have a little turn for satire,
   And yet methinks the older that one grows
Inclines us more to laugh than scold, though laughter
Leaves us so doubly serious shortly after.

Oh, mirth and innocence! Oh, milk and water!
   Ye happy mixtures of more happy days!
In these sad centuries of sin and slaughter
   Abominable Man no more allays
His thirst with such pure beverage. No matter,
   I love you both, and both shall have my praise:

Oh, for old Saturn's reign of sugar candy! –
Meantime I drink to your return in brandy.
(79–80)

That 'the good old times' (mourned in *The Age of Bronze*) have in fact gone for good, is clear from *The Vision of Judgement*, Byron's answer to Southey's poem of the same name. This is a savage attack on a man, an age, and an ethos: Byron referred to his 'finest Carravagio style', and certainly the general tone is much darker, whatever the light relief.[28] Byron laughs and scolds mercilessly, and underneath both is the sad sobriety of one who knows he is not penning light verses. The asides, the disclaimers ('Tis every tittle true, beyond suspicion, /And accurate as any other vision') merely serve to point up the mournful absurdity that is the poem's theme. This is very much not an anti-poem, even though it is so directly launched against another poet, another poem; it is, by virtue of that very fact, a determined attempt to re-establish true poetic value, and for Byron that means true moral value. Southey's heresy lay in his assumption of orthodoxy: he had failed his age. He had done so in a particularly absurd way, in the pompous hexameters he had written to herald George III's arrival in heaven. Southey's poem was obnoxious to Byron's poetical, personal, critical, aesthetic, moral sensibilities: *The Vision of Judgement* was Byron's stinging rebuke, the supreme example of a parody that transcends the genre, establishing itself as the authentic voice. The title itself is stark and terrifying, subverting Southey's poem and sustaining Byron's claim to greatness: the judgement of Southey's own title is turned back on its author, his vision ridiculed. As for Byron's own vision, that finds its fullest expression in *Don Juan* – and again, Southey's unlaid ghost lurks behind the poem as an awful warning.

Goethe was to proclaim, after reading Byron, that 'English poetry is already in possession of something we Germans totally lack: a cultured comic language.'[29] Byron comments in *Don Juan* that 'The days of comedy are gone, alas!' (XIII, 94). Although the point he goes on to develop is more akin to that made by Hazlitt in his dissection of the state of English comedy, the wider sentiment implied in that line reverberates throughout the bulk of this sprawling, uneven poem. Against it, providing the tensions on which the poem depends, we should set the couplet at the beginning of the fourth canto:

And the sad truth which hovers o'er my desk
Turns what was once romantic to burlesque.
                                (IV, 3)

Goethe was, I think, right in what he said, and what is of prime
interest in reading *Don Juan* is seeing how Byron sets about
establishing a language that is both 'cultured' and 'comic'. That, it
seems to me, is his supreme achievement, one that grows out of his
other satires, but which sets all these late works apart from the Popean
couplets of, say, *English Bards and Scotch Reviewers*.[30] We have
already seen how increasingly in *Childe Harold* the problem of
expression became paramount: this was not simply the recurrent
poetic difficulty of capturing experience in words. It was something
more specific than that, for it really involved the forging of a language
that was idiosyncratic, individual, attentive to Byron's own particular
needs (and *Childe Harold* shows how various, how conflicting these
were), and at the same time representative, answering to the challenge
of the age. Just as Byron's life (and death) had that quality of
engagement with the world on more than an insular level – his and
Shelley's political concerns make Wordsworth's revolutionary experiences seem relatively marginal – so his poetry reflects that
European engagement, that sense of things having to fit together,
however problematic the jigsaw might seem. It is for this reason – in
any case the poem insistently asserts it – that the bland bromides of
Helen Gardner will not do.[31] To say that *Don Juan* 'began as a farce
and developed into a comedy'; to say that 'satire is a major element in
Don Juan; but so is romance'; to say that the poem demonstrates a
'fundamental good humour' – all this is to reduce the poem, to make
it manageable. Manageable is what it refuses to be.

As Byron says at the end of Canto XIV:

Were things but only called by their right name
Caesar himself would be ashamed of fame.
                                (XIV, 102)

The right name is the one that Byron endlessly searches for: words,
after all, 'are things, and a small drop of ink, /Falling like dew upon a
thought, produces /That which makes thousands, perhaps millions,
think' (II, 88). He might protest that he deals 'only in generalities', but
his generalities derive their force from what he calls his 'repertory of

facts'. Keats was to scoff at Byron for 'describing what he sees, whereas I describe what I imagine'.[32] It was a false dichotomy, and Keats was wrong to scoff, for what Byron saw was not seen by many. This in itself accounts for the poem's length — Byron's vision (that is the word to use) is perceptive, but also amazingly wide and extensive. Nor could he rest within the artificial confines of Dr Johnson's panoramic, but armchair, sweep from China to Peru: he had to make that journey, and learn for himself the altered perspectives as he went. It was only then that he could justify his talk of calling things by the right name — his was a relativist's position ('Changeable too, yet somehow *idem semper*' XVII, 11), as he said, 'So that I almost think that the same skin/For one without has two or three within'. He might laugh at his shifts, make a joke out of them — 'But if a writer should be quite consistent/How could he possibly show things existent?' (XV, 87). He then compounds the joke by contradicting himself, making it a personal need as well as a response to the truth of things 'as they really are':

> If people contradict themselves, can I
>   Help contradicting them and everybody,
> Even my veracious self? But that's a lie:
>   I never did so, never will. How should I?
> He who doubts all things nothing can deny.
>   Truth's fountains may be clear, her streams are muddy
> And cut through such canals of contradiction
> That she must often navigate o'er fiction.
>
> (XV, 88)

If, in *Beppo*, Byron had made play with his own persona, he moves very much more to the centre of the poem in *Don Juan*. There can be no doubt about our awareness of his presence in the poem: he is there in practically every line. As with Wordsworth, Coleridge and Keats, the poet's character is an important factor for Byron; but his perception is that character is not a fixed entity, it is something constantly changing and developing, as it confronts different circumstances. This does not mean that there are no fixed truths, rather that one has to be honest about the limits to knowledge.

Honesty is the keynote of the poem. The dedication, in its force and compression, is quite extraordinarily brilliant.[33] Southey is again the butt, the poet Laureate and therefore 'representative of all the race': his epical pretensions are as absurd as his political backsliding.

Coleridge's more abstruse flights into metaphysics earn a sharp rebuke, but Southey's yearnings for sublimity are mocked out of court, in a superbly diminishing sexual innuendo:

> You, Bob, are rather insolent, you know,
>   At being disappointed in your wish
> To supersede all warblers here below,
>   And be the only blackbird in the dish.
> And then you overstrain yourself, or so,
>   And tumble downward like the flying fish
> Gasping on deck, because you soar too high, Bob,
> And fall for lack of moisture quite a dry Bob.
>
> (Dedication, 3)

For a poem which is to be about the greatest libertine ever (and yet an oddly passive hero), this is a nicely calculated stroke. Byron can proceed to make the contrast between himself and all these latter-day poetasters:

> For me, who, wandering with pedestrain Muses,
>   Contend not with you on the wingèd steed,
> I wish your fate may yield ye, when she chooses,
>   The fame you envy and the skill you need.
>
> (Dedication, 8)

He sets himself firmly in the honest tradition of Milton, representative of true sublimity because, amongst other things, of Milton's lack of cant: Byron's own verse is to be 'honest' and 'simple'. In a sense, the dedication itself is simple in its directness: *Don Juan* is anything but, for honesty there is not a simple matter. As we have come to expect, it is partly a question of decorum. Perversely (or so it seems) Byron chooses to write an epic poem, not because it is the poem people expect, but because it is the poem the age requires. By turning 'what was once romantic to burlesque', by subverting common epic assumptions whilst appearing to uphold them ('the regularity of my design /Forbids all wandering as the worst of sinning', he absurdly boasts, before we realise the absurdity), Byron concocts a poem that has no one single English forbear.

    The opening stanza of the first canto demonstrates well enough the relationship between poet, public and poem that Byron establishes:

I want a hero, an uncommon want,
　　When every year and month sends forth a new one,
Till after cloying the gazettes with cant,
　　The age discovers he is not the true one.
Of such as these I should not care to vaunt;
　　I'll therefore take our ancient friend Don Juan.
We all have seen him in the pantomime
Sent to the devil somewhat ere his time.

　　　　　　　　　　　　　　　　　　　　(I, 1)

Helen Gardner might regard this as 'good-humoured' or farcical
(even Paul West returns repeatedly to the notion of Byron as farceur);
but the poem displays all the good humour of a man who laughingly
cries 'Oops' as he sticks the knife in before apologetically pulling it
out. The offhandedness of the opening is deliberately disarming. The
reader might think he knows where he stands, he might suppose there
is some genial relationship — that 'we', that 'our' suggest a knowing
conspiracy. But the age's lack is also the poet's need ('want' explodes
several lines later, like so many of Byron's delayed charges) — and not
simply any poet: by declaring his differences from other poets, he
draws attention to himself as an epic poet with his own ideas of
decorum. But more than that — he is a particular sort of man, the
gentlemanly dandy we have encountered in *Beppo*. By the end of the
first canto this persona has established itself.

　　Don José and his lady quarrelled. Why,
　　　　Not any of the many could divine,
　　Though several thousand people chose to try.
　　　　'Twas surely no concern of theirs nor mine.
　　I loathe that low vice curiosity,
　　　　But if there's anything in which I shine,
　　'Tis in arranging all my friends' affairs,
　　Not having, of my own, domestic cares.

　　　　　　　　　　　　　　　　　　　　(I, 23)

He is the perfect vehicle for gossip; and that is the tone of much of the
early part of the poem, the chatter of the inveterate gossip who hits at
truths almost by accident, who betrays himself without knowing it,
the breathless rush of verbiage revealing because it is both highly self-
conscious and yet hardly conscious of itself at all.

I had my doubts, perhaps I have them still,
    But what I say is neither here nor there.
I knew his father well and have some skill
    In character, but it would not be fair
From sire to son to augur good or ill.
    He and his wife were an ill-assorted pair,
But scandal's my aversion. I protest
Against all evil speaking, even in jest.

For my part I say nothing, nothing, but
    This I will say (my reasons are my own)
That if I had an only son to put
    To school (as God be praised that I have none),
'Tis not with Donna Inez I would shut
    Him up to learn his catechism alone.
No, no, I'd send him out betimes to college,
For there it was I picked up my own knowledge.

                              (I, 51–2)

Examples of this tone abound. It depends for its effectiveness on our accepting the poet on his own terms: his self-effacement is a cunning ploy whereby we do not realise what is happening, his terms are so treacherous. He can refer apparently mockingly to his 'chaste Muse', but in the next line his address to his 'still chaster reader' makes us wonder whose side he is on. For the license he wishes to take is a poetic one, and yet the concept of chastity is one he has been ridiculing with his attack on so-called Platonic love – it is hard to erase from our minds that attack only a few stanzas earlier:

Oh Plato, Plato, you have paved the way
    With your confounded fantasies to more
Immoral conduct by the fancied sway
    Your system feigns o'er the controlless core
Of human hearts than all the long array
    Of poets and romancers.

                              (I, 116)

Most gossips have their blind spots, and Byron plays on this factor; about Julia at one point he says

I'm really puzzled what to think or say,
She kept her counsel in so close a way.

This puzzlement, which might not at first seem to owe very much to the bafflement of the 'Epistle to Augusta' and *Childe Harold*, has an important extension canvassed later in the first canto — and this canto is surprisingly all-embracing in the concerns it bodies forth. The gossip's private lack of knowledge becomes the common man's bewilderment (as he says later, he is merely trying 'to build up common things with commonplaces', XIV, 7), in an age which suddenly seems to be bursting out in all directions.

> Man's a strange animal and makes strange use
>   Of his own nature and the various arts,
> And likes particularly to produce
>   Some new experiment to show his parts.
> This is the age of oddities let loose,
>   Where different talents find their different marts.
> You'd best begin with truth, and when you've lost your
> Labour, there's a sure market for imposture . . .

> This is the patent age of new inventions
>   For killing bodies and for saving souls,
> All propagated with the best intentions.
>   Sir Humphry Davy's lantern, by which coals
> Are safely mined for in the mode he mentions,
>   Timbuctoo travels, voyages to the poles
> Are ways to benefit mankind, as true
> Perhaps as shooting them at Waterloo.

> Man's a phenomenon, one knows not what,
>   And wonderful beyond all wondrous measure.
> 'Tis pity though in this sublime world that
>   Pleasure's a sin and sometimes sin's a pleasure.
> Few mortals know what end they would be at,
>   But whether glory, power or love or treasure,
> The path is through perplexing ways, and when
> The goal is gained, we die you know — and then?
>   (I, 128; 132–3)

Of course Byron has no answer to that question, but once asked it is not easily forgotten, darkly underlining as it does not merely the perplexity, but the absurdity that stands as the frame of the action. And so the argument is pushed a stage further — the persona's lack of knowledge becomes the age's perplexity, and that in turn becomes the bafflement of every individual when forced up against eternal verities which refuse to be verified. It is typical of Byron that this canto should end on the literary note with which the poem began, that the epic decorum he invokes should be emphasised as a moral quality; he is in effect inverting that decorum by appealing to truth (something not to be found in most epics), whilst at the same time believing in Milton, Dryden, Pope as opposed to Wordsworth, Coleridge, Southey. What can be known will be known, and that knowledge can be furthered only by a sensitivity to the past as well as the present. *Childe Harold* had already taught Byron that, and the knowledge was not always comforting. It is a complex lesson, because against the ravages of time there are some monuments that survive, reminding us of those that haven't. In the same way, the poetry that has survived has its own lessons to teach, which no amount of revolutionary poetics will subvert: that poetry represents a sanity, a restorative healthiness which is in danger of suffocation. Fortunately Byron has won a victory of sorts, accepting his losses for what they are:

> No more — no more — oh never more, my heart,
>   Canst thou be my sole world, my universe!
> Once all in all, but now a thing apart,
>   Thou canst not be my blessing or my curse.
> The illusion's gone forever, and thou art
>   Insensible, I trust, but none the worse.
> And in thy stead I've got a deal of judgement,
> Though heaven knows how it ever found a lodgement.
>
> (I, 215)

That judgement is essential to the poet in this whirling world:

> Well—well, the world must turn upon on its axis,
>   And all mankind turn with it, heads or tails,
> And live and die, make love and pay our taxes,
>   And as the veering wind shifts, shift our sails.
> The King commands us, and the doctor quacks us,
>   The priest instructs, and so our life exhales,

> A little breath, love, wine, ambition, fame,
> Fighting, devotion, dust – perhaps a name.
>
> (II, 4)

There is a superb conjunction there of acceptance and regret, of necessary compromise and possible hope. Byron is one of the few poets who knows the true value of a list, and of conjunctions and particles.

It is not that judgement has ousted feeling: the relationships between Juan and Julia, and Juan and Haidée, show how much Byron is prepared to invest in an emotion that has every appearance of being romantic. To undercut it subsequently is not necessarily to deny it at the time, but it inevitably qualifies it. What is happening when Juan, leaving Spain for the first time, reads Julia's letter (in itself a moving document) and vomits as he does so, is too complex to be passed off merely as a re-definition of 'lovesickness':

> No doubt he would have been much more pathetic,
> But the sea acted as a strong emetic.
>
> (II, 21)

It is a virtuoso explanation of the relation between life and art, between experience as lived and experience as recreated on paper. When the same letter is used for lots to be drawn (to decide who shall be eaten first), the reader might well wish that the poet had grown 'inarticulate with reaching' (II, 20).

Pace John Wain, Byron is not a timid poet:[34] constantly he takes risks, daring us to object (it is not, though, until Canto XIV that his scorn becomes unbridled – 'as the effect is fine /And keeps the atrocious reader in suspense'), urging us to accept his premise that literature has in fact served us ill by pretending to truths it cannot sustain. The cannibalism in the boat is rightly revolting – Byron knows when a joke turns sour. Byron can face facts starkly, as in his account, in sinuous, flexible verse, of drowned men:

> And first one universal shriek there rushed,
>   Louder than the loud ocean, like a crash
> Of echoing thunder, and then all was hushed,
>   Save the wild wind and the remorseless dash
> Of billows; but at intervals there gushed,
>   Accompanied with a convulsive splash,

A solitary shriek, the bubbling cry
Of some strong swimmer in his agony.
(II, 53)

That 'strong' makes the agony worse. In a similar way, the facts of love are acknowledged, along with the poets' desertion of their duty:

All tragedies are finished by a death,
    All comedies are ended by a marriage.
The future states of both are left to faith,
    For authors fear description might disparage
The worlds to come of both, or fall beneath,
    And then both worlds would punish their miscarriage.
So leaving each their priest and prayer book ready,
They say no more of death or of the lady.
(III, 9)

This stanza alone says much about the relation between the two modes, as between death and marriage, and about the ways in which literature has not confronted the logic of its conclusions. This is what Byron finds so sickening, so appalling, that when he declares his need to speak the truth, he has to see it as an act of immorality (XII, 40). It is a distinctive mark of Byron's vision that he is always looking round the corner, beyond those neat finalities of marriage and death. If there were sadly good reasons for the poem's unfinished state, it was an appropriate state for it to be left in, for Byron's peering into the dark can have no limits. The question is insistent: 'and then?'

Byron wins the right to ask this question by virtue of his simultaneous flaunting and flouting of epic convention, and by virtue of his studied carelessness. Having the best of both worlds is granted to few poets, perhaps because few demand it. Byron asks so nicely, the Muse can hardly refuse. One of his greatest moments is the attack on War, which starts in Canto VII: it becomes an attack on Love, on Glory, on all human aspirations. At this point the self-questionings of Hamlet assume their allusive importance, and we recall the worms of decay in the skull at the start of *Childe Harold*, Canto II. 'To be or not to be! That is the question', he echoes (IX, 14); 'The time is out of joint, and so am I' (IX, 41). The image of the skull hovers menacingly over the cantos on War, for here is the ultimate reminder of absurdity, here at the centre of the poem is the end, the 'bourn from which no traveller returns':

Death laughs. Go ponder o'er the skeleton
  With which men image out the unknown thing
That hides the past world, like to a set sun
  Which still elsewhere may rouse a brighter spring.
Death laughs at all you weep for. Look upon
  This hourly dread of all, whose threatened sting
Turns life to terror, even though in its sheath.
Mark how its lipless mouth grins without breath!

Mark how it laughs and scorns at all you are!
  And yet was what you are. From ear to ear
It laughs not. There is now no fleshy bar
  So called. The Antic long hath ceased to hear,
But still he smiles. And whether near or far
  He strips from man that mantle (far more dear
Than even the tailor's), his incarnate skin,
White, black, or copper — the dead bones will grin.

And thus Death laughs. It is sad merriment,
  But still it is so; and with such example
Why should not Life be equally content
  With his superior in a smile to trample
Upon the nothings which are daily spent
  Like bubbles on an ocean much less ample
Than the eternal deluge, which devours
Suns as rays, worlds like atoms, years like hours?

                                        (IX, 11–13)

This will not be gainsaid by anything elsewhere in the poem. As
Byron manoeuvres his hero across Europe, he adopts the mask,
between 'fool and sage', of a Hamlet, forever questioning, forever
fooling, conscious of the ghost stalking after him, demanding
retribution in 'this vile age of chaff' (XIII, 97): 'List, oh list!/Alas,
poor Ghost!' Byron knows that the ghost is saying back, 'Alas, poor
Hamlet'. What Byron has won, in *Don Juan*, is what so many of the
other major Romantic poets were anxious to achieve — the dramatisation of self in poetry. He has achieved this and satisfied, surprisingly,
Arnold's *desiderata* for a poetry adequate to its age. This sense of
adequacy is a direct result of Byron's pushing to its logical conclusions
what had been an increasingly pressing hint in other poets' work: to
write about the self required a sense of one's own ridiculousness.
Wordsworth, Coleridge, Southey, Keats had all acknowledged this
fact. It was left to Byron to celebrate it.

5 'Confusion and Nonsense': Tennyson and Clough

I

When Bulwer-Lytton opined in 1838 that 'when the multitude ceased to speak of Lord Byron, they ceased to speak about poetry itself', it was not the satires he had in mind.[1] Byron's value, for those Victorians prepared to grant him any value at all, lay in his early work, in the posturings and self-communings of the *Tales*, of *Manfred*, of the passionate lyrics: the so-called Spasmodic poets discovered in such verse, once they had reduced it to manageable proportions, a model of how to cope with their own fevered imaginations. The over-riding concept of literature as a moral force would not allow many Victorians to nod their approval at *Beppo* or *Don Juan* (so blinkered was their idea of morality): the combination of Byron's personal failings and laxities with verse that itself was not only lax but irreverently comic was sufficient deterrent.

There were, as there always are, exceptions. There were qualifications, as there were bound to be in an age which saw poets and critics alike hopelessly confused as to what was and what was not permissible in poetry. The argument, which involved the connection between the Victorians and their predecessors, was complex, tortuous and seemingly endless. I cannot here give anything like an adequate account of the issues involved, the passions raised, the conflicts and contradictions which lay behind the gradual establishment of an accepted pantheon of Victorian poets – one accepted to this day as consisting of Tennyson, Arnold and Browning. What interests me is the place of Arthur Hugh Clough in this debate and in this pantheon (he is often excluded altogether). Rather than try to give a complete account of Clough in a limited space, I particularly want to look at Clough's relationship to his age, to the poetic traditions that were available to him. It is not simply a matter of conscious influences at work: from this perspective it might be possible to suggest a

116 Poetry and Humour from Cowper to Clough

relationship between Clough and, say, Byron, that would have surprised Clough if put to him in those terms. Such relationships matter when we are trying to see the development of an overall pattern (or at least one possible pattern, one possible development) in a very complicated period (so complicated that it almost defies the notion of period).[2]

Tennyson's *Poems* of 1842 provide an instructive test case of what was expected of poetry: his own anxieties and double vision are reflected in the critics' unease. One reviewer in particular unwittingly manages to have the best (or the worst) of both worlds. John Sterling anticipates Matthew Arnold's call for a poetry that is adequate to its age; he also questions what seem to him the essentially utilitarian assumptions that lie behind the guilt oozing out of 'The Palace of Art'. His review is a curious balancing act, the more so in that he brings into his performance Scott, Byron, Crabbe and Wordsworth.

Sterling begins his essay with a survey of the present state of society, which is all bustle and advance amidst the whirling, scalding steam of mechanisation and talk. He is very conscious that this society, radically different in character from anything previously experienced, requires a different sort of poetry to accommodate it:

Now, strangely as our time is racked and torn, haunted by ghosts, and errant in search of lost realities, poor in genuine culture, incoherent among its own chief elements, untrained to social facility and epicurean quiet, yet unable to unite its means in pursuit of any lofty blessing, half-sick, half-dreaming, and whole confused – he would be not only misanthropic, but ignorant, who should maintain it to be a poor, dull, and altogether hopeless age, and not rather one full of great though conflicting energies, seething with high feelings, and struggling towards the light with piercing though still hooded eyes.[3]

The two writers who have come closest to the ideal are Scott and Byron. But Scott's 'wholesome sense and dear felicity' are offset by his obsession with the past rather than the present. Byron is closer, even in his typically 'romantic' vein: 'it is but a small though a profound and irrepressible part of our far-spread modern mind that he has so well embodied in his scornful Harolds and despairing Giaours'. After this grudging praise it comes as a surprise to see what Sterling goes on to say:

We have indeed one of his works, the only one, which is a splendid attempt at a creative survey of modern life, and contains all the essential elements of such performance. And in spite of the puerile egotisms and dawdling prate into which the poem so often wanders, the first five cantos of *Don Juan*, forming in point of bulk about half, have more of fiery beauty and native sweetness in them than anything we know of in our modern literature. There is also a wide range and keenness of observation; and were some trivialities struck out, as they so easily might be, no capital defect would remain but the weakness of speculative culture visible in Lord Byron's philosophical excursions. In the latter half of the poem, and unhappily when he is on English ground, the lax shapelessness of structure, the endless slipshod, yawny loungings, and vapid carelessness of execution, become very disagreeable in spite of passages rich with imperishable beauty, wit, and vigour, such as no other modern Englishman or woman could have approached. On the whole, with all its faults, moral and poetic, the earlier portion of this singular book will probably remain, like the first half of *Faust*, the most genuine and striking monument of a whole recent national literature. But the weakness as to all deeper thought, and the incomplete groundplan, place it somewhat lower than could be wished.

We could say that Sterling has missed the point entirely, and that a spruced-up *Don Juan* would be a denial of the poem's chief strengths. In fact we begin to wonder what it is in the poem that Sterling so admires, when the qualifications come crowding in: wit and vigour are contained by beauty and native sweetness, the sense of the poet's own self is reduced to puerile egotism. Sterling has certainly failed to see the connection between that self and the way the poem works. Nonetheless, he sees the connection of the poem with the age, and so strong is Sterling's desire for such a marriage, he welcomes it in spite of everything. The problems increase as the argument proceeds, for Sterling's view of this age is not all comprehensive and wide-eyed:

The still unadulterated purity of home among large circles of the nation presents an endless abundance of the feelings and characters, the want of which nothing else in existence can supply even to a poet.

The promise of the age, like Byron's masterpiece, is reduced to comforting domestic pieties, to a belief, genuinely held, in 'the power of self-subjection combined with almost boundless liberty'. Against 'brooding doubt and remorse' is set (significant image, this, indeed) 'the gas-jet flame of faith irradiating its own coal-mine darkness'. If, then, we were surprised at Byron's place in the argument, Crabbe's might startle us even more:

> Of all our recent writers the one who might seem at first sight to have most nearly succeeded in this quest after the poetic *Sangreal* is Crabbe. No one has ranged so widely through all classes, employed so many diverse elements of circumstance and character.

There is, of course, a large 'but'. It transpires that Sterling's demands for an 'eager sweetness, a fiery spirituous (*sic*) essence, yet bland as honey' are as sentimental as Rupert Brooke's nostalgic yearnings for tea at Grantchester. Sterling has nothing to say about Crabbe's irony, his mordant satire; the critic's sobriety can applaud what Crabbe's contemporaries (Wordsworth, Coleridge, Hazlitt above all) deplored:

> . . . it even may be said that few parts of them but would have found an appropriate place in some of the reports of our various commissions for inquiring into the state of the country.

Again, the 'but': Crabbe's honest Augustan virtues are not enough. Suddenly, Sterling's position becomes transparent:

> In poetry we seek, and find a refuge from the harshness and narrowness of the actual world. But using the very substance of this Actual for poetry, its positiveness, shrewdness, detailedness, incongruity, and adding no new peculiar powers from within, we do no otherwise than if we should take shelter from rain under the end of a roof-spout.

Clearly Byron and Crabbe (and Wordsworth) pose too powerful a threat to such a creed.

Tennyson, *mirabile dictu*, bursts on to the stage, with his priorities in the right place: the fig leaf of 'beautiful imagery' is there is to make acceptable the 'thoroughly speculative intellect'. But even Tennyson is not blameless, St Simeon Stylites is dismissed with contempt:

. . . his loathsome, yet ridiculous attempts at saintship, all founded on an idea of the Divinity fit only for an African worshipping a scarecrow fetish made of dog's bones, goose-feathers, and dunghill-rags. This is no topic for Poetry: she has better task than to wrap her mantle round a sordid, greedy lunatic.

Not merely those modern critics interested in the development of the dramatic monologue would argue for the importance of *Simeon*. It is the extreme instance of what lurks below the surface of several of these poems, an awareness not simply of poetry's obligations to society, but also of the possibilities of breaking through that very decorum that, as Sterling demonstrates, is still a critical shibboleth in 1842. But decorum is by now a concept even more than usually loaded. Tennyson might well have felt aggrieved after his agonisings in 'The Palace of Art' (prompted by R. C. Trench's comment that 'we cannot live in Art'), that Sterling should turn round and say most definitely that we can live in Art. The poem is for Sterling a 'folly' precisely because it will not accept what art can do: Tennyson is no better than Simeon, or 'some crack-brained sot repenting in the stocks'.

Sterling's confusions are representative. It is small wonder that we can chart in Victorian poetry a move from Romantic introspection 'focused on the poet's consciousness', as Walter Houghton puts it, to an introspection based on self-consciousness.[4] (Houghton makes a distinction between the earlier question 'What shall I do?' and the essentially Victorian one of 'Who am I?'; this seems to me rather too neat, in that the two questions are complementary, as 'The Palace of Art' makes clear.) So that, ironically enough, Sterling's eager emphasis on the age's powers of 'self-subjection' (paralleling his scorn for Byron's egotism) is undermined in poetic practice by the very confusions he unwittingly reflects and generates. The young Arthur Hugh Clough, whilst still a precocious schoolboy at Rugby, had lamented 'the great egotism, or subjectivity, of our poetical literature of the present day' as compared to Homer, where 'we see nothing of the writer's self, and he is but the medium through which we view an object'.[5] And yet (the irony operates here too), his 'profound doubts', as Houghton observes, '. . . drove him inward and developed a subtlety and complexity of self-consciousness that perhaps only Coleridge equalled among 19th century poets.'[6]

II

The late 1840s were extraordinarily eventful. The Brontës, Dickens, Mrs Gaskell, Thackeray all demonstrated within a few years that the English novel — what Sterling had dismissed as the 'looser and readier form of prose romance' — could indeed address itself to the 'poetic representation' (Sterling's phrase) of the time, and a lot more besides. Such activity was bound to have an effect on poets already beating their breasts about their role and function. Not everyone had taken Sterling's 'bland as honey' view of Tennyson's 1842 volume: there was considerable pressure on him to produce poetry with something more direct to say to an age of alarming transition. In 1847 Tennyson obliged (thogh that was not how all his readers saw it) with *The Princess*, whose topicality is apparent when we relate it to, say, Charlotte Brontë's tackling of the problem of female independence in *Jane Eyre*.[7] Then in December 1848 appeared a poem by Clough, with a title hardly calculated to win potential readers: *The Bothie of Tober-na-vuolich: A Long Vacation Pastoral*. Clough's poem is a fascinating challenge, as much to us as it was to his contemporaries. The two best recent studies of Clough both face this challenge and then shy away from it. Walter Houghton, in a generally admirable account, observes that what above all keeps *The Bothie* 'fresh and alive' is 'its sheer charm, or whatever it is that makes it one of the most delightful poems in English literature.'[8] Robindra Biswas likewise talks of 'that complex charm — that final unsatisfactory word on which all appreciative readers must fall back . . .[9] Both these formulations seem a retreat from Charles Kingsley's commendation of the way in which 'the *bizarrerie* of the subject was so charmingly expressed in the *bizarrerie* of the style.'[10] If we are to be more precise about the character of Clough's first long poem, the nature and quality of its success, then we need to see it in the context of his shorter poems of about the same time, in the context, too, of his own views as to what poetry should be.

Clough's relation to the poetic traditions open to him is interesting in its complexities and combinations. His very alertness to tradition should temper any eager claims on his behalf for outstanding innovation, for unlooked-for modernity. In any case our own perspectives are in themselves still undefined: if Robindra Biswas can say that 'the dominant critical tradition was, of course, a post-Romantic one',[11] Jerome Buckley can chart a very strong streak of

anti-Romanticism that itself has claims to dominance.[12] John
Sterling might have agreed with Biswas that critical and creative
effort alike was directed towards 'asserting the prestige . . . of poetry
against the forces of Utilitarianism, science, and the practical temper
of an industrial and mercantile society'. He would certainly have
agreed that the problem was basically how a Romantic view of
poetry's value could be 'adjusted to an increasingly intractable,
insistent and disturbing world of fact'. And Arnold's high seriousness
echoes not simply Sterling, but Newman, Carlyle and Mill, all of
whom found it hard to accommodate anything less than the sublime.
Clough shared with the major figures of his day the belief in the
primarily moral function of poetry. Where he differs is in his
eclecticism, his realisation that he can learn both from the Romantics
(his praise for Wordsworth's 'truly human, homely and frugal life in
the cottage at Grasmere' is significant), and from the poets of the
seventeenth and eighteenth centuries whom Arnold dubbed 'classics
of our prose rather than of our poetry'.

As R. G. Cox has shown, there was something of a 'minority
tradition' which asked of poetry more than the Romantics seemed to
be offering.[13] The 'most frequent charge . . . is a lack of thought', a
charge levelled both at the Romantics and at their minor successors in
the late 1820s, when poetry enters curious doldrums, blown off
course by conflicting winds. Even as late as 1861 Elizabeth Barrett
Browning can be blamed for her egotism ('true originality will never
be attained by a self-conscious, morbid, restless assertion of the value
of a man's own individuality'), and the buck is passed back to
Wordsworth. Those who escape the charge of egotism are, like
Southey in 1839, charged with escapism:

> Suspicion of satire, wit, the play of mind, a confusion of seriousness
> with solemnity, a conception of poetic style which emphasised
> verbal melody and sonority at the expense of the vitality of the
> rhythms and tones of speech . . . make it difficult to bring
> effectively into his poetry the normal adult consciousness, if not
> directly, the concerns and interests, of the age.

Cox suggests that Browning is the one exception, and Browning for
his pains is charged by Arnold with a 'confused multitudinousness'.
Cox makes no mention of Clough, and argues, rather bleakly, for the
slight effect of this body of anti-Romantic criticism: 'there were
almost no examples they could point to of contemporary poets

possessing the qualities they felt to be needed'. The poet Henry
Taylor, who made similar anti-Romantic noises in his Introduction
to *Philip van Artevalde* (1834), hardly exemplified, in his own poetry,
an ideal that could be grasped and followed.

It was, in fact, Clough who eventually, in theory and practice,
made the right connections. As the so-called 'minority tradition' had
more or less worked itself out by the 1830s, his isolation from the
main stream of thought is all the more apparent. He, too, attacked
Browning's 'reckless, decomposite manner – dashing at anything
and insisting that it will do',[14] but he had Dryden's example to extol
in its place, an example important for its denotative precision of
language. *Fraser's Magazine* complained in 1853 of the modern poet's
'inability, or carelessness, about seeing any object clearly' (Arnold of
course was to put it better);[15] it was what Clough regarded as
Wordsworth's sentimental failing along the same lines that made him
prefer Crabbe to Keats and Shelley.

Clough, like his contemporaries, is very conscious of the age's
demands.

> But we have not yet in England, I imagine, had anyone to give us a
> manner suitable to our new matter. There has been a kind of
> dissolution of English; but no one writer has come to reunite and
> revivify the escaping components. We have something new to say,
> but do not know how to say it. . . . Have we any one who speaks
> for our day as justly and appropriately as Dryden for his? Have we
> anything that will stand wear and tear as well and be as bright and
> unobsolete in a hundred and fifty years, as Alexander's feast is
> today?[16]

This was a brave question, bravely put, for Clough could see the
possibility that the novel might achieve the wholeness of response
which poetry seemed to be denying itself. He could see, too, that a
return merely to eighteenth-century modes and forms was no answer.
Whilst he was interested in the tensions that arose between the 'ease
and familiarity and closeness to common language' and the need to
'exceed and transcend common language', he acknowledged 'how
little expression of personal and individual feeling do we find in the
pages of Dryden'.[17] If, then, Dryden's age was important for its
'austere love of truth', Clough could see more than was in fact there in
Alexander Smith's *Life Drama*, simply because it seemed to him to
answer the question, should not poetry 'deal more than at present it

usually does, with general wants, ordinary feelings, the obvious rather than the rare facts of human nature?'[18] The dangers are obvious, in this professed liking for (it is actually more like adulation of) a mediocre, but much trumpeted, Spasmodic poet: content, as with Arnold, can become the central concern, and we end up with the false dichotomy between form and content that is at the base of Arnold's view of the Romantics, of his distrust of Keats, even of Shakespeare. But Clough is able to qualify this emphasis on content: Dryden is important for his language, just as the point of copying out pages of Goldsmith is a stylistic one. To see the object as it really is requires the ability to write about it appropriately. In this recognition we can see that Sterling's tight-lipped concept of decorum has given way to something more open, and much more scrupulous. Scrupulosity, Clough learns, is inseparable from a broad and vigorous sense of humour.

Although *Ambarvalia* (a volume of poems written by Clough and a friend, Thomas Burbidge) was not published until 1849, after *The Bothie*, the poems it contained – and others, published even later – were for the most part written before the bright star of *The Bothie* flashed across the sky. It is hard to escape a sense, as we read through these poems, of oppression and earnestness, a rather dispiritingly querulous note of unease. The opening poem of *Ambarvalia* sets the tone that is to predominate:

> The human spirits saw I on a day,
> Sitting and looking each a different way;
> And hardly tasking, subtly questioning,
> Another spirit went around the ring
> To each and each: and as he ceased his say,
> Each after each, I heard them singly sing,
> Some querulously high, some softly, sadly low,
> We know not, – what avails to know?
> We know not, – wherefore need we know?
> This answer gave they still unto his suing,
> We know not, let us do as we are doing.

Most readers would readily place this in the mid-nineteenth century – it seems to reflect the age's morbid anxieties, the search for knowledge that is undefined and ultimately futile. But the poem's conclusion is surprising in its neatness, as though the complacency of our response is suddenly jolted by a shift in mood and manner. The final words of the questioning spirit offer another perspective:

> Truly, thou know'st not, and thou need'st not know;
> Hope only, hope thou, and believe alway;
> I also know not, and I need not know,
> Only with questionings pass I to and fro,
> Perplexing those that sleep, and in their folly
> Imbreeding doubt and sceptic melancholy;
> Till that, their dreams deserting, they with me
> Come all to this true ignorance and thee.

There is, in these lines, an alertness both to perplexity and to ignorance that is, in the final turn, strangely and disturbingly moving. It does not suggest how the other poems might develop: what it does is to instil in us an awareness of Clough's grasp of paradox. The doubt and melancholy that he mocks are part of his own wider vision of an ignorance that is 'true'.

It is nonetheless also true that Clough strives in many of these poems for an affirmative view that may, at this distance, strike us as hollow and sentimental. An argument for Clough's sense of humour gets little support from the distinction he makes in 'Light words they were . . .' between a self-complacent society gathering ('the best at best / By frivolous laugh and prate conventional / All too untuned for all she thought to say — ') and a lady of principle who determines to challenge their frivolity. She speaks out: 'God in her spoke, and made her heard'. This seems a typically censorious, Victorian attack on levity; and there are several poems that either make similar points, or reach towards a religious sublime that has no room for humour. But then, after a celebration of domestic virtues ('The Silver Wedding! . . .'), we have thrown out at us a poem which appears to challenge the assumptions Clough himself has been expecting us to make:

> Why should I say I see the things I see not,
>   Why be and be not?
> Show love for that I love not, and fear for what I fear not?
> And dance about to music that I hear not?
>   Who standeth i' the street
>   Shall be hustled and justled about;
> And he that stops i' the dance shall be spurned by the dancer's feet,

Shall be shoved and be twisted by all he shall meet,
    And shall raise up an outcry and rout;
    And the partner, too, —
    What is the partner to do?
While all the while 'tis but, perchance, an humming in mine ear,
    That yet anon shall hear,
    And I anon, the music in my soul,
    In a moment read the whole . . .
. . .
Alas! alas! alas! and what if all along
    The music is not sounding?

Clough explores the distinction between two possible types of music, 'one loud and bold and coarse', 'the other, soft and low', and clearly prefers the second. But it cannot be left simply as a matter of preference. These disarming questions about seeing what we are meant to see reverberate throughout the poem, just as Clough's sense of isolation from the crowd drives him inwards, away from the hustle and bustle. This is no Keatsian formulation of unheard melodies being sweeter: Clough is already beginning to tease himself and his reader ('But listen, listen, listen — if haply be heard it may; /Listen, listen, listen, — is it not sounding now?'). He insists, though, that the teasing is to be distinguished from 'vain Philosophy' and pours scorn on those who take delight in their own 'superior science',

    Part in forevision of the attentive look
    And laughing glance that may one time reward them,
    When the fresh ore, this day dug up, at last
    Shall, thrice refined and purified, from the mint
    Of conversation intellectual
    Into the golden currency of wit
    Issue — satirical or pointed sentence,
    Impromptu, epigram, or it may be sonnet,
    Heir undisputed to the pinkiest page
    In the album of a literary lady.

But in this very act of scorning such wit, he is preparing the ground for his own variety of satire. It is a satire that is direct and forceful, with an authority derived from the moral strength which combats the hypocrisy of the age. Again, we have to rub our eyes, and realise afresh the implicit shock of this attack:

Duty – that's to say complying
  With whate'er's expected here;
On your unknown cousin's dying,
  Straight be ready with the tear;
Upon etiquette relying,
Unto usage nought denying,
Lend your waist to be embraced,
  Blush not even, never fear;
Claims of kith and kin connection,
  Claims of manners honour still,
Ready money of affection
  Pay, whoever drew the bill.
With the form conforming duly,
Senseless what it meaneth truly,
Go to church – the world require you,
  To balls – the world require you too,
And marry – papa and mamma desire you,
  And your sisters and schoolfellows do.
Duty – 'tis to take on trust
What things are good, and right, and just;
  And whether indeed they be or be not,
  Try not, test not, feel not, see not:
'Tis walk and dance, sit down and rise
  By leading, opening ne'er your eyes;
Stunt sturdy limbs that Nature gave,
And be drawn in a Bath chair along to the grave.

'Tis the stern and prompt suppressing,
  As an obvious deadly sin,
All the questing and the guessing
  Of the soul's own soul within:
    'Tis the coward acquiescence
      In a destiny's behest,
    To a shade by terror made,
    Sacrificing, aye, the essence
      Of all that's truest, noblest, best:
    'Tis the blind non-recognition
      Either of goodness, truth or beauty,
    Except by precept and submission;
      Moral blank, and moral void,
      Life at very birth destroyed,

> Atrophy, exinanition!
> Duty!—
> Yea, by duty's prime condition
> Pure nonentity of duty!

We might well feel here that Clough's vantage point is too clearly defined, in that he spells out what could be inferred from the savage ironies of the opening lines, with their Carlylean recognition of wealth's and mechanisation's attractions for a society which sees itself in terms of an aimless dance. It is as though Clough finds he cannot suppress his feelings any longer: the poem is an outburst, impassioned and subtle, but in the end limited by its determination to hit the nail on the head. It would be wrong, though, to leave the poem at that. The manner of the first half of the poem returns in later verse, and needs to be distinguished from the light verse of the day, of the early Tennyson: it stands half-way between an eighteenth-century precision of speech and the idiosyncrasies of the full dramatic monologue. Furthermore it allows Clough to move on to one of the most interesting performances in *Ambarvalia*, the 'Blank Misgivings of a Creature moving about in Worlds not realised' (comparable to Tennyson's 'Supposed Confessions', but infinitely superior).

In this sequence, Clough explores the self-consciousness he had earlier thought such a failing in poetry. He is not yet sufficiently confident to view himself with an amused detachment; it is rather a bemused world-weariness, a self-exasperation that yet steers clear of the Spasmodic school of self-indulgence. Inevitably, we recall *Childe Harold*. Clough's poem begins:

> Here am I yet, another twelvemonth spent,
> One-third departed of the mortal span,
> Carrying on the child into the man,
> Nothing into reality. Sails rent,
> And rudder broken, — reason impotent, —
> Affections all unfixed; so forth I fare
> On the mid seas unheedingly, so dare
> To do and to be done by, well content.

The Wordsworthian belief in growth, in progression, no longer has much force. As another poem shows ('Is it true ye gods who treat us'), poetry itself, 'the vision and the faculty divine' (already gravely mocked in 'On Latmos') cannot be guaranteed to offer anything when set beneath the precise gaze of reason. The odd thing about this poem is its ending. The 'too quick despairer' of Arnold's lament for Clough, *Thyrsis*, turns out to be rather a jaunty character:

> Oh say it, all who think it,
> Look straight, and never blink it!
> If it is so, let it be so,
> And we will all agree so;
> But the plot has counterplot,
> It may be, and yet be not.

When Clough has attained this detachment he is in a position to move on from 'honest doubt' to something more particular. He displays here a nonchalance which is refreshing in its openness to either possibility, in its refusal to care too much. There is almost a sense of relief in the realisation that in the end none of this may matter. That realisation seems to me not by any means a typically Victorian insight – on the contrary, it has its ancestry, if anywhere, in Byron.

III

The distinctive quality of Clough's developing vision – it reaches its first high point in *The Bothie* – can be tested against Tennyson's performance in his poems up to and including *The Princess* of 1847. Tennyson agonised over the choices open to him as a poet, and yet was sufficiently sure in his solutions to introduce, into a number of the 1842 poems, contemporary situations, conversational, prosaic diction, exploration of characters who give themselves away by what they say and do. Frequently Tennyson introduces not merely such recognitions of his age and its turmoils, but also touches of humour. These are not always subtle. Sometimes it is a matter of imitating political fable in ballad form, as in 'The Goose' or 'Mechanophilus'; sometimes, as in 'The Gardener's Daughter' and other such 'English Idylls', a matter of being deliberately prosaic; sometimes it is harmless playing, as in 'Will Waterproof's Lyrical Monologue'. Leigh Hunt saw through the device with which Tennyson prefaced 'Godiva', a device to give the poem a casual modernity ('I waited for the train at Coventry; /I hung with grooms and porters on the bridge'). Hunt thought it mere 'boyishness';[19] but Tennyson's unease spills over to illuminate *The Princess*, which he called 'A Medley'.

Tennyson, in *The Princess*, and Clough, in *The Bothie*, are tackling the question of women's place in society. In both poems, significantly, there is a lot of laughter, a lot of undergraduate high jinks which could well nowadays put people off. We are reminded, certainly in *The Princess*, that talk of social inequalities is often going to be no more than talk: the young bloods who act out the drama are perhaps going to learn very little from it. Just as the poem is, in form, a game, a charade, so the theme of female emancipation is, in the end, not going to be taken very seriously. As Tennyson wrote to S. E. Dawson: 'You have seen amongst other things that if women ever were to play such freaks, the burlesque and the tragic might go hand in hand'.[20] If we applaud Tennyson's openness to stylistic incongruities deliberately employed, it is less easy to accept his biased view of the initial proposition, that women should attempt to assert themselves, even if in doing so they are driven to setting up a wholly female college, its doors shut firmly against the male world. Tennyson's apologetic tone ('it is, after all, only a medley') extends from the theme to the style and back again; the conclusion, spoken by the poet (as opposed to the various protagonists who, improbably, relate different parts of the story in turn) emphasises Tennyson's equivocation:

> Yet how to bind the scattered scheme of seven
> Together in one sheaf? What style could suit?
> The men required that I should give throughout
> The sort of mock-heroic gigantesque,
> With which we bantered little Lilia first:
> The women – and perhaps they felt their power,
> For something in the ballads which they sang,
> Or in their silent influence as they sat,
> Had ever seemed to wrestle with burlesque,
> And drove us, last, to quite a solemn close –
> They hated banter, wished for something real,
> A gallant fight, a noble princess – why
> Not make her true-heroic – true-sublime?
> Or all, they said, as earnest as the close?
> Which yet with such a framework scarce could be.
> Then rose a little feud betwixt the two,
> Betwixt the mockers and the realists:
> And I, betwixt them both, to please them both,
> And yet to give the story as it rose,

I moved as in a strange diagonal,
And maybe neither pleased myself nor them.

In *The Princess* Tennyson's ambitions are immense: he is trying to
make sense of the present, but also of its relationship to the past and to
a possibly golden future ('This fine old world of ours is but a
child /Yet in the go-cart. Patience! Give it time /To learn its limbs:
there is a hand that guides'); whilst at the same time trying to say
something about women in Victorian society. His self-imposed brief
is ultimately beyond him: the poem lacks focus, and whilst the
Prologue might set the more romance-like elements in a solid
framework of social event and niceties ('Sir Walter Vivien all a
summer's day /Gave his broad lawns until the set of sun /Up to the
people . . .'), it serves to undercut what force that romance might
have had. We might be cheered by Tennyson's determination to
celebrate an actual 'feast of the Mechanics' Institute' at Maidstone in
July 1842, by his spirited attempt to capture the variegated scene with
all its modern inventions ('Strange was the sight, and smacking of the
time'), but it verges on the false jollity of a holiday camp:

> here were telescopes
> For azure views; and there a group of girls
> In circle waited, whom the electric shock
> Dislinked with shrieks and laughter: round the lake
> A little clock-work steamer paddling plied
> And shook the lilies: perched about the knolls
> A dozen angry models jetted steam:
> A petty railway ran . . .
> . . . so that sport
> Went hand in hand with Science; otherwhere
> Pure sport: a herd of boys with clamour bowled
> And stumped the wicket; babies rolled about
> Like tumbled fruit in grass . . .
>
> (Prologue, 67–83)

The aristocratic observers of this idyllic scene ('ambrosial' is a word
tossed in to remind us of our true bearings) are eventually 'satiated',
and decide to compose a poem about women, spurred on by Lilia
'wild with sport', who has her own ideas of women's place –

> O I wish
> That I were some great princess, I would build
> Far off from men a college like a man's . . .
>   (Prologue, 133–5)

But the drift the poem will take is clear enough. Lilia is outnumbered by the men, and has in any case got the poet ranged against her. She is subsumed into a roseate view of English maidenhood.

> Petulant she spoke, and at herself she laughed;
> A rosebud set with little wilful thorns,
> And sweet as English air could make her, she.
>   (Prologue, 152–4)

It is hardly likely, with such bias, that the female case will get much of a hearing. But it will provide some amusement. And if the hero-prince is prone to fits and seizures, unable to tell shadow from substance ('For all things were and were not' seems to anticipate Clough's dichotomy, but the line's function is very different), then that is further calculated to make the whole thing seem preposterous. This is not some Hamletesque, brooding hero in doubt (we have to wait for *Maud* for that), but a cataleptic clown.

The basic plot 'grates', like Cyril, 'on rusty hinges'. The hero's beloved has locked herself away in a college for women, seduced by feminist notions. The hero, with Cyril and Florian, decides that in order to enter the apparently impregnable fortress, they must all dress up as women. This of course provides much opportunity for sexist mirth, especially when an amenable relative slips them past the sentries and falls prey to the usual familial feelings:

> I am sad and glad
> To see you, Florian. *I* give thee to death
> My brother! it was duty spoke, not I.
> My needful seeming harshness, pardon it.
> Our mother, is she well?
>   (II, 286–9)

The irony is not lost on us, nor the obvious drift the poem is about to take. Well might the poet have wished for Shakespearian skills to tell this tale, in which the man, dressed as a woman, rides out with his beloved, and unknowing, Ida. Tennyson pushes the whole thing over into farce, as his hero is forced to sing, 'maidenlike as far/As I could ape their treble'; his companion Cyril is less prudent, and launches into 'a careless, careless tavern-catch/Of Moll and Meg, and strange experiences/Unmeet for ladies'. The game seems to be up, but even in the ensuing chase our hero seems to enjoy himself ('secret laughter tickled all my soul'). Princess Ida is not amused. Battle cannot be averted by careless male titters. If we are less than convinced by the arguments on femininity put forward by the men, then that is no wonder; no wonder, either, that the victorious females immediately become Florence Nightingales of the battlefield, with 'the tender ministries/Of female hands and hospitality'. The proud Princess Ida acknowledges defeat, and herself 'a Queen of farce!' Of course, the argument is more complicated than this résumé suggests: if it were not, the poem's basic lack of action would be intolerable (which it is not, provided we are in no hurry). But the essential point remains: Tennyson does not take his story within a story seriously, even in comic terms. Humour is used at the expense of the argument. *The Princess* is no *Lysistrata*. If the poem begins in optimism, in complacent acceptance of the right relation between lord and servant, it ends in a quiet optimism that accepts not only that, but also the right relation between man and woman. The old values are reasserted in conventional terms. Significantly the winds of change from France have still to cross the channel:

> Too comic for the solemn things they are,
> Too solemn for the comic touches in them,
> Like our wild Princess with as wise a dream
> As some of theirs — God bless the narrow seas!
> (Conclusion, 67–70)

This 'Tory member's elder son' does not seem to be an isolated voice in the poem.

IV

Tennyson's 'Medley' reflects, rather than resolves, the age's confusions; his conscious use of humour is to deflate an 'issue of the day' that he himself cannot take seriously. We emerge from the poem as we are meant to, as from a dream. Lilia symbolically removes her scarf from the old statue, the scarf she had wildly, sportively thrown round it to turn it into a female warrior bold: it is, after all, no more than a gesture.

Clough's *Bothie* might seem, initially, to be offering rather a similar sort of medley. That seems to have been a line taken by some of his contemporaries, whose praise upset an Arnold determined to 'refuge myself with Obermann in his forest against your Zeit Geist'.[21] Arnold was to object to *Ambarvalia* on rather different grounds, based on 'a growing sense of the deficiency of the *beautiful* in your poems'.[22] It is instructive to take Arnold's injunction, prompted by *Ambarvalia*:

> Reflect too, as I cannot but do here more and more, in spite of all the nonsense some people talk, how deeply *unpoetical* the age and all one's surroundings are. Not unprofound, not ungrand, not unmoving: — but *unpoetical* . . .[23]

and to set this alongside Kingsley's observation, prompted by *The Bothie*:

> He found the sublime and the ridiculous hand in hand, as they usually are, not only in Cockneyized Highlands, but everywhere else, we suspect, on this earth; and, like greater men than himself, he has not been ashamed to draw them into the same picture.[24]

William Rossetti put it rather differently when he referred to the 'strong and complete . . . aspect of *fact*' pervading the poem, and said that its 'completeness' was a sign of its 'peculiar modernness', its 'recognition of every-day fact'.[25] But the basic point was the same. Further, just as Kingsley could see the intimate connection between subject and style, William Whewell acknowledged the benefits of the much-maligned hexameter as the proper 'vehicle of a representation of the realities of life'.[26] Even Arnold's original protestations got watered down until he could see the poem as 'serio-comic', and therefore with 'a right to be grotesque . . . grotesque *truly*'.[27]

Any argument in defence of Clough based on the grotesque is bound to recall one possible contemporary response to Browning's poetry: it would certainly be grossly unfair to Browning if we were not to acknowledge what he had achieved, and was to achieve, in his vision of the world's 'multitudinousness'. But Clough was doing something rather different, and was scarcely aware of Browning's poetry until late in life. So that the contemporary response to *The Bothie* could mislead us. It is not a poem we have any right to expect from Clough in 1848, just after he has resigned his Oriel Fellowship in disgust. *The Bothie* is a poem of tremendous resilience, a poem of assurance and surprise. Clough seems to have worked out of his system all the nagging doubts of his shorter poems, and seized on that crucial element of detachment that had emerged in a mere handful of poems. The self-consciousness has changed: R. H. Hutton put the matter rather well, in relation to *Amours de Voyage*:

> Clough's genius was, if I may say so, a genius for moving buoyantly under a great weight of superincumbent embarrassment. . . . It would hardly be possible, I think, to convey in any rhythm more effectively the impression of an eager, cordial, and embarrassed speech.[28]

In the case of *The Bothie*, it is the buoyancy we most immediately notice: but Hutton's analysis is masterly in its insight, and in the connection it makes back to the eighteenth-century tradition, and ahead to the much more complex poetry of *Amours de Voyage*.

As with *The Princess*, we could say that *The Bothie* is in essence a joke – a much more literary one, with its mock epic tone, its use of the reviled hexameter, its Oxford reading-party setting; but Clough, unlike Tennyson, seems in little doubt as to what he is doing. Whilst *The Princess* is interesting as a document of its time, *The Bothie* is interesting because it is a confidently achieved poem. Quite where this confidence comes from is a mystery, and this no doubt accounts for the resort to 'charm' on the part of admiring, but bemused, critics. Barbara Hardy has suggested, in her essay on Clough's self-consciousness, how he tends to steer clear of satire because of his 'profound and sober respect for life' – in this she compares him to George Eliot – but the comparison could also be made backwards with Wordsworth.[29] Clough could appreciate the moral purposes of satire – hence his understanding of Crabbe – but it should be clear when we read *The Bothie* that satire is not his concern. On the other hand Barbara Hardy's remark that Clough is 'too impassioned and too uncertain to be praised as an ironist' needs qualification even in the context of *The Bothie*, whose triumph is precisely in the relationships it establishes between the knowledge of self and the knowledge of community, explored confidently and wonderingly.[30] In *The Princess* a dream atmosphere is deliberately cultivated and calculated to make us keep our distance from it as reality; there are times in *The Bothie* when we get a rather similar whiff of another, alien world that could well be that of the dream. But it calls to mind, not Tennyson, but Wordsworth, and his other world of dreams, of insights and incomprehensibilities.

A sense of reality, though, is what the poem asserts to begin with, paradoxically couched in terms that are familiar to classical scholars — the Homeric games, the exuberance, the formulaic repetition of phrases — familiar, too, in the use of slang and consciously racy speech ('*Shady* in Latin, said Lindsay, but *topping* in Plays and Aldrich'); but the terms and the use to which they are put force us also into a sense of the unfamiliar. We cannot call, for example, the opening lines mock-epic quite, in any accepted sense of the term, although mock-epic as a concept lurks behind them. Hutton's 'buoyancy' is a useful term to remember here, provided we ally it to the precision already seen in Clough's shorter poems, a precision not simply denotative, but emotional in that it subtly suggests, along with the rhythmic cadences, a solemnity that will be seen to justify itself together with a lively good-humouredness that calls the solemnity into question without destroying it. This seems to me a remarkable instance of the creative potentialities of Clough's vision, gently hinted at:

It was the afternoon; and the sports were now at the ending.
Long had the stone been put, tree cast, and thrown the hammer;
Up the perpendicular hill, Sir Hector so called it,
Eight stout gillies had run, with speed and agility wondrous;
Run too the course on the level had been; the leaping was over:
Last in the show of address, a novelty recently added,
Noble ladies their prizes adjudged for costume that was perfect,
Turning the clansmen about, as they stood with upraised elbows,
Bowing their eye-glassed brows, and fingering kilt and sporran.
It was four of the clock, and the sports were come to the ending,
Therefore the Oxford party went off to adorn for the dinner.

Social points are being made here, unobtrusively but firmly, just as the richly erotic qualities of the poem's development are hinted at here in the noble ladies' eyeing and appraising the kilts and the sporrans — 'fingering' is brilliant.

Whereas Tennyson never seems certain how much to allow to the boisterous youthfulness of his protagonists at Sir Walter's, Clough gives a very clear sense of what these strange people are like, Oxonians marooned in the Highlands, carrying with them their own

cultivated proprieties, black and white ties and all, but all of them, in
their way, like Adam the tutor, 'with sense and feeling beneath it'.
Sense and feeling are what the poem explores, and just as the 'cheery,
cigar-loving Lindsay,/Lindsay the ready of speech, the Piper, the
Dialectician', in three weeks 'had created a dialect new for the party',
so Clough finds himself not merely cultivating the 'dialect of the
tribe', but redefining it. Similarly the characters are redefined both by
the Highland setting, and by the classical superimpositions: Airlie,
'effulgent as god of Olympus', immaculate, scrupulously dressed,
'like a god, came leaving his ample Olympian chamber'.

The first part of the poem is devoted to scene-setting, the local
gentry, priests, 'Members of Paliament many, forgetful of votes and
blue-books/Here, amid heathery hills, upon beast and bird of the
forest/Venting the murderous spleen of the endless Railway Com-
mittee'. (How facile, in retrospect, seem Tennyson's contemporary
references.) There is a truly Homeric feast (but again with neat
touches to distinguish the layers of society – 'Sherry, not overchoice,
for the gentry'), which is summed up in the epic line, 'So to the viands
before them with laughter and chat they beset them'. This conjunction of laughter and chat is central to the poem's structure. The
movement of the poem is contained in speeches and laughter, and
above the laughter of the merrymakers can be heard the poet's own
laughter, as he relishes the absurdity whilst acknowledging the
Muses' presence:

Spare me, O great Recollection! for words to the task were unequal,
Spare me, O mistress of Song! nor bid me remember minutely
All that was said and done o'er the well-mixed tempting toddy . . .

                                                           (I, 82–4)

Clough is too good a classicist not to know that knowledge and
memory go hand in hand: this is a poem about both. It is no rhetorical
accident that in his plea to the Muse to spare him, he likens the
hubbub of speech to a 'suddent torrent in time of speat in the
mountain'; even Sir Hector's 'garrulous tale' is 'wild as the torrent';
what might at this juncture seem a merely lively remembrance of epic
simile accrues to itself reverberations later in the poem, when the
central sexual imagery of discovery and knowledge is couched in
similar terms. Clough's sense of paradox is nice: 'Left to oblivion be it,
the memory, faithful as ever . . .'

This unobtrusive wryness gives way to something more threatening to the social well-being of the gathering when the toast is offered: 'My friends! are you ready? the Strangers'. The Oxonians naturally expect Adam the tutor to reply: there is consternation when, egged on by Adam, Philip Hewson assumes the role. Hewson has been mentioned once so far; we know nothing about him. At this crucial, social moment, Clough begins to elaborate on the tensions with which the poem is to concern itself. If 'laughter and chat' have so far predominated – and will do so still in many ways – Hewson is there to redefine the terms:

> Philip Hewson a poet,
> Hewson a radical hot, hating lords and scorning ladies,
> Silent mostly, but often reviling in fire and fury
> Feudal tenures, mercantile lords, competition and bishops,
> Liveries, armorial bearings, amongst other matters the Game-laws:
> He could speak, and was asked – to by Adam, but Lindsay aloud cried
> (Whisky was hot in his brain), Confound it, no, not Hewson,
> A'nt he cock-sure to bring in his eternal political humbug?
> However, so it must be, and after due pause of silence,
> Waving his hand to Lindsay, and smiling oddly to Adam,
> Up to them rose and spoke the poet and radical Hewson.
> I am, I think, perhaps the most perfect stranger present.
> I have not, as have some of my friends, in my veins some tincture,
> Some few ounces of Scottish blood; no, nothing like it.
> I am therefore perhaps the fittest to answer and thank you.
>
> (I, 124–38)

This is beautifully ironic: the qualifications in his speech, along with that essential recognition as to his 'perfect strangeness', give way to what seems a triumphant speech of reconciliation. English and Scots, 'better friends . . . for that old fighting . . . inasmuch as we know each other the better,/We can now shake hands without pretending or shuffling'. His speech is greeted with delighted uproar, 'a great tornado of cheering', but before that has 'died wholly away' he adds 'his doubtful conclusion':

> I have, however, less claim than others perhaps to this honour,
> For, let me say, I am neither game-keeper, nor game-preserver.
>   So he said, and sat down, but his satire had not been taken.

He is indeed, the most perfect stranger, an embarrassment to everyone, a man who values integrity beyond social decorum. Clough can see his excesses, but he can see, above all, how much Hewson matters. At the end of Part I, a mysterious guest accosts him: 'Young man, if ye pass through the Braes o' Lochaber/See by the loch-side ye come to the Bothie of Tober-na-vuolich'. The drift of the poem, emotionally, argumentatively, geographically, is towards the Bothie. As yet its significance we cannot know; but we feel the substance of the shadow already cast over the poem.

Typically, the pastoral connotations of the poem are reinforced at the start of the second part — 'Et certamen erat, Corydon cum Thyrside, magnum' — only to be altered out of all recognition. This *certamen* is no light affair: it is another paradox that the section should open with such emphasis on light and playfulness, placid bathing pool and amber torrent framed together, like the bathers Philip and Arthur.

Morn, in yellow and white, came broadening out from the
   mountains,
Long ere music and reel were hushed in the barn of the dancers.
Duly in *matutine* bathed before eight some two of the party,
Where in the morning was custom, where over a ledge of granite
Into a granite bason the amber torrent descended.
There two plunges each took Philip and Arthur together,
Duly in *matutine* bathed, and read, and waited for breakfast:
Breakfast, commencing at nine, lingered lazily on to noon-day.

(II, 1 – 8)

When they are all reassembled, discussion turns to women, and it is Philip who makes the running (now, incidentally, not 'silent mostly', but 'the eloquent speaker'), with his attack on the pretensions of Lady Augustas and Floras, hot-house products who ape the qualities of true pastoral, which is a matter of 'out-of-doors' beauty wedded to labour. He launches into a marvellous speech (acknowledging the scorn it will be greeted with) on the connection between beauty and work: his ideal is a 'capless, bonnetless maiden,/Bending with three-pronged fork in a garden uprooting potatoes'. He cannot fully account for the effect the sight of such a person has had on him: but 'a new thing was in me'. It certainly seems an improvement on the 'dull farces of escort'. If we have been reminded of Wordsworth's redefinition of pastoral in poems like 'Michael' and 'The Bróthers', we are reminded now of Blake's 'Proverbs of Hell', by Philip's peroration:

Better a crust of black bread than a mountain of paper confections,
Better a daisy in earth than a dahlia cut and gathered,
Better a cowslip with root than a prize carnation without it.

(II, 65–7)

The sober tutor Adam can scarcely get in his 'That I allow' before Philip is off again 'with the bit in his teeth'. Philip's view, of course, is an idealised inversion, a Rachel or a 'Dora beloved, of Alexis', inviting the mockery and laughter of his companions: Arthur, for instance, who asks 'Is not all this the same that one hears at common-room breakfasts, /Or perhaps Trinity wines, about Gothic buildings and Beauty?' The architectural analogy is taken up by Hobbes, 'contemplative, corpulent, witty', with a fantastically absurd extension of the notion, worth quoting for what it tells us, not simply of the flexibility of the verse, but also of the body of thought behind the poem:

Philip shall write us a book, a Treatise upon *The Laws of Architectural Beauty in Application to Women;*
Illustrations, of course, and a Parker's Glossary pendent,
Where shall in specimen seen be the sculliony stumpy-columnar,
(Which to a reverent taste is perhaps the most moving of any,)
Rising to grace of true woman in English the Early and Later,
Charming us still in fulfilling the Richer and Loftier stages,
Lost, ere we end, in the Lady-Debased and the Lady-Flamboyant:
Whence why in satire and spite too merciless onward pursue her
Hither to hideous close, Modern-Florid, modern – fine-lady?
No, I will leave it to you, my Philip, my Pugin of women.

(II, 144–54)

The tutor takes a more solemnly responsible view, mindful of Philip's youth, and of the need to search for the good – good not absolute, but 'That which is good for ourselves, our proper selves, our best selves.' The tutor's speech is interesting, especially in the context of the overall discussion: it is an index of Clough's control over his diverse material (the debate ranges widely, from duty to equality) that he can encompass Philip's idealistically realistic attitudes, the mockery of Hobbes and Arthur, and Adam's cautious wisdom set against Philip's headlong impetuosity. The poem becomes a quest, as some of the party head for the 'Bothie of what-did-he-call it', for Philip's best and proper self. Clough is managing a dramatisation of one of the central quests of his day; it is a major achievement to create a work so essentially exterior and dramatic, in a form that is harmonic rather than melodic, a form sanctioned by classical antecedent but not anticipated by it.

Another classical ingredient emerges in the third part: Clough makes use of choric devices as news begins to filter back. Philip does not return with the others, and Lindsay the Piper's report is received by the tutor in stunned silence —

> Why, Hewson we left in Rannoch,
> By the lochside and the pines, in a farmer's house, — reflecting —
> Helping to shear, and dry clothes, and bring in peat from the peat-
> stack.
> And the Tutor's countenance fell, perplexed, dumb-foundered
> Stood he, — slow and with pain disengaging jest from earnest.
>
> (III, 101 – 5)

Again, the tutor's role in the poem is underscored by this last line — in the midst of whirling activity, the flames of rumour lapping at his feet, he stands pained. Philip's talk has, after all, turned into action. And underneath the ensuing reports that Arthur and Lindsay eagerly supply, with slang crowding itself out as each man vies with the other, as they recount in significant detail their battling in the torrents ('How to the element offering their bodies, downshooting the fall, they/Mingled themselves with the flood and the force of imperious water') prior to the discovery of Philip embracing the golden-haired Katie — underneath all this jocularity (and irony at Philip's expense) lies the heavy burden of the tutor's pain. Jest and earnest are uncomfortably close. Philip, it transpires, has given himself entirely to a Katie whose love for him cannot match his capacity for giving. He is seen alone in the mountains, musing on the impossibility of their relationship, reverting again and again to the cry 'Would I were dead, I keep saying, that so I could go and uphold her!' Perhaps a spirituality will serve where physical desire is so frustrated; and whilst Philip muses, and writes in desperation to his tutor, Katie dances with Airlie. Philip and Katie part company, and Clough lets us know how he views the relationship:

Yea! for the first time in life a man complete and perfect,
So forth! much that before has been heard of. – Howbeit they parted.
                                                        (IV, 123–4)

In his letter, Philip tries to explain that in some inexplicable way a
glance from another girl in passing seemed to tell him everything,
seemed to condemn his frivolity, his trance-like state, his possession.
He tries to 'hide himself from himself' – a crucial phrase, in view of
Adam's earlier talk about what was good and proper for ourselves.
From this relationship, Philip turns in self-disgust to one with 'O
strange! O marvel, marvel of marvels' – Lady Maria. But it is not
simply self-disgust; his letters display his turbulent mind, his
sophistries that justify his recklessness:

And I find myself saying, and what I am saying, discern not,
Dig in thy deep dark prison, O miner! and finding be thankful;
Though unpolished by thee, unto thee unseen in perfection,
While thou art eating black bread in the poisonous air of the cavern,
Far away glitters the gem on the peerless neck of a Princess,
Dig, and starve, and be thankful; it is so, and thou hast been aiding.
                                                        (V, 63–7)

The cynicism here is the more disturbing because Philip cannot
himself decide whether he believes what he says. He can echo
sophistically the tutor's remark, 'we can't know all things at twenty',
but the sadder echo is of the tutor's pained distinction between jest
and earnest: Philip, too, wonders 'in irony is it, or earnest?' The larger
irony is rammed home by Adam's reply – Philip is indulging in the
pastoral absurdities he had earlier scorned, sporting now with
Amaryllis in the shade.

The second part of the poem traces Philip's discovery of himself,
painful and slow, through his relationship with Elspie – the girl he
had seen in passing, whose look had been so significant and
inscrutable. Philip has gained the Bothie of Tober-na-vuolich. But he
is now cautious, exulting in the accident that has brought him there,
but no longer relying on outward forms as guides. This is essentially a
moral teething, the more perplexing because of its hidden, unaccountable movements. Philip's words recall Clough's most explicit
short poem of the erotic, 'Natura Naturans' – what is there stated in
lyric, slightly uneasy terms, is here put with the full force of dramatic
introspection:

I was as one that sleeps on the railway; one, who dreaming
Hears through his dream the name of his home shouted out; hears and
      hears not, —
Faint, and louder again, and less loud, dying in distance;
Dimly conscious, with something of inward debate and choice, —
      and
Sense of claim and reality present, anon relapses
Nevertheless, and continues the dream and fancy, while forward
Swiftly, remorseless, the car presses on, he knows not whither.

                                                        (VI, 60—6)

That Philip's dream can form the basis of a sound reality is clear
from Adam's sanction of the relationship. But the relationship has to
discover itself: both Philip and Elspie have to confront and conquer
their confusions, confusions which require essential scrupulosity to be
observed. Elspie keeps returning to potent sexual imagery, as the
images of river and bridge from earlier in the poem begin, like the
two lovers, to merge and coalesce.

            Well, — she answered,
And she was silent some time, and blushed all over, and answered
Quietly, after her fashion, still knitting, Maybe, I think of it,
Though I don't know that I did: and she paused again; but it may be,
Yes, — I don't know Mr. Philip, — but only it feels to me strangely
Like to the high new bridge, they used to build at, below there,
Over the burn and glen on the road. You won't understand me.
But I keep saying in my mind — this long time slowly with trouble
I have been building myself, up, up, and toilfully raising,
Just like as if the bridge were to do it itself without masons,
Painfully getting myself upraised one stone on another,
All one side I mean; and now I see on the other
Just such another fabric uprising, better and stronger,
Close to me, coming to join me: and then I sometimes fancy, —
Sometimes I find myself dreaming at nights about arches and
      bridges, —
Sometimes I dream of a great invisible hand coming down, and
Dropping the great key-stone in the middle: there in my dreaming,
There I feel the great key-stone coming in, and through it
Feel the other part — all the other stones of the archway,
Joined into mine with a strange happy sense of completeness. But,
      dear me,

This is confusion and nonsense. I mix all the things I can think of.
And you won't understand, Mr. Philip.

(VII, 53 – 74)

Philip understands. But the Lawrentian nature of their passion has still
to be worked through, the keystone of the arch put in place, the sheer
force of feeling grasped without being held in check. Yet Clough
avoids, miraculously in his time, the earnestness of Lawrence, even if
he cannot always avoid the sentimental (Philip is rather prone to the
ready tear): what makes the last three sections of *The Bothie* so
peculiarly moving and affecting is their combination of gravity – not
with its usual opposite gaiety – but with humorous, amazed com-
passion. Each attains that knowledge of self which is insurance against
submission to the other. Elspie's declaration of belief in Philip, along
with her acknowledged fear, is answered by Philip's laughter – 'So,
my own Elspie, at last you are clear that I'm bad enough for you'. It is
only when knowledge, not only of self, but of the other, is
sufficient and assured that marriage is possible, and, with it, the trek
(modelled on Tom Arnold's journey) to New Zealand. Philip's name
at the last has its full meaning revealed, just as in the process his self-
conscious self discovers itself, paradoxically, by subjugation:

There he hewed, and dug; subdued the earth and his spirit;
There he built him a home; there Elspie bare him children,
David and Bella; perhaps ere this too an Elspie or Adam;
There hath he farmstead and land, and fields of corn and flax fields;
And the Antipodes too have a Bothie of Tober-na-vuolich.

(IX, 196 – 200)

The qualifications supplied by the protagonists, and by Adam the
tutor, are sufficient for us not to see in this conclusion any easy
escapism, nor wry irony at Philip's expense. It is a movingly
affirmative poem, the more so because it has taken the greatest pains
to be open and honest.

Just as it seems an abdication of our responsibilities as readers to sum
it all up as 'charming', so I do not think we can account for *The
Bothie*'s manifold complexities by a simple resort to the word
'humour'. *The Bothie* may, after all, be like *The Princess*, a 'medley'.
But it is a much less self-conscious one, and a much more realistic
reflection of the turbulences that lead to that final emigration: a finely
wrought balance is in the end achieved. I suggest that this is possible

because of Clough's confidence within the poem, a confidence that shows itself especially in the way he can move from local to larger irony, from ribald comedy to intensely sexual seriousness, from the wryly amused observation of a social scene to the dramatised participation in actions that mirror the bewildered recognition of the closeness of jest and earnest. 'Confusion and nonsense' can, after all, complete and underpin the union both Philip and Elspie seek.

6 The Sound of Distant Laughter: Clough

I

Clough sent an early draft of *Amours de Voyage* to J. C. Shairp, who wrote:

> The state of soul of which it is a projection I do not like. It strikes me as the most Werterish (not that I ever read Werter) of all you have yet done. There is no hope, nor strength, nor belief in these; — everything crumbles to dust beneath a ceaseless self-introspection and criticism which is throughout the one only inspiration. The gaiety of manner where no gaiety is, becomes flippancy. . . . The Ambarvalia, if Werterish, was honest serious Werterism — but this is Beppoish or Don Juanish (If I remember them right). The Hexameters still do not go down with me. They give me a sense of Travestie — which is their place I think . . . I won't flatter; but you were not made, my dear Clough, to make sport before The Philistines in this way, but for something else.[1]

Clough was not surprised at Shairp's reaction: it was what he had expected. 'You don't at all sting, I assure you . . . Gott und Teufel, my friend, you don't suppose all that comes from myself!'[2] But there was also disappointment in Clough's question: 'do you not, in the conception, find any final Strength of Mind in the unfortunate fool of a hero?' None of his contemporaries seemed to grasp the point of the poem: like Arnold, most of then wanted to forget it, not talk about it. It was nine years later, in 1858, that Clough sent the poem, with some hesitation, to the *Atlantic Monthly*.

Shairp, of course, meant to sting with his Byronic references; and although Walter Houghton seems to accept unquestioningly Clough's admiration for Byron, there are grounds for wondering how welcome the comparison would be to Clough. But that is another matter. Shairp's complete bemusement is transparent in his ability to see the poem as both 'Werterish' and 'Don Juanish' — and in his inability to see either the contradictions or the connections. To refer to Byron in an attempt to describe Clough's achievement is not altogether misguided — the two poets share qualities in ways that can still be surprising. Byron is still prey today to the smothering embrace of sentimental critics; rather similarly, those who in Clough's day responded at all to, say, the hexameters of *Amours de Voyage*, employed those very terms that had characterised discussion of humour in poetry for much of the eighteenth and early nineteenth centuries: 'it changes from grave to gay without desecrating what should be solemn, or disenchanting that which should be graceful'.[3] Even Barbara Hardy wants to have her cake and eat it: of *The Bothie* she can say that the 'irony strengthens rather than undermines the final pastoral salute to a new society, to marriage, work and fertility' — and yet, 'Clough is too impassioned and too uncertain to be praised as an ironist.'[4] Of *Amours de Voyage*, the levity 'is undermining'; and the very use of the term 'levity' is reminiscent of the moral debate on wit and humour in the eighteenth century. One of Clough's virtues is that he manages to turn the tables on that debate, that he revives the concept of wit in poetry.

Something of this had been emerging in *The Bothie*; its importance in *Amours de Voyage* is central, and has been well put by John Goode, in one of the best pieces on Clough that there is:

> One wants above all to use the word 'wit' about Clough's best poetry, and by this I mean that we are aware of a sophisticated verbal mode of discrimination among values.[5]

This surely makes the connection backwards to Byron, whilst reminding us of the great gulf between the early eighteenth century and the mid-nineteenth century: in other words Clough's (and Byron's) task is all the harder in that 'wit' can no longer rely on an accepted set of values (hence the incomprehension of much of the contemporary response). As Goode puts it, 'by the 1840s the stability of relationship between language and meaning has disappeared'.[6] I would have said that it had started to disappear quite some time before that, and that we see in Clough the continuation of a process already well under way in Byron's best poetry. Just as Byron, in *Don Juan* especially, is searching desperately for the right way of naming things, so Clough in *Amours de Voyage*, is concerned, like his hero

Claude, with naming things. The complex irony of the process is revealed in the comparison he makes with Adam (it is significant that Adam the Tutor is central to *The Bothie*, and that Clough had already written a poem about Adam and Eve):

So in fantastic height, in coxcomb exaltation,
Here in the Garden I walk, can freely concede to the Maker
That the works of his hand are all very good: his creatures,
Beast of the field and fowl, he brings them before me; I name them;
That which I name them, they are, – the bird, the beast, and the
    cattle.
But for Adam, – alas, poor critical coxcomb Adam!
But for Adam there is not found an help-meet for him.

(I, 7)

In naming things, Claude / Adam has not begun to understand: 'like Iago', he 'can be nothing at all, if it is not critical wholly'. This is one of the major issues of the poem – how can one be oneself, whilst at the same time recognising the existence of others? Biswas is mainly right when he says that if we can pin the poem down to a particular theme, it is 'the vindication of the life of thought' – but the conditional is important, and with it the qualifications crowd in. As Coleridge had recognised, 'thought' is 'I thinking', and that 'I' is also feeling. This, too, was a truth that Byron, very differently, acknowledged.

It would be wrong to overemphasise the Byronic connection; but the emphasis in the other direction, towards Eliot and Prufrock, Uncle Tom Cobley and all, is worse. Michael Timko has said of *Amours de Voyage* that Clough's main purpose

is the exposé of a self-centred prig unable to realise, as does Philip in the *Bothie*, the necessity of striking a balance between theory and practice, between independence of, and unity with his fellow men.[7]

Claude might not, indeed, be a Werther or a Childe Harold; but the poem cannot be summed up as a 'serio-comic analysis of a Victorian dilettante'. It is true that Clough himself referred to the poem as 'tragi-comedy or comi-tragedy' – but the equivocation over where to put the emphasis is significant. Clough had protested to Shairp about Shairp's immediate identifying of the hero with the poet, and perhaps he protested too much: letters of the time show how much of Clough there is in Claude, and that reveals the inadequacy of Timko's account. The perspectives are constantly shifting. Claude is both observer and observed: the dramatisation of conflict in *The Bothie* has become the central motivating force of *Amours de Voyage*. Biswas catches the flavour of the poem (and its technique – no mere super-added pleasure', these hexameters and elegiacs, but essential expressions of the poem's 'crisis in meaning') when he talks of 'this oscillating, helplessly open poetry'.[8] This is Clough's distinction, as it had been Blake's, Wordsworth's, Keats's, Byron's. Few Victorians would accept such openness. Clough knows only too well the constraints on openness: the voyage outwards, 'unto the perfecter earth' is also a voyage inwards.

> *'The world that we live in*
> *Whithersoever we turn, still is the same narrow crib;*
> *'Tis but to prove limitation, and measure a cord, that we travel;*
> *Let who would 'scape and be free go to his chamber and think;*
> *'Tis but to change idle fancies for memories wilfully falser;*
> *'Tis but to go and have been.' – Come, little bark! let us go.*
>
> (I, introductory elegiacs)

Emerson observed that 'Travelling is a fool's paradise';[9] Imlac in *Rasselas* (and Johnson in *The Rambler*) had made a similar point. But even Imlac had acknowledged the experiential need for the journey to be made, in that limitation has to be proved before it can be accepted. *Amours de Voyage* is a poem about the implications of travel; the tourist in particular is mocked. But even here there is ambiguity and qualification – it is, after all, by his Murray's *Guide* under his arm that Claude is partially defined. The more searching definition depends, breathtakingly, on his having journeyed, as Clough himself had, to Rome at a crucial stage in its history. That relationship between personal and historical circumstance is the nub of the poem: this is primarily why Prufrock gets in the way of our view of the poem. Byron's travelling heroes Childe Harold and Don Juan provide better clues as to the type of poem *Amours de Voyage* might be.

The poem's structure – five cantos made up entirely of letters, each canto framed by elegiac stanzas that form a counterpoint of commentary and irony to set against the irony within the letters themselves – has, perhaps not surprisingly, led many to see *Amours de*

Voyage in terms of an embryonic novel. It is one way out of the critical problems the poem raises, and it exonerates us from too scrupulous a regard for the texture of the poetry. But it is precisely the texture that matters. In *The Bothie* Clough had been able to play off the anti-heroic elements against the recognisably heroic, epic qualities of the structure. Even there, though, he employed indirection and evasions which undermined any neat categorisation which might have temptingly offered itself: in *Amours de Voyage* the indirection, the evasions take over the poem more or less entirely. Whereas in *The Bothie* letters from Philip had received carefully considered replies from the tutor, so that some sort of choric comment was always available (even when merely speculative – as with Philip's contemporaries and their frank puzzlements), in *Amours de Voyage* letters are sent into a void. We never see the replies, other than in the way they are reflected in the protagonists' own letters. It is a poem about substance and shadow, about shadowy relationships which are none the less valuable for being shadowy. It is a poem of multiple ironies, which depend for their effect and meaning on the fact that it is a poem, and not a novel. *Amours de Voyage* is built on letters, on correspondence (Claude and Mary, the two figures of the central relationship, do not exchange letters with each other); it explores the deeper implications of what it means to correspond.

This theme is broached in Claude's first letter to Eustace: already, whatever the connections, the differences between *Amours de Voyage* and *The Bothie* begin to strike us. Whilst there is the same rather hesitant gait, the racy speech, that Clough had discovered in his earlier use of the hexameter, we have here that greater complexity of self-embarrassment noted by R. H. Hutton, set in, and partially explained by, the turbulent context of Rome. Rome's past is overlaid with gewgaws, its present theatened from within (Clough's own views on Mazzini's Republic deny any easy identification with the republican cause), and from without by the French. Claude's attitudes are defined from line to line, his absurdities half apparent to himself and yet in themselves necessary adjuncts of his character (as Georgina is to say in her first letter to Louisa about Claude: 'Very stupid, I think, but George says so *very* clever'). His pomposity is clear, his inconsistency too; but also his need for *rapport*, not merely with 'Eustatio', but with Rome and its self-denying continuities.

Dear Eustatio, I write that you may write me an answer,
Or at the least to put us again *en rapport* with each other.

Rome disappoints me much, — St Peter's, perhaps, in especial;
Only the Arch of Titus and view from the Lateran please me:
This, however, perhaps, is the weather, which truly is horrid.
Greece must be better, surely; and yet I am feeling so spiteful,
That I could travel to Athens, to Delphi, and Troy, and Mount Sinai,
Though but to see with my eyes that these are vanity also.
   Rome disappoints me much; I hardly as yet understand, but
Rubbishy seems the word that most exactly would suit it.
All the foolish destructions, and all the sillier savings,
All the incongruous things of past incompatible ages,
Seem to be treasured up here to make fools of present and future.
Would to Heaven the old Goths had made a cleaner sweep of it!
Would to Heaven some new ones would come and destroy these
   churches!
However, one can live in Rome as also in London.
Rome is better than London, because it is other than London.
It is a blessing, no doubt to be rid, at least for a time, of
All one's friends and relations, yourself (forgive me!) included, —
All the *assujettissement* of having been what one has been,
What one thinks one is, or thinks that others suppose one;
Yet, in despite of all, we turn like fools to the English.
Vernon has been my fate; who is here the same that you knew him, —
Making the tour, it seems, with friends of the name of Trevellyn.
                                                            (I, 1)

The self-conscious humour, the self-assertion and self-assurance all
come through in these lines, with each comma in its place as Claude
tries to establish his own position. It is typical of him at this stage to
use the French word so knowingly, as though by thus making it seem
foreign it can actually be distanced, that fact the word half-conceals:
the subjection, the constraint Claude is anxious to throw off is thrown
back at him in the self-advertisement of the word, just as the commas
and qualifications are efforts at liberation and reminders of the narrow
crib. (Dickens observes parenthetically in *Bleak House* that 'the
fashionable intelligence is weak in English, but a giant refreshed in
French'.) The tensions already explored in the framing elegiac lines
which open the poem are dramatised here and held in suspense, as the
aspiration towards nobler things is set against the turn, after all, to the
English. Claude would like to be above Vernon and the Trevellyns
(and fate), but he is, like them, 'making the tour'. Already, at the very
start of his next letter, the process of adjustment has to be

acknowledged, even if it is with an air of distaste and superiority: 'Rome disappoints me still; but I shrink and adapt myself to it'.

In *The Bothie* Clough had explored a relationship in which it was important to define yourself by not submitting to the other; the natural imagery, so glorious a part of the overall pattern of the poem, had underlined this movement towards growth and fulfilment. The paradox had been that, in the end, some subduing of the spirit was necessary. Clough slips this notion in to the last few lines of the poem and leaves it there for us to ponder as a wry comment on the poem's basic optimism. In *Amours de Voyage* the idea of submission is a much more central one. On the wider historical plane it involves Rome's struggle against France; on the personal plane, so intimately related, it involves Claude's struggle against himself and his vulnerability to Mary Trevellyn. The idea is complicated by the part played by fate (as Claude sees it initially): if the poem seems to tread so circumspectly, it is because it is so conscious of circumstance. Long before Hardy, and with less uncompromising rigidity, Clough sees the ironies and satires of circumstance.

Circumstance is an instructive word: it involves what is there, around us (seen abstractly by Claude as 'a tyrannous sense of a superincumbent oppression'), but it also involves our attitude, our stance, to what is there. As Claude writes to Eustace:

> Curious work, meantime, re-entering society: how we
> Walk a livelong day, great Heaven, and watch our shadows!
> What our shadows seem, forsooth, we will ourselves be.
> Do I look like that? You think me that: then I *am* that.
>
> (I, 4)

So that what Claude had seen from his lofty superiority as shrinkage and adaptation is in fact a necessity. Cowper had laughed at his shadow on the wall in the midday sun; Clough may be laughing at Claude as he watches his shadow. But there is an essential truth in Claude's rather desperate observation. Later on in the poem, when Claude is made aware of his social predicament ('the foolish family Vernon /Made some uneasy remarks, as we walked to our lodging together, /As to intentions, forsooth, and so forth' – the uneasy play on words gives itself away), he declares:

> How could I go? Great Heavens! to conduct a permitted flirtation
> Under those vulgar eyes, the observed of such observers!
>
> (III, 13)

Claude cannot, simply, be his own observer. There are always other eyes watching: if he thinks he can escape the implications by dismissing the vulgarity of the eyes that watch him, he cannot escape the gaze of poet and reader. This kind of irony runs through the poem: people are always on the move, to see, or to escape being seen. As the ironically lyrical lines of the elegiacs at the end of the third canto remind us, after Claude's confident declaration ('Tibur I shall not see; – but something better I shall see'):

> *Therefore farewell, ye hills, and ye, ye envineyarded ruins!*
> *Therefore farewell, ye walls, palaces, pillars and domes!*
> *Therefore farewell, far seen, ye peaks of the mythic Albano,*
> *Seen from Montorio's height, Tibur and AEsula's hills . . .*
> *Therefore farewell, ye plains, and ye hills, and the City Eternal!*
> *Therefore farewell! We depart, but to behold you again!*
>
> (III, concluding elegiacs)

A. Alvarez has referred to Clough's 'subtly polished language of manners'.[10] This is misleading, in that one of the things Claude is rebutting is the very notion of 'manners' – in his agonising over what role he should play in the fighting, he asks

Am I prepared to lay down my life for the British female?
Really, who knows? One has bowed and talked till, little by little,
All the natural heat has escaped of the chivalrous spirit.
Oh, one conformed, of course; but one doesn't die for good manners.

(II, 4)

The irony is at Claude's expense, as we see in his next letter. His detachment from the scene (mirroring Clough's own very extraordinary detachment from the events in Rome, as revealed in his letters) is caught well here, and it is hard to miss the echo of the earlier point he had made about manners; he too is a victim to the things and conventions he despises.

Weary of wondering, watching, and guessing, and gossiping idly,
Down I go, and pass through the quiet streets with the knots of
National Guards patrolling, and flags hanging out at the windows,
English, American, Danish, – and, after offering to help an
Irish family moving *en masse* to the Maison Serny,
After endeavouring idly to minister balm to the trembling

Quinquagenarian fears of two lone British spinsters,
Go to make sure of my dinner before the enemy enter.

(II, 5)

The language is polished certainly, but not in the way Alvarez seems
to be suggesting. If *Amours de Voyage* is a poem about manners, it is a
poem essentially against manners. With that cold, almost cynically
self-preserving juxtaposition whereby other people's fears are reduced by the claims of the stomach — shockingly so in that they are
essentially decorous claims — we are taken back, imagistically, to
Claude's quotation from Horace. This quotation, in its dislocations,
captures his own ambivalences when weighing up the claims of
country and ideals against the claims of the precious self:

Dulce it is, and *decorum*, no doubt, for the country to fall, — to
Offer one's blood an oblation to Freedom, and die for the Cause; yet
Still, individual culture is also something, and no man
Finds quite distinct the assurance that he of all others is called on,
Or would be justified, even, in taking away from the world that
Precious creature, himself. Nature sent him here to abide here,
Else why sent him at all? Nature wants him still, it is likely.
On the whole, we are meant to look after ourselves . . .

(II, 2)

Mary Trevellyn had observed of Claude at the end of Canto I, 'but
I think him terribly selfish'. Selfishness itself is a two-edged concept
(as we learn from Fanny Price's dilemma in *Mansfield Park*); Adam
the tutor, in *The Bothie*, had tempered Philip's enthusiasms by urging
him, in anticipation of Arnold, to do what was good for his best and
proper self, and Philip's quest had been towards that good. It is a
relativist concept, involving what elsewhere is defined by Clough in
Amours de Voyage as 'poise and retention' (and, incidentally, ac-
curately seized upon by Alvarez as a clue to the poem's meaning).
Poise starts off as a social concept, one of manners — all these people
have their own versions of poise, which come out in the way they
talk. But the combination and juxtaposition of 'poise and retention'
lift it out of the social plane on to the moral plane. It occurs initially in
one of the most stunning and most stunned letters Claude writes to
Eustace. Claude's flirtation with the political events around him —
drinking coffee as fighting goes on in the city — suddenly gives way to
a direct confrontation with violence. 'Flirtation' is the word to use

here, for Claude's response to these events is an index to his later
response to Mary, and his feelings for her. The tone he adopts has lost
the confidence of the opening letters, even though he retains, at least
initially, some of the bluster: again, the qualifications, the with-
drawals and retractions, the uncertainties as to what has actually been
seen, are reflected in the syntax and rhythms of speech. His words
flow and yet choke on themselves, just as consciousness grasps a two-
way movement, likened to the wave of the tide in a stream; the
narrative past gives way, in the flurry of action witnessed, to the
narrative present, and then back again into the past. This is a virtuoso
performance of a very remarkable kind — it demands full quotation.

So, I have seen a man killed! An experience that, among others!
Yes, I suppose I have; although I can hardly be certain,
And in a court of justice could never declare I had seen it.
But a man was killed, I am told, in a place where I saw
Something; a man was killed, I am told, and I saw something.
    I was returning home from St. Peter's; Murray, as usual,
Under my arm, I remember; had crossed the St. Angelo bridge; and
Moving towards the Condotti, had got to the first barricade, when
Gradually, thinking still of St. Peter's, I became conscious
Of a sensation of movement opposing me, — tendency this way
(Such as one fancies may be in a stream when the wave of the tide is
Coming and not yet come, — a sort of poise and retention);
So I turned, and, before I turned, caught sight of stragglers
Heading a crowd, it is plain, that is coming behind that corner.
Looking up, I see windows filled with heads; the Piazza,
Into which you remember the Ponte St. Angelo enters,
Since I passed, has thickened with curious groups; and now the
Crowd is coming, has turned, has crossed that last barricade, is
Here at my side. In the middle they drag at something. What is it?
Ha! bare swords in the air, held up! There seem to be voices
Pleading and hands putting back; official, perhaps; but the swords are
Many, and bare in the air. In the air? They descend; they are smiting,
Hewing, chopping — At what? In the air once more upstretched! And
Is it blood that's on them? Yes, certainly blood! Of whom, then?
Over whom is the cry of this furor of exultation?
    While they are skipping and screaming, and dancing their caps on
        the points of
Swords and bayonets, I to the outskirts back, and ask a
Mercantile-seeming bystander, 'What is it?' and he, looking always

That way, makes me answer, 'A Priest, who was trying to fly to
The Neopolitan Army,' – and thus explains the proceeding.
    You didn't see the dead man? No; – I began to be doubtful;
I was in black myself, and didn't know what mightn't happen; –
But a National Guard close by me, outside of the hubbub,
Broke his sword with slashing a broad hat covered with dust, – and
Passing away from the place with Murray under my arm, and
Stooping, I saw through the legs of the people the legs of a body.

                                                                (II, 7)

As escape from this chilling episode, Claude goes off to the Coliseum,
'which at the full of the moon is an object worthy a visit.' He can cope
with objects, relics of the past. But his own poise has been shaken.
    To make the point explicitly, the connection between this event
and his love for Mary (typically, Claude repeatedly puts responsibility for the statement, and therefore the fact, of his love, on to
Eustace), Clough gives to Claude, not long after this episode (the
bridge between the two is effected by Georgina's 'Only think, dearest
Louisa, what fearful scenes we have witnessed!'), the very words he
had used about the crowd's movement:

There are two different kinds, I believe, of human attraction:
One which simply disturbs, unsettles, and makes you uneasy,
And another that poises, retains, and fixes and holds you.
I have no doubt, for myself, in giving my voice for the latter.
I do not wish to be moved, but growing where I was growing,
There more truly to grow, to live where as yet I had languished.

                                                                (II, 11)

Of course, such poise and retention, however desirable, is not easy to
attain. It is one thing to cling selfishly

            to our rocks, like limpets; Ocean may bluster,
Over and under and round us; we open our shells to imbibe our
Nourishment, close them again, and are safe, fulfilling the purpose
Nature intended, – a wise one, of course, and a noble, we doubt not.

                                                                (II, 2)

But such clinging is incompatible with true growth: as Claude cries,
twice, 'Let us not talk of growth; we are still in our Aqueous Ages'.
He recalls the voyage from Marseilles to Civita Vecchia, and the

imagery of water − which permeates the poem − is set off against the poise he had seen in the images of stream and tide. Unlike the Byronic Childe Harold, Claude can see little hope in Nature's grand Ocean:

'This is Nature,' I said: 'we are born as it were from her waters,
Over her billows that buffet and beat us, her offspring uncared-for,
Casting one single regard of a painful victorious knowledge,
Into her billows that buffet and beat us we sink and are swallowed.'

(III, 2)

In turn, against this is to be set the later ambiguity of freedom within constraint, constraint within freedom, which allows man to accept action that involves circumscription.

But for assurance within of a limitless ocean divine, o'er
Whose great tranquil depths unconscious the wind-tost surface
Breaks into ripples of trouble that come and change and endure
    not, −
But that in this, of a truth, we have our being, and know it,
Think you we men could submit to live and move as we do here?

That, again, is undercut by the abrupt dismissal of the other, female half of the equation:

Ah, but the women, − God bless them! they don't think at all about
    it.

(III, 6)

Poise and retention are necessary, and necessarily difficult, concepts. Amongst other things, they involve the contradictory impulses within the self − self-possession, and self-denial. We are back with the notion of juxtaposition, one that itself has started its life in the poem on the level of excuse, in Canto I, as Claude, having had to 'shrink and adapt' himself to Rome, finds even more alarmingly and snobbishly, that against his better self − or at least what he thinks of as his 'own self ' − he actually gets on with the Trevellyns, in spite of 'the slightly mercantile accent.' He knows there are 'thousands as pretty and hundreds as pleasant' −

Well, I know, after all, it is only juxtaposition, −
Juxtaposition, in short; and what is juxtaposition?

(I, 11)

It is typical of Claude to hide behind an abstraction, one that he can depend on and yet question; as the elegiacs at the end of Canto I put it with precision,

> *So through the city I wander and question, unsatisfied ever,*
> *Reverent so I accept, doubtful because I revere.*

In these lines we get the poise and retention rarely allowed to Claude in his dramatised moments: these elegiacs serve, in a way, the choric function of Adam in *The Bothie*.

If juxtaposition has seemed, when introduced there by Claude, an evasion, the very questioning of the use he makes of it lends it integrity. This is explored in the very rich passage which follows, in the next letter to Eustace. The nonchalant, chatty tone gives way to a recreation of the freedom he has only loosely spoken of in the previous letter — it is a freedom to be himself, to suffer the pain which that involves. The image is extravagant, witty, poetic, securely placed at the very end of the first canto, not without its own ironies, but crucial for our belief in Claude as someone who matters.

> But I am in for it now, — *laissez faire*, of a truth, *laissez aller*.
> Yes, I am going, — I feel it, I feel and cannot recall it, —
> Fusing with this thing and that, entering into all sorts of relations,
> Tying I know not what ties, which, whatever they are, I know one thing,
> Will, and must, woe is me, be one day painfully broken, —
> Broken with painful remorses, with shrinkings of soul, and relentings,
> Foolish delays, more foolish evasions, most foolish renewals.
> But I have made the step, have quitted the ship of Ulysses;
> Quitted the sea and the shore, passed into the magical island;
> Yet on my lips is the *moly*, medicinal, offered by Hermes.
> I have come into the precinct, the labyrinth closes around me,
> Path into path rounding slyly; I pace slowly on, and the fancy,
> Struggling awhile to sustain the long sequences, weary, bewildered,
> Fain must collapse in despair; I yield, I am lost, and know nothing;
> Yet in my bosom unbroken remaineth the clue; I shall use it.
> Lo, with the rope on my loins I descend through the fissure; I sink, yet
> Inly secure in the strength of invisible arms up above me;
> Still, wheresoever I swing, wherever to shore, or to shelf, or
> Floor of cavern untrodden, shell-sprinkled, enchanting, I know I

Yet shall one time feel the strong cord tighten about me, —
Feel it, relentless, upbear me from spots I would rest in; and though
    the
Rope sway wildly, I faint, crags wound me, from crag unto crag re-
Bounding, or, wide in the void, I die ten deaths, ere the end I
Yet shall plant firm foot on the broad lofty spaces I quit, shall
Feel underneath me again the great massy strengths of abstraction,
Look yet abroad from the height o'er the sea whose salt wave I have
    tasted.

                                                            (I, 12)

Claude has moved an amazing distance within the space of two
letters: he has effectively established the terms whereby the rest of the
action — or non-action — is to be judged. The passage I have quoted is
particularly interesting in its combination of (literally) deep seriousness of romantic aspiration, and recognition of folly and bewilderment. Mention of Ulysses inevitably recalls Tennyson, mention of
the island, Arnold, and once again Clough's distinctiveness announces itself: we get here a sublime account and recreation of the
balance he yearns for, a re-enactment of the implications of
juxtaposition which re-emerge towards the end of the poem. Again,
an adequate account of the movement of this verse cannot rest in the
use of the term 'humour'. The flickering surface yields glances of light
at each turn of the line, just as, on the larger scale of the poem as a
whole, the bewilderments and confusions of the protagonists can
seem funny, even farcical, just as their language can reveal them,
whilst they search for the language that will make that revelation
unnecessary. Claude cries out despairingly in Canto I, as he worries
about the Roman past, the conglomeration of Christian and
heathen — 'Utter, O some one, the word that shall reconcile Ancient
and Modern!'. When he cries thus, it has its humorous point; but in
retrospect it has its desolate emptiness, for the word does not exist.
Juxtaposition is one possible word, but it is the great massy
abstractions underneath it that count, and which cannot ultimately be
caught. As he says, half-jokingly in Canto III,

            Take from me this regal knowledge;
Let me, contented and mute, with the beasts of the field, my brothers,
Tranquilly, happily lie, — and eat grass, like Nebuchadnezzar!

                                                            (III, 10)

Whenever he thinks in naturalistic terms, it is as an escape from the burden of knowledge –

> And, to escape from our strivings, mistakings, misgrowths, and
>   perversions,
> Fain could demand to return to that perfect and primitive silence,
> Fain to be enfolded and fixed, as of old, in their rigid embraces.
>
> (III, 7)

If 'rigid' gives the game away there, there is something deeply ironic – and consciously so, clearly – in the silence he yearns for. It is, after all, a complete negation, not merely of all that he wants to escape, but of the talk that gives him life.

Claude may at times yearn for silence, but he knows he cannot have it for long: the surrounding turbulence is sufficient reminder of that reality. This does not prevent his feeling ashamed of talking, for the very fact that it can offer itself as an alternative to action – whether political or physical – points uncomfortably to the falseness of his position. The dangers of observing scrupulously the dictates of his conscience at its finest moments are clear to Claude: the notion that action is factitious can be seen as itself factitious. The letters to Eustace constitute a desperate recognition that process and change continue, demanding confrontation. Claude can cry '*Hang* this thinking, at last! '; but without such complex thinking he would cope even less well with the pressures from without and from within. A sensibility as finely honed as Claude's is never going to be able to rest in certainties. As he says at the start of Canto II, 'I, who avoided it all, am fated, it seems, to describe it'. If he would much rather retreat into the quietness of a monastery, he has to learn that such escape is not for him: 'The Fates, it is clear, are against us'.

Just how much they are against Claude and Mary emerges at the beginning of the fourth canto, when Claude wakes up to the fact that he has missed the others at Florence; the rest of the poem becomes a chapter of missed opportunities. Clough's achievement is remarkable in that he has written a love poem in which neither party discloses the true level of feeling which prompts his or her behaviour. Indirection and qualification characterise the poem's emotions: the attempt to 'see things, not try to evade them' involves what is bound to seem evasion, for as Claude declares

Fact shall be fact for me, and the Truth the Truth as ever,
Flexible, changeable, vague, and multiform, and doubtful.

(V, 5)

When truth is seen in such terms, there can be little credence put in
abstracts like Love and Faith. The political events in Rome reinforce
the same point, for the City's fall is seen as a reflection of his own
inaction and his loss of Mary. Claude does not want to think in the
grand terms of tragedy, either for Rome or for himself. But it is
precisely the eschewing of such gestures that makes us conscious of
the implicit tragic quality of what has happened, and failed to happen:

Rome is fallen, I hear, the gallant Medici taken,
Noble Manara slain, and Garibaldi has lost *il Moro*; —
Rome is fallen; and fallen, or falling, heroical Venice.
I, meanwhile, for the loss of a single small chit of a girl, sit
Moping and mourning here, — for her, and myself much smaller.

(V, 6)

The sad absurdity of the contrast is moving in its starkness. Claude is
an impressive creation because of his ability to look at himself, to
impose on his antics a gaze that is dispassionate and essentially comic.
From his greater height, Clough can be compassionate, mellowing
the humour with a grim sense of life's ironies. The poem ends with
Claude and Mary going off in opposite directions. They have both
submitted in their own ways to the compelling necessities of
circumstance.

Amours de Voyage is a difficult and elusive poem. It has little of the
light airiness of *The Bothie*; its denser textures forbid any extraction of
the narrative from the letters that embody that narrative. But I do not
think Clough would have been able to write such a poem if he had
not first written *The Bothie*. The earlier poem anticipates some of
Clough's later concerns, and in fact suggests how those concerns
might be coped with in a sufficiently flexible verse-form. Clough has
found, in Claude, a perfect characterisation of his own inner conflicts;
in the structure of the poem he discovers the ideal means of
combining a personal crisis with larger political events of telling
immediacy. *Amours de Voyage* depends for its effect very much on
varieties of tones of voice caught and held in flux. The voices are not
those we often find in poetry: they are the voices of an age and a class,
observed with all the truth and humour Clough has at his command.

When Claude scoffs at the Horatian ideal of decorous patriotism, Clough is pointedly reminding us of his own assault on decorum. In many ways this poem, with its astute and delicate balancing of the opposing claims of thought and action, seems to me Clough's major achievement. I value it especially for its combination of deep feeling and ironic detachment, a sense of life's tragedy and a constant resort to the wit that makes the tragedy bearable. Clough does not repeat the formula: *Dipsychus* is very much a poem which recognises the need for humour above all. But there is something rather desperate about the need.

II

Dipsychus is Clough's last major poem. It is the hardest to come to terms with, to accept in the way it seems to ask to be accepted. This is not to deny its importance or its interest, for it contains some of the most brilliant poetry Clough ever wrote. Although *Amours de Voyage* had grown out of Clough's personal experiences in Rome, he had managed to dramatise and externalise the conflicts. *Dipsychus* was written not long afterwards, and was even more personal in origin. The fact of this intimate reflection of his own doubts and difficulties helps, perhaps, to explain some of the problems of a poem that is never really finished. Not content with the creation of characters who can enact the inner confusions of his own mind, Clough writes a modern, inverted form of *Faust*: not only does Dipsychus eventually get round to calling the Spirit Mephistopheles, but in the original draft Dipsychus was called Faustulus. Clough certainly denies himself the opportunity for subtle characterisation that had been the distinguishing mark of his two earlier major poems. But his letters demonstrate his need to resolve the conflicts that had dogged him for so long: it was necessary for him to get away from his own 'hidings' from himself, and the Faust legend might make things manageable. Any resolution he had was hardened by the promptings of his future wife, Blanche Smith, who was horrified when she chanced upon the manuscript of *Dipsychus*. In fact, her role in Clough's later years was distressingly prominent, in that Clough's clinging on to her values of purity and innocence proved the undoing of his own scrupulosity.

His whole being had centred on inner turmoil, on a recognition that he consisted of different, opposing selves, which required acknowledgement and exposure; under Blanche's tutelage he was encouraged to think of one self only, that which corresponded most closely to Blanche's own self-confessed and prized idealism. By the time Blanche discovered *Dipsychus* amongst his papers in 1853, Clough was quite prepared to submit to her moral authority. Two months later, she was able to say, composedly and complacently, 'I do think somehow you have a higher idea of what things ought to be . . . you never shock me now'.[11] *Dipsychus* shows Clough moving towards a resolution, trying to iron out the contradictions. It may well be that such a move is incompatible with such contradictions, that in fact Clough had achieved the perfect balance, the sense of flux and stasis, in *Amours de Voyage*, and that *Dipsychus* is the record of an attempt at a more complete resolution, bound to fail because of the very nature of the conflict. Certainly Clough felt uneasy about the poem: it was never properly finished, and the brief continuation lacks conviction. Even within the body of the poem as it stands, Clough offers several explicit suggestions that the poem is not entirely under his control. We might be able to explain this fact by reference to Clough's life; but I am more interested here in seeing what happens within the poem, and in seeing it in relation to his other work. There are strong grounds for suggesting that, whatever its shortcomings, *Dipsychus* is Clough's most ambitious poem; and, as Blanche saw, his most shocking.

The poem is framed by a Prologue and an Epilogue, each of which consists of a conversation between the poet and his uncle. These conversations are useful pointers to the self-consciousness, and the self-conscious literariness, of the poem, in that they show us Clough considering himself as a poet.

> 'I hope it is in good plain verse', said my uncle; 'none of your hurry-scurry anapaests . . . *Simplex duntaxat et unum*. But you young people think Horace and your uncle old fools . . .'

The poet concedes that Horace and his uncle are right, but urges that the ear has to be cultivated. His uncle concludes:

> 'Well, well, . . . *sunt certi denique fines*, no doubt. So commence, my young Piso, while Aristarchus is tolerably wakeful, and do not waste by your logic the fund you will want for your poetry.'

This discussion of metrical technique is deceptively bland, for it does in fact look ahead to some of the chief concerns of the poem, and these naturally go far beyond any considerations merely of metre. 'Good plain verse' is on one level what we get, especially from the Spirit: the Horatian decorum is honoured. But it is honoured as much in the breach as in the observance, for the poem contains an astonishing variety of verse forms and rhythms which match the varieties of experience within the poem. The simplicity invoked by the uncle turns out to be much more slippery than Horace would have expected. Anyone who has read the poem and then goes back to the Prologue might well wonder how reliable it is as a reflection of the poem's spirit. The opposition of poetry to logic in that final sentence is certainly an indication of the central dilemma in one of its forms; and the necessary acknowledgement of boundaries is echoed in the debate in Scene VI as to where the moral line should be drawn. But the opposition is not an easy one, the boundaries are hard to draw. The effect of this is retrospectively ironical: the apparent agreement and harmony between uncle and poet is not something which the poem supports.

Likewise the Epilogue emphasises divisions, and denies the simplicity urged at the outset.

'I don't very well understand what it's all about', said my uncle. 'I won't say I didn't drop into a doze while the young man was drivelling through his later soliloquies. But there was a great deal that was unmeaning, vague, and involved; and what was most plain was least decent and least moral.'

'Dear sir', said I, 'says the proverb – "Needs must when the devil drives", and if the devil is to speak – '

'Well', said my uncle, 'why should he? Nobody asked him. Not that he didn't say much which, if only it hadn't been for the way he said it, and that it was he who said it, would have been sensible enough.'

'But, sir', said I, 'perhaps he wasn't a devil after all. That's the beauty of the poem; nobody can say. You see, dear sir, the thing which it is attempted to represent is the conflict between the tender conscience and the world. Now, the over-tender conscience will, of course, exaggerate the wickedness of the world; and the Spirit in my poem may be merely the hypothesis or subjective imagination, formed – '

The uncle has had enough of such explanation. His instincts tell him that something is wrong with the poem when his nephew has to launch into the theory of it all. Their conversation becomes a debate on the faults of the public school ethos instilled by Arnold at Rugby, with the uncle taking the view that such education unfitted youths for the world. The uncle turns out to be an enlightened man, and his unease with moral posturing has its effect on the way we respond to Dipsychus, whom he has found rather unsatisfactory. For his bafflement as to the poem's meaning is something we readers can often share. The main point of the Epilogue seems to be to give us some support.

Within the poem itself there are several places where a particular tone of voice is brought into question. Dipsychus recites part of Clough's 'Easter Day' poem, written at Naples the previous year, and the ever-present Spirit comments:

> Hm! and the tone then after all
> Something of the ironical?
> Sarcastic, say; or were it fitter
> To style it the religious bitter?

Dipsychus replies, 'Interpret it I cannot. I but wrote it.' The same point is made in Scene VII, when Dipsychus again tries to recite part of the same poem. The Spirit observes, 'Well, now it's anything but clear / What is the tone that's taken here', and Dipsychus gives the same response. There are times, like these, when Clough and Dipsychus seem one and the same person. This is bound to present problems of balance in that if there is not sufficient distance between creator and creation then it is going to be impossible to be objective, especially about something as tortured as a divided soul engaged in debate with a tempting spirit. But at these particular points, the blurring acts as a comment on the poet himself. For Dipsychus to deny his knowledge of what the poem means, how it is to be read, might seem disingenuous. But the repetition of this episode is important in the poem's structure, for that structure itself is insisting, much of the time, on its own openness. Just as Dipsychus is uncertain of himself, 'bewildered, baffled, hurried hence and thence / All at cross-purpose even with myself', so Clough seems uncertain which direction the poem should take, hence the apologetics of the Epilogue, the inconclusiveness of the poem and yet the desire to conclude and round off. On the one hand we are constantly being reminded that this is a highly complicated and variegated poem (the

Spirit will comment on Dipsychus' hexameter and rhymes, rather as Byron continually makes play with the fact that he is writing a poem); on the other hand there is an attempt to move beyond this level of reading to something more positive. That is where the real problems arise, for positives in *Dipsychus* are hard to come by.

The basic theme of the poem is really a continuation of what had absorbed Clough in *Amours de Voyage*, the relation between action and thought. But whereas in *Amours de Voyage* there had been a full working out, psychologically, of Claude's dilemma, towards his eventual espousal of knowledge as the one thing to be trusted, in *Dipsychus* there seems to be a more desperate sense of impossibilities. Dipsychus, the central figure, is an epitome of self-doubt, 'still resting on [him] self', and attended by a Spirit who taunts his communings, his intellectual and emotional blockage which prevents any action at all. As his name implies, and as he tells us himself, Dipsychus is divided against himself: the Spirit is there to appeal to his baser self, primarily, to force him to see the folly of such behaviour in the world as it really is. In the face of the Spirit's jaunty cynicism, Dipsychus for much of the poem seems to cut a sorry figure. His aspirations are mocked by the hedonistic promptings of the Spirit, who is well aware of the delights of the minute. These lines are an effective attack on spiritual, poetic and moral superiority:

> Our lonely pious altitudes
> Are followed quick by prettier moods.
> Who knows with what ease devotion
> Slips into earthlier emotion?
>
> (I, 74–7)

Dipsychus sees himself as an innocent child of Eden, forced to listen to the Spirit's poisonous talk:

> Why did I ever one brief moment's space
> To this insidious lewdness lend chaste ears,
> Or parley with this filthy Belial?
>
> (IIA, 9–11)

But the Spirit's dismissal of practically everything Dipsychus says in the opening scenes of the poem is so triumphant in its logic that it is hard not to applaud the Spirit. Dipsychus indeed seems a prig, reluctant to engage with the world, hiding behind moral pretexts

which act as escape routes from the cosmopolitan world the Spirit
knows and understands. At this stage in the poem, significantly,
Dipsychus has none of the argumentative brilliance which makes
Claude's agonisings so credible. The absurdity of Dipsychus' fears of
the world's contamination is evident, almost without the scoffing
presence of the Spirit.

> Ah me, me!
> Clear stars above, thou roseate westward sky,
> Take up my being into yours; assume
> My sense to own you only; steep my brain
> In your essential purity. Or, great Alps,
> That wrapping round your heads in solemn clouds
> Seem sternly to sweep past our vanities,
> Lead me with you — take me away; preserve me!
> — Ah, if it must be, look then, foolish eyes —
> Listen fond ears; but, oh, poor mind, stand fast!
>
> (II, 54–63)

We seem to have, at this stage in the poem, a very direct opposition
between otherworldliness (the over-tender conscience) and the basic
sensuality of the Spirit. It was this that particularly upset Blanche
Smith.

But such polarities are not really Clough's concern for long. When
the Spirit begins to explain his own position, we can see that he has a
certain desperate truth on his side. There is a sense of mischievous
revelling in what he says and how he says it:

> I know it's mainly your temptation
> To think the thing a revelation,
> A mystic mouthful that will give
> Knowledge and death — none know and live!
> I tell you plainly that it brings
> Some ease; but the emptiness of things
> (That one old sermon Earth still preaches
> Until we practise what she teaches)
> Is the sole lesson you'll learn by it —
> Still you undoubtedly should try it.
> 'Try all things' — bad and good, no matter;
> You can't till then hold fast the latter.
> If not, this itch will stick and vex you

> Your live long days till death unsex you —
> Hide in your bones, for aught I know,
> And with you to the next world go.
> Briefly — you cannot rest, I'm certain,
> Until your hand has drawn the curtain.
> Once known the little lies behind it,
> You'll go your way and never mind it.
> Ill's only cure is, never doubt it,
> To do — and think no more about it.
>
> (IIA, 20—41)

This passage can cause some uneasiness, though, and not simply because *Amours de Voyage* has taught us to distrust unthinking action. Beneath the jolly repartee lies a cynicism that Clough is not entirely endorsing: it gives itself away by its very neatness and glibness. This is all the more necessary when Dipsychus presents such insubstantial opposition. The Spirit astutely realises that Dipsychus is not really answering his argument on the correct terms: by reducing everything to a fear of sexual commitment he is distorting the complexities of the issue. There can be little doubt but that the Spirit has all the best tunes to begin with, but he, too, is being judged. This is why it is difficult to keep our bearings. In the continuation of this particulr scene, for instance, the Spirit bursts into song, reminding us how much of the poem's world is represented by song and dance and colour. Earlier, in the first scene, the Spirit tried to capture the ebullience of the setting:

> Aye! what a crowd! and what a noise!
> With all these screaming half-breeched boys.
> *Partout* dogs, boys, and women wander —
> And see, a fellow singing yonder;
> Singing, ye gods, and dancing too —
> Tooraloo, tooraloo, tooraloo, loo;
> Fiddle di, diddle di, diddle di da
> *Figaro sù, Figaro giù —*
> *Figaro quà, Figaro là!*
> How he likes doing it! Ah, ha, ha!
>
> (I, 59—68)

His own song now seems a guarantee of the rightness of his instincts. As the poem progresses this might appear retrospectively to be too sanguine a view of the Spirit's attitude. But for the moment the

variety and sense of life are all with the Spirit. After he has sung a few
lines of 'It was a lover and his lass', and elicited a lugubrious response
from Dipsychus, the Spirit cannot contain himself. It does not seem
too fanciful to hear an echo of 'The Idiot Boy' in these lines:

> O Joseph and Don Quixote! This
> A chivalry of chasteness is,
> That turns to nothing all, that story
> Has made out of your ancient glory!
>
> (IIA, 55–8)

As I have been suggesting, it is a mistake to see the Spirit and
Dipsychus as opposites, purely and simply. One of the fundamental
truths about their relationship emerges soon after this scene, when
Dipsychus senses that the Spirit is leaving him, and cries out 'O folly,
folly, what have I done? Ah me!'; the Spirit stays, fully aware that he
is necessary to Dipsychus. He can say much later (XI, 137) 'What
could you do, if I should go away?' The two of them need each other:
the Spirit needs Dipsychus, the ideal victim for his argumentative and
spiritual machinations; Dipsychus needs the Spirit as a salutary,
masochistic corrective to his own self-communings. Because of the
way they reflect each other's needs, there are times when they seem to
be adopting rather similar poses. When Dipsychus decides that the
only solution is to get married, to retire into the safety of
conventional domesticity, the Spirit is quite prepared to help him:
such readiness is alarming to a Dipsychus who had viewed the process
in abstract terms:

> O welcome then, the sweet domestic bonds,
> The matrimonial sanctities; the hopes
> And cares of wedded life; parental thoughts,
> The prattle of young children, the good word
> Of fellow men, the sanction of the law,
> And permanence and habit, that transmute
> Grossness itself to crystal. O, why, why,
> Why ever let this speculating brain
> Rest upon other objects than on this?
>
> (IIA, 79–87)

The Spirit reminds him of the realities which are not only sensual and
coarse. They are both natural and artificial, for they involve an

acknowledgement of the body, and of society. It transpires that Dipsychus' yearnings for the bonds of matrimony are matched for their conventional nature by the Spirit's urgings of the claims of good society. The Spirit's bouncy assurances are scarcely undermined by Dipsychus' morose doubts about the social manners he wishes to escape from. At this point, as later, the poem turns on the action of seeing things as they are (it had been a Byronic motif, too); Dipsychus objects to the 'consideration' involved in social behaviour, as opposed to acting according to 'one's humour'. The Spirit's answer is interesting:

> That is, act
> On a dispassionate judgement of the fact;
> Look all your data fairly in the face,
> And rule your conduct simply by the case.
> (III, 44–7)

The Spirit is advocating a detachment which contrasts sharply with the vacillations we associate with Dipsychus: there is something of the sweet reason of the eighteenth century about the Spirit, rather at odds with his urging of instinct elsewhere. Here it is Dipsychus who is standing up for instinct, for 'the green and vernal spontaneity', something with which the Spirit is usually identified. As the Spirit pushes on with his argument, doubts begin to creep in as to his logic. He claims that the social scene can obliterate 'all grosser thoughts completely' – thereby apparently satisfying one of Dipsychus' requirements; he goes on from there to suggest that the whole fabric of good society is essential to survival, to the clarity which is his main concern. The Spirit is really uttering sentiments that we associate with the object of attack in the early poem on 'Duty'.

> I really seem without exaggeration
> To experience the True Regeneration;
> One's own dress too, one's manner, what one's doing
> And saying, all assist to one's renewing –
> I love to see in these their fitting places
> The bows, and forms, and all you call grimaces.
> I heartily could wish we'd kept some more of them,
> However much they talk about the bore of them.
> Fact is, your awkward parvenus are shy at it,
> Afraid to look like waiters if they try at it.

'Tis sad to what democracy is leading;
Give me your Eighteenth Century for high breeding.
Though I can put up gladly with the present,
And quite can think our modern parties pleasant.
One shouldn't analyse the thing too nearly;
The main effect is admirable clearly.
Good manners, said our great aunts, next to piety;
And so, my friend, hurrah for good society.

                                    (III, 91—108)

It is this kind of progression which makes any reading of the poem
unsettling. By the time we arrive at the fourth scene, the famous song
of Dipsychus in the gondola, with its appeal to ease and placidity and
comfort, could almost have come from the Spirit. It is as though
Dipsychus' tone of voice has dramatically altered, to accommodate
itself to what the Spirit has been saying. The lilting rhythm, reflecting
the effortless, almost imperceptible motion through the water, seems
to identify Dipsychus with the Spirit. But Dispychus' desire is for an
escape from the world and its commotions: his hedonism differs from
the Spirit's.

Afloat; we move. Delicious! Ah,
What else is like the gondola?
This level floor of liquid glass
Begins beneath it swift to pass.
It goes as though it went alone
By some impulsion of its own.
How light it moves, how softly! Ah,
Were all things like the gondola!

How light it moves, how softly! Ah,
Could life, as does our gondola,
Unvexed with quarrels, aims, and cares,
And moral duties and affairs,
Unswaying, noiseless, swift, and strong,
For ever thus — thus glide along!
How light we move, how softly! Ah
Were all things like the gondola!

                                    (IV, 3—18)

The Spirit takes up the refrain, quite happy to condone the belief that if only we could eliminate 'This interfering, enslaving, o'ermastering demon of craving,/This wicked tempter inside us to ruin still eager to guide us,/Life were beatitude, action a possible pure satisfaction'. But it is not that simple. Dipsychus craves a spiritual solitude which will acknowledge nothing beyond the ideal; his sense of life's beauty and perfection is different from the Spirit's. Once again, the Spirit's retort has an ironic realism which makes Dipsychus' rather pathetic pleas ('O let me love my love unto myself alone,/And know my knowledge to the world unknown'), with its unconvincing spirituality, appear less than effective as argument. This is one of the great ironies of the poem, that the thinker is usually outwitted by the worldly Spirit.

> This lovely creature's glowing charms
> Are gross illusion, I don't doubt that;
> But when I pressed her in my arms
> I somehow didn't think about that.
>
> This world is very odd, we see;
> We do not comprehend it;
> But in one fact can all agree
> God won't, and we can't mend it.
>
> Being common sense, it can't be sin
> To take it as we find it;
> The pleasure to take pleasure in;
> The pain, try not to mind it.
>
> (IV, 110–21)

The appeal to common sense is one that will reverberate through the rest of the poem. The prominence of this elusive concept is an indication of the magnitude of Dipsychus' problem: for its ambiguity unsettles him, just as does the ambiguity of 'instinct' and 'nature'. Dipsychus does not have in his dialectic the language to cope with such subtleties. He remains static in his arguments, whereas the Spirit flits about, constantly outflanking him; so that when Dipsychus returns to the gondola song, it is finally to acknowledge that 'Life is not as the gondola', and the Spirit has had enough of it anyway. One couplet in particular merits comment:

Over still waters mildly come
The distant laughter and the hum.
                    (IV, 287)

So long as it is distant such noise is acceptable, the placidity of the
gondola will not be disturbed. This is the romantic dream (of 'vague
romantic girls and boys'), in which reality is accommodated as a fact,
but not as anything actually impinging on the dream. The Spirit's
reiterated point is that the noise and commotion cannot be ignored:
we are all part of the dance. The related point is that the Spirit's own
laughter provides a running commentary on Dipsychus' romantic
aspirations, provides a threat to his ideal, insubstantial world.

Quite how significant this is emerges in the next scene, when
Dipsychus' dreams have changed. The confusion and oddity of the
world, already announced by the Spirit, have now become part of
Dipsychus' dream world; his song shows how potent the Spirit's
influence has become. This song is one of the high points in the poem:
Clough demonstrates his lyric mastery in combination with a
macabre sense of futility. If we see Dipsychus as a conglomeration of
extremes, a ragbag of disparate views, a representative of the
breakdown of normal values and connections, then the poem comes
into its own here, as Dipsychus assumes the attitudes that naturally fill
his mind's vacuum once long-held beliefs are destroyed by superior
logic. The dream and its utterance is the logical extension of all that
the Spirit has so far said.

> I dreamt a dream; till morning light
> A bell rang in my head all night,
> Tinkling and tinkling first, and then
> Tolling; and tinkling; tolling again.
> So brisk and gay, and then so slow!
> O joy, and terror! mirth, and woe!
> Ting, ting, there is no God; ting, ting –
> Dong, there is no God; dong,
> There is no God; dong, dong!
>
> Ting, ting, there is no God; ting, ting;
> Come dance and play, and merrily sing –
> Ting, ting a ding; ting, ting a ding!
> O pretty girl who trippest along,
> Come to my bed – it isn't wrong.

> Uncork the bottle, sing the song!
> Ting, ting a ding: dong, dong.
> Wine has dregs; the song an end;
> A silly girl is a poor friend
> And age and weakness who shall mend?
> Dong, there is no God; Dong! . . .
>
> (V, 7–26)

It is important for our belief in Dipsychus that this revelation is given to him at this point. But there is cruel irony in the fact that when Dipsychus thinks he has won through to some sort of pragmatic victory, and plunges into the sea in an ecstasy of engagement which is at the same time escape, he is in fact back with his old idealistic fervour. The Spirit keeps his aloof, practical distance:

> Come, no more of that stuff,
> I'm sure you've stayed in long enough
>
> . . .
>
> Pleasant perhaps. However, no offence,
> Animal spirits are not common sense.
>
> (V, 222–7)

Dipsychus' inability to keep up with the Spirit is nicely illustrated in the rather curious sixth scene, which centres on an insult delivered to Dipsychus by 'a German brute'. The Spirit thinks that Dipsychus should retaliate, even if only verbally. It is a question of social decorum as much as anything, and once that point is made by the Spirit we are reminded of how conventional a figure he can be. Clough seems to be on dangerous ground here, for the Spirit is really making a fuss about nothing. But he cleverly turns it into an attack on Dipsychus and his hopelessly absurd attitudes which reveal themselves as lofty, empty platitudes. The Spirit can point to the underlying weakness of Dipsychus' position: if he is not going to take action in this instance, then how will he behave on more important occasions? He wrings from Dipsychus an admission that he is confused by the episode. Dipsychus believes that he can bleed 'for other's wrongs /In vindication of a Cause' (what Claude had been unable to do); but his lofty abstractions are soon knocked down by the Spirit, who launches into an attack on pious charity (like Mrs Jellyby's in *Bleak House*) that does not begin at home. Again, the point is strongly made: what Dipsychus can cope with has to be at a distance. His plunge into the sea had been no more than the public schoolboy's early morning cold bath.

The second half of the poem describes a somewhat different movement. Dipsychus indulges in long soliloquies, which are clearly meant to be taken with some seriousness. By Scene IX he has more or less agreed to throw in his lot with the Spirit, and the battle is, to that extent, won and lost. Clough has changed his tactics here. We do not get in this scene the swift exchange of ideas that made the early scenes of the poem almost Byronic in their sparkling wit (a wit actually acknowledged by Dipsychus); instead we have a total concentration on Dipsychus, with the voice of the Spirit heard only towards the end of the scene. The tone has altered drastically, as Dipsychus confronts his own destiny. The fact that it is seen in these terms seems to jar, as though Clough were trying to make heroic claims for his anti-hero. The problem of action is still there, as it had been in *Amours de Voyage*. Instinct urges action, rather than staying on the edge, watching the waltz ('Life loves no lookers-on at his great game'). But the 'age of instinct [like the age of comedy] has, it seems, gone by'. Clough tries to confront the distortions of the age in an interesting passage which lifts the poem on to another level, almost makes it a different kind of poem. There is a grim humour in these lines quite different from the wit displayed elsewhere in the poem. It is really the first and only time that the melancholic Dipsychus is allowed to be taken really seriously.

> Ah, if I had a course like a full stream,
> If life were as the field of chase! No, no;
> The age of instinct has, it seems, gone by,
> And will not be forced back. And to live now
> I must sluice out myself into canals,
> And lose all force in ducts. The modern Hotspur
> Shrills not his trumpet of 'To Horse, To Horse!'
> But consults columns in a railway guide;
> A demigod of figures; an Achilles
> Of computation;
> A verier Mercury, express come down
> To *do* the world with swift arithmetic.
> Well, one could bear with that; were the end ours,
> One's choice and the correlative of the soul,
> To drudge were then sweet service. But indeed
> The earth moves slowly, if it move at all,
> And by the general, not the single force.

At the [huge] members of the vast machine,
In all those crowded rooms of industry,
No individual soul has loftier leave
Than fiddling with a piston or a valve.
. . .
Oh, could I shoot my thought up to the sky,
A column of pure shape, for all to observe!
But I must slave, a meagre coral-worm,
To build beneath the tide with excrement
What one day will be island, or be reef,
And will feed men, or wreck them. Well, well, well.

(IX, 103−45)

The role of humour and wit from here onwards is not so consistent. As Clough tries to elevate Dipsychus into a convincingly positive character, with values that matter (even if they are being undermined by events) he realises that he cannot afford to keep Dipsychus as the mere butt of the Spirit's wit. The plight of Dipsychus is a genuine one. The Spirit still keeps up his taunts, some of them effective; but he too has to resort to long soliloquies, as though that were the only way to answer Dipsychus. His demolition work can still be brusque:

Come, my pretty boy,
You have been making mows to the blank sky
Quite long enough for good. We'll put you up
Into the higher form . . .

(XI, 112−15)

We are back with the initial problem. Try as he will, Clough cannot really turn Dipsychus into a tragic hero. The vision that he has in the next scene seems like a last-minute attempt to offer some positive view, and it is not in fact knocked down by the Spirit. But it has no substance: the religiose terms of reference carry little weight when religion has already taken such a beating, and when the Spirit has started to call himself the Shepherd and the Way. The anarchic tendencies of the poem whenever the Spirit is around are too strong to be counterbalanced by an insubstantial vision, snatched out of the hat in desperation. Dipsychus seems to think that his submission is temporary, a means 'to gain time /And arms and stature'. In this he is evidently self-deceived. The Spirit's common sense has won the day: Dipsychus is embraced by a vision of the 'positive and present', with

his 'feet upon the ground'. The Spirit can say triumphantly, now that
the lost sheep has been recovered, 'Little Bo Peep, she lost her sheep!'
The connection between the nursery rhyme and the Christian
connotations of the Shepherd and the Way is the final irony.

Dipsychus is a kaleidoscopic, vertiginous poem. At one point,
Dipsychus complains of the 'whole mass/O' the motley facts of
existence flowing by!'. Clough reflects this sense of movement and
flux in the varieties of verse form he adopts. He seems to pour into the
containing vessel of the poem's basic structure as many different types
of verse as he is capable of. Dipsychus has a great urge to rush into the
sea's embrace, but in fact he finds himself overwhelmed by the 'great
floods of the fiend . . . I come into deep waters/Where no ground
is!'. Like a drowning man, Dipsychus as surrogate for Clough sees his
whole poetic life flash before him in all its bewildering confusion and
diversity. It is all very well for the Spirit to reiterate that our task is
'To see things simply as they are'; but the poem demonstrates that
nothing simply is. For the Spirit, of course, the facts are as he sees
them:

> Why will you walk about thus with your eyes shut,
> Treating for facts the self-made hues that float
> On tight-pressed pupils, which you know are not facts?
> To use the undistorted light of the sun
> Is not a crime; to look straight out upon
> The big plain things that stare one in the face
> Does not contaminate; to see pollutes not
> What one must feel if one won't see; what *is*,
> And will be too, howe'er we blink, and must
> One way or other make itself observed.
>
> (XI, 124–33)

But the whole drift of the poem suggests that more than looking is
required: Dipsychus himself realises that to look is in a way more
contaminating than to act. Acting and seeing both involve being true
to the self:

> To thine own self be true, the wise man says.
> Are then my fears myself? O double self!
> And I untrue to both.
>
> (X, 62–4)

It is the fate of Dipsychus that he cannot reconcile his various selves. His grasp on life is fragmentary. To the extent that the poem itself is fragmentary, it could be argued that Clough is using it as an image for his subject's loss of centre. That might provide a defence of the poem for those who feel it needs defending against charges of looseness. The issue is made difficult, though, not so much because of the astonishing shifts, but because of Clough's apparent attempts to give to Dipsychus a more credible, breast-beating role than he has had in the first part of the poem. In this *Dipsychus* differs from the two other major poems, each of which manages to get the right balance between humour and seriousness. By pushing things that much further, by taking the argument to its extremes, Clough shows his daring and assurance. But once at the extremes, he seems to want to draw back from the implications; by then it is too late, and the poem tugs insistently in two different directions. The humour has become such a potent and dangerous element in the structure that it takes over, and we can never be quite sure that Clough condones that. The Spirit takes Dipsychus off with a gleeful laugh into a world of laughter and noise: it seems to be a victory for cynicism, for necessity ('Not I will, but I must', as Claude had discovered). Indeed the overall tone of the poem can be seen, at times, as one of desperation. But that is not quite how the poem impresses itself on us. Openness is carried so far, and then Clough seems to want to draw things together. But he has denied himself the means of doing so.

Clough's work as a whole is a remarkable testimony to the strength of the tradition I have been charting. He stands out from the other Victorian poets because in two poems, and partially in a third, he confronts the problem of his own self in all its divisions. In doing so he is accepting the Romantic challenge which was itself ambiguous: the claims of the spirit, of the imagination, could not be sustained for long before the underlying tensions began to show through. The exploration of Dipsychus' aspirations is an extension of what the Romantic poets had felt, even at their most sublime moments. Clough manages to combine the various strands of what we think of as Romanticism as no one else had: there are touches of Wordsworth, Keats and Byron in him. This achievement was made possible by his growing awareness of the uses to which he could put his strong sense of wit and humour. It was not simply a question of coming to terms with his multiple selves: those selves required definition in the context of an age that was itself finding it hard to know which way it was going. The poet's responsibilities were increasingly identified with the age's, and Clough saw the poet as addressing himself to those responsibilities. But the certainties of the Romantics had gone, the self-confidence could not be reasserted. For Clough the only way to be true to what he saw within himself, and outside, was to employ all the varieties of humour at his disposal. In each of his major poems he carved out a unique mode to express a unique vision. In so doing he was challenging what the Victorians had come to think of as the proper realms of poetry. If it is a final irony that in *Dipsychus* Clough seems to draw back from the implications of his extremes, that should not be taken as the final word. For even in *Dipsychus* Clough's challenge to decorum in the name of comedy and humanity is perfectly clear. That is his claim to greatness.

Notes

(Unless otherwise stated, all the books listed were published in London.)

ABBREVIATIONS

MP	Modern Philology
PMLA	Publications of the Modern Language Association of America
RES	Review of English Studies
SEL	Studies in English Literature

CHAPTER 1: 'THE PECULIAR PROVINCE': THEORIES OF HUMOUR

1. Quoted in Kenneth Hopkins, *Portraits in Satire* (1958), p. 239.
2. John E. Jordan, *Why the Lyrical Ballads?* (Berkeley, Los Angeles, London, 1976), p. 129.
3. Quoted in Hopkins, op. cit., p. 198.
4. The following books are particularly useful, and I have drawn on them for some of the material in this chapter: Stuart M. Tave, *The Amiable Humorist* (Chicago, 1960); David Farley-Hills, *The Benevolence of Laughter* (1974); Richard Boston, *An Anatomy of Laughter* (1974); Robert B. Martin, *The Triumph of Wit* (Oxford, 1974).
5. trans. T. S. Dorsch, in *Classical Literary Criticism* (Harmondsworth, 1965), pp. 35–6.
6. ibid., p. 37.
7. ibid., p. 82.
8. ibid., p. 87.
9. *Leviathan*, Chapter VI.
10. See especially *Sensus Communis: An Essay on the Freedom of Wit and Humour* (1709); *Soliloquy, or Advice to an Author* (1710).
11. *The Benevolence of Laughter* (1974), p. 19.
12. Isaac Barrow, *Against Foolish Talking and Jesting* (1678); Addison, especially *Spectator*, No. 381.
13. *Letters*, ed. Bonamy Dobrée, VI (1932), pp. 2691–3.
14. *Critical Works*, ed. E. N. Hooker, I (1939), pp. 282–3.
15. *Lectures*, II (1820 edition), p. 384.
16. *Preface to Shakespeare* (1765).
17. Laurence Sterne, *Letters*, ed. Lewis P. Curtis (Oxford, 1935) p. 163; William Cowper, *Correspondence*, ed. Thomas Wright, II (1904), pp. 26–7.
18. Henry Mackenzie, *Mirror*, No. 100 (1780).

19. See especially Upali Amarasinghe, *Dryden and Pope in the early nineteenth century* (Cambridge, 1962).
20. *Essay on Pope*, I (1772), p. 344.
21. Wordsworth, Preface to *Lyrical Ballads* (1800); Hazlitt, *On Poetry in General* (1818).
22. Hazlitt, *Complete Works*, ed. P. P. Howe, V (London and Toronto, 1930), p. 68.
23. ibid., VI (1931), p. 38.
24. ibid., VI, p. 70.
25. ibid., VI, p. 5.
26. *Letters of Charles and Mary Lamb*, ed. E. V. Lucas, II (1935), p. 167.
27. Hazlitt, *Complete Works*, XX (1934), p. 363.
28. ibid., VI (1931), p. 23.
29. ibid., XVII (1933), p. 152.
30. *Works*, ed. Percy Fitzgerald, IV (1886), p. 287.
31. ibid., IV, pp. 290–1.
32. ibid., VI, p. 236.
33. *Works*, ed. D. Masson, XI (Edinburgh, 1890), p. 263.
34. *Critical and Miscellaneous Essays*, I (1899), p. 12.
35. *Leigh Hunt's Literary Criticism*, ed. L. H. and C. W. Houtchens, (New York, 1956), p. 559.
36. ibid., p. 146.
37. ibid., p. 158.
38. ibid., p. 535.

CHAPTER 2: LAUGHING SONGS: BLAKE AND WORDSWORTH

In this chapter I have quoted from the following editions:
Blake, *Poetry and Prose*, ed. Geoffrey Keynes (1927).
Wordsworth, *Poetical Works*, ed. E. de Selincourt and H. Darbishire, 5 vols (Oxford, 1940–9).

1.   *Henry Crabb Robinson on Books and their Writers*, ed. Edith J. Morley, I (1938), p. 85.
2.   Quoted in *Blake: The Critical Heritage*, ed. G. E. Bentley Jr (London and Boston, 1975), p. xvii.
3.   ibid., p. 131.
4.   Francis Jeffrey, *Edinburgh Review* (Nov. 1814); *Blake: The Critical Heritage*, p. 2.
5.   ibid., p. 196.
6.   ibid., p. 226.
7.   ibid., p. 54.
8.   Hazard Adams, *William Blake: A Reading of the Shorter Poems* (Seattle, 1963), p. 11.
9.   ibid., p. 60.
10. Anne Mellor, *Blake's Human Form Divine* (1974).
11. Robert F. Gleckner, *The Piper and the Bard* (1959).
12. See Martha Winburn England, 'Apprenticeship at the Haymarket?', *Bulletin of*

New York Public Library, LXXII (1969), pp. 440–64, 531–50; reprinted in revised form in David V. Erdman and John E. Grant (eds.), *Blake's Visionary Forms Dramatic* (Princeton, 1970), pp. 3–29.

13. Northrop Frye, *Fearful Symmetry* (Princeton, 1947), p. 191.
14. David V. Erdman, *Blake: Prophet against Empire* (Princeton, 1954), p. 92.
15. Bernard Blackstone, *English Blake* (1949), p. 26.
16. Quoted in Deborah Dorfman, *Blake in the Nineteenth Century* (New Haven and London, 1969), p. 50.
17. Stephen Maxfield Parrish, *The Art of the Lyrical Ballads* (Cambridge, Mass., 1973); Jared Curtis, *Wordsworth's Experiments with Tradition: the Lyric Poems of 1802* (Ithaca and London, 1971); Mary Jacobus, *Tradition and Experiment in Wordsworth's Lyrical Ballads (1798)* (Oxford, 1976).
18. Hazlitt, *Complete Works*, ed. P. P. Howe, XI (1932), p. 87.
19. ibid., XI, pp. 90–1.
20. ibid., XI, p. 91.
21. ibid., XI, p. 91.
22. ibid., XVII (1933), p. 118.
23. Mary Jacobus, *Tradition and Experiment*, p. 272.
24. ibid., p. 240.
25. R. F. Storch, 'Wordsworth's Experimental Ballads: The Radical Uses of Intelligence and Comedy', *SEL*, XI (1971), 622.
26. Mary Jacobus, 'Southey's Debt to *Lyrical Ballads* (1798)', *RES*, n.s. XXII, (1971), 20–36.
27. The lines were altered to:

> Though but of compass small and bare
> To thirsty suns and parching air.

28. R. F. Storch, 'Wordsworth's Experimental Ballads', *SEL*, XI (1971), 638. For other articles on humour in *Peter Bell*, see A. E. H. Swaen, 'Peter Bell', *Anglia*, XLVII (1923), 136–84; George L. Marsh, 'The "Peter Bell" Parodies of 1819', *MP*, XL (1943), 267–74; Frederick Garber, 'Wordsworth's Comedy of Redemption', *Anglia*, LXXXIV (1966), 388–97; John E. Jordan, 'The Hewing of "Peter Bell"', *SEL*, VII (1967), 559–603. See also Jordan, 'Wordsworth's Humor', *PMLA*, LXXIII (1958), 81–93.
29. Stephen M. Parrish, '*Michael* and the Pastoral Ballad', in Jonathan Wordsworth (ed.), *Bicentenary Wordsworth Studies* (Ithaca and London, 1970), pp. 50–75.

CHAPTER 3: THE ACCOMMODATING SELF: COWPER TO KEATS

In this chapter I have quoted from the following editions:
Thomson, *The Seasons* and *The Castle of Indolence*, ed. James Sambrook (Oxford, 1972).
Gray, *The Poems of Thomas Gray, William Collins, Oliver Goldsmith*, ed. Roger Lonsdale (1969).
Cowper, *Poetical Works*, ed. H. S. Milford, 4th ed. revised (1967).
Southey, *Poems*, ed. Maurice H. Fitzgerald (1909).

Coleridge, *Complete Poetical Works*, ed. E. H. Coleridge, 2 vols (Oxford, 1912).
Wordsworth, *The Prelude* (1805 text), ed. J. C. Maxwell (Harmondsworth, 1971).
Keats, *The Poems of John Keats*, ed. Miriam Allott (1970).

1. Carlyle, *Critical and Miscellaneous Essays*, II (1899), p. 133.
2. Hazlitt, *Complete Works*, ed. P. P. Howe, VIII (1931), p. 209.
3. ibid., V (1930), p. 91.
4. ibid., V (1930), p. 153.
5. ibid., XI (1932), p. 75.
6. ibid., XI (1932), p. 77; IV (1930), p. 113.
7. Coleridge, Preface to *Poems on Various Subjects* (1796). See Kathleen Coburn, *The Self-Conscious Imagination* (1974).
8. *The Notebooks*, ed. K. Coburn, I (1957), item no. 62.
9. *The Letters of William and Dorothy Wordsworth*, ed. E. de Selincourt, 2nd ed. revised Chester L. Shaver, I (Oxford, 1967), p. 470.
10. *Letters and Journals*, ed. R. E. Prothero, II (1904), p. 351.
11. *Byron's Letters and Journals*, ed. Leslie A. Marchand, I (1973), p. 114.
12. See especially George Kitchin, *A Survey of Burlesque and Parody in English* (Edinburgh and London, 1931).
13. See David Farley-Hills, *The Benevolence of Laughter* (1974).
14. 'Hymn to the Penates', 71–2.
15. *Collected Letters of Samuel Taylor Coleridge*, ed. Earl L. Griggs, I (Oxford, 1956), p. 279.
16. See Max F. Schulz, *The Poetic Voices of Coleridge* (Detroit, 1963).
17. See Ford J. Swetnam, Jr., 'The Satiric Voices of *The Prelude*', in Jonathan Wordsworth (ed.), *Bicentary Wordsworth Studies* (Ithaca and London, 1970), pp. 92–110.
18. Cowper to John Newton, 6 August 1785.
19. *The Keats Circle*, ed. Hyder Edward Rollins, 2nd ed., II (Cambridge, Mass., 1965), pp. 208–9.
20. *The Letters of John Keats*, ed. Hyder Edward Rollins, I (1958), pp. 266–7.
21. ibid., I, p. 374.
22. *Byron's Letters and Journals*, ed. Leslie A. Marchand, V (1976), p. 165.
23. *The Letters of John Keats*, I, p. 43.
24. ibid., I, p. 242.
25. ibid., I, p. 242.
26. ibid., II, p. 61.
27. ibid., I, p. 237.
28. ibid., I, p. 184.
29. ibid., I, p. 292.
30. ibid., I, p. 403.
31. ibid., II, pp. 58–109.
32. ibid., I, pp. 275–83.
33. See especially Albert Gérard, *English Romantic Poetry* (Berkeley, 1968); Stuart M. Sperry, *Keats the Poet* (Princeton, 1973).
34. *The Letters of John Keats*, II, p. 174.
35. ibid., II, pp. 162–3.
36. *The Keats Circle*, II, p. 134.
37. Georgia S. Dunbar, 'The Significance of the Humor in "Lamia"', *Keats–*

Shelley Journal, VIII (Winter 1959), 17–26; Martin Halpern, 'Keats and the "Spirit that Laughest"', *Keats–Shelley Journal*, XV (Winter 1966), 69–86.
38. Dunbar, op. cit., p. 21.
39. *The Letters of John Keats*, II, p. 159.
40. See John Gittings, *John Keats* (Harmondsworth, 1971), pp. 534–41.

CHAPTER 4: 'THE ELOQUENCE OF INDIFFERENCE': BYRON

In this chapter I have quoted from the following editions:
Byron, *The Poetical Works*, ed. Frederick Page, revised John Jump (1970).
Byron, *Don Juan*, ed. T. G. Steffan, E. Steffan and W. W. Pratt (Harmondsworth, 1973).

1. See Leslie A. Marchand, *Byron: A Biography*, I (1957), p. 148.
2. Jerome J. McGann, *Fiery Dust: Byron's Poetic Development* (Chicago and London, 1968), especially pp. 3–28.
3. *The Letters of John Keats*, ed. Hyder Edward Rollins, II (Cambridge, Mass., 1958), p. 67.
4. *Byron's Letters and Journals*, ed. Leslie A. Marchand, I (1973), p. 132.
5. ibid., I, p. 215.
6. ibid., I, p. 237.
7. ibid., I, p. 247.
8. Andrew Rutherford, *Byron: A Critical Study* (Edinburgh and London, 1961), p. 101. See also McGann, *Fiery Dust*, Ch. 2, and Robert F. Gleckner, *Byron and the Ruins of Paradise* (Baltimore, 1967), pp. 39–90, 225–97.
9. For a full discussion of Byron and decorum, see G. M. Ridenour, *The Style of Don Juan* (Yale, 1960).
10. For a development of this, see Bernard Beatty, 'Lord Byron: poetry and precedent', in R. T. Davies and B. G. Beatty (eds.), *Literature of the Romantic Period, 1750–1850* (Liverpool, 1976), pp. 114–34.
11. Paul West, *Byron and the Spoiler's Art* (1960), p. 58.
12. 'Byron', in M. H. Abrams (ed.), *English Romantic Poets*, 2nd ed. (London, Oxford, New York, 1975), p. 268.
13. Quoted in *Byron: The Critical Heritage*, ed. Andrew Rutherford (1970), pp. 36, 40.
14. ibid., p. 45.
15. For *Childe Harold* as a 'quest' poem, see John Holloway, *The Proud Knowledge* (London and Boston, 1977), pp. 132–7.
16. Quoted in Bernard Blackstone, *Byron: A Survey* (1975), p. 81.
17. See McGann, *Fiery Dust*, pp. 31–66.
18. See Blackstone, *Byron: A Survey*, pp. 83–4.
19. W. W. Robson, 'Byron and Sincerity' in M. H. Abrams (ed.), *English Romantic Poets* (London, Oxford, New York, 1975), pp. 275–302; Patricia Ball, *The Heart's Events: The Victorian Poetry of Relationships* (1976), pp. 20–31.
20. *Byron's Letters and Journals*, ed. Leslie A. Marchand, V (1976), pp. 265.
21. *Letters and Journals*, ed. R. E. Prothero, V (1904), p. 82; VI (1904), p. 67.
22. *Don Juan*, VII, 2.
23. *Byron's Letters and Journals*, ed. Leslie A. Marchand, V (1976), p. 265.

24. ibid., VI (1976), p. 31.
25. *Letters and Journals*, ed. R. E. Prothero, V (1904), pp. 591–2.
26. ibid., V, pp. 591–2.
27. Blackstone, *Byron: A Survey*, p. 93; Rutherford, *Byron: A Critical Study*, p. 216.
28. *Correspondence*, ed. John Murray, II (1922), p. 203.
29. E. M. Butler, *Byron and Goethe* (1956), p. 49.
30. Paul West, in *Byron and the Spoiler's Art* (1960) p. 16, comments curiously that there is no development or improvement of style between *English Bards* and *Don Juan*.
31. Helen Gardner, 'Don Juan', in Paul West (ed.), *Byron: A Collectiin of Critical Essays* (1963), pp. 113–21.
32. *The Letters of John Keats*, ed. Hyder Edward Rollins, II (Cambridge, Mass., 1958), p. 200.
33. For a full discussion of the dedication, see G. M. Ridenour, *The Style of Don Juan*, pp. 1–18.
34. John Wain, 'The Search for Identity', in Paul West (ed.), *Byron: A Collection of Critical Essays* (1963), pp. 157–70.

CHAPTER 5: 'CONFUSION AND NONSENSE':
TENNYSON AND CLOUGH

In this chapter I have quoted from the following editions:
Tennyson, *The Poems of Tennyson*, ed. Christopher Ricks (1969).
Clough, *The Poems of Arthur Hugh Clough*, ed. A. L. P. Norrington (1968).

1. Bulwer-Lytton, *England and the English* (1833), quoted in Jerome Buckley, *The Victorian Temper* (New York, 1951), p. 20.
2. I have not tried to give anything like a complete account of Clough, and have deliberately steered clear of biographical considerations. See especially Walter E. Houghton, *The Poetry of Clough* (New Haven and London, 1963); Robindra K. Biswas, *Arthur Hugh Clough: Towards a Reconsideration* (Oxford, 1972).
3. *Quarterly Review*, LXX (Sept. 1842), quoted in *Tennyson: The Critical Heritage*, ed. John Jump (1967), p. 103.
4. Houghton, op. cit., p. 57.
5. Houghton, op. cit., p. 63.
6. Houghton, op. cit., p. 57.
7. See John Killham, *Tennyson and 'The Princess': Reflections of an Age* (1958); Bernard Bergonzi, 'Feminism and Femininity in *The Princess*', in Isobel Armstrong (ed.), *The Major Victorian Poets: Reconsiderations* (1969), pp. 35–50.
8. Houghton, op. cit., p. 100.
9. Biswas, op. cit., p. 267.
10. *Fraser's Magazine*, XXXIX (Jan. 1849), quoted in *Clough: The Critical Heritage*, ed. Michael Thorpe (1972), p. 40.
11. Biswas, op. cit., p. 201.
12. Buckley, *The Victorian Temper*, p. 30.

13. R. G. Cox, 'Victorian Criticism of Poetry: The Minority Tradition', *Scrutiny*, XVIII (June, 1951), pp. 2–17.
14. Quoted in Biswas, op. cit., p. 225.
15. Quoted in Cox, op. cit., p. 8.
16. *Selected Prose Works of Arthur Hugh Clough*, ed. Buckner B. Trawick (Alabama, 1964), p. 96.
17. ibid., p. 106.
18. ibid., p. 144.
19. *Church of England Quarterly Review* (Oct. 1842), p. 582.
20. Quoted in *The Poems of Tennyson*, ed. Christopher Ricks (1969), p. 743.
21. *The Letters of Matthew Arnold to Arthur Hugh Clough*, ed. H. F. Lowry (1932), p. 95.
22. ibid., p. 66.
23. ibid., p. 99.
24. *Fraser's Magazine*, XXXIX (Jan. 1849), in *Critical Heritage*, p. 40.
25. *The Germ*, No. 1 (Jan. 1850), in *Critical Heritage*, p. 56.
26. *North British Review* (May, 1853), in *Critical Heritage*, p. 65.
27. *On Translating Homer* (1860–1).
28. *Fortnightly Review*, XXXIX (June, 1883), quoted in Biswas, op. cit., p. 271.
29. 'Clough's Self-Consciousness', in Isobel Armstrong (ed.), *The Major Victorian Poets: Reconsiderations* (1969), p. 268.
30. ibid., p. 273.

CHAPTER 6: THE SOUND OF DISTANT LAUGHTER: CLOUGH

In this chapter I have quoted from the following edition:
The Poems of Arthur Hugh Clough, ed. A. L. P. Norrington (1968).

1. *The Correspondence of Arthur Hugh Clough*, ed. F. L. Mulhauser, I (Oxford, 1957), p. 275.
2. ibid., p. 276.
3. Walter Bagehot in *National Review*, XIII (Oct. 1862), in *Critical Heritage*, p. 173.
4. 'Clough's Self-Consciousness', in Isobel Armstrong (ed.), *The Major Victorian Poets: Reconsiderations* (1969), pp. 269, 273.
5. '*Amours de Voyage*: The Aqueous Poem', in Isobel Armstrong (ed.), op. cit., p. 291.
6. ibid., p. 302.
7. *Innocent Victorian: The Satiric Poetry of Arthur Hugh Clough* (Columbus, 1966), p. 138.
8. Biswas, op. cit., p. 318.
9. Quoted in Goode, op. cit., p. 279.
10. A. Alvarez, 'Convictions of Excellence', *New Statesman* (3 Feb. 1962), pp. 163–4.
11. Quoted in Biswas, op. cit., p. 441; see especially chapter X.

Index